Piety and Persecution in the French Texts of England

MEDIEVAL AND RENAISSANCE
TEXTS AND STUDIES

VOLUME 420

———

THE FRENCH OF ENGLAND TRANSLATION SERIES
(FRETS)

VOLUME 6

Piety and Persecution in the French Texts of England

Translated, with Notes and Introduction by
Maureen B. M. Boulton

FRETS Series Editors
Thelma Fenster and
Jocelyn Wogan-Browne

Tempe, Arizona
2013

Published with the assistance of Fordham University.

THE ARIZONA CENTER FOR
MEDIEVAL &
RENAISSANCE
STUDIES

Published by ACMRS (Arizona Center for Medieval and Renaissance Studies)
Tempe, Arizona
© 2013 Arizona Board of Regents for Arizona State University.
All Rights Reserved.

Library of Congress Cataloging-in-Publication Data

Piety and persecution in the French texts of England / translated, with notes and
introduction by Maureen B. M. Boulton.
    pages cm. -- (Medieval and Renaissance Texts and Studies ; Volume 420) (The
French of England Translation Series (FRETS) ; Volume 6)
  Includes bibliographical references and index.
  ISBN 978-0-86698-468-3 (acid-free paper)
 1. French literature--To 1500--History and criticism. 2. Jesus Christ--History of
doctrines--Middle Ages, 600-1500. 3. Apocryphal infancy Gospels. I. Boulton, Maureen
Barry McCann, 1948-
  PQ1463.G95P54 2013
  840.9'001--dc23
                                                                          2013018359

Front Cover:
The cover illustration, taken from Bodleian Library, MS Selden Supra 38, f. 24r (reproduced with permission), shows the child Jesus sitting on a sunbeam, and below a child who has fallen off, while at the right another child reports the disaster to his father.

∞
This book is made to last. It is set in Adobe Caslon Pro,
smyth-sewn and printed on acid-free paper to library specifications.
Printed in the United States of America

Table of Contents

Series Editors' Preface — vii

Acknowledgments — ix

Abbreviations — xi

Introduction — 1

Suggestions for Further Reading — 49

Note on the Treatment of Text and Translation — 59

1. Robert Grosseteste, *The Castle of Love (Le Chasteau d'amour)* — 61
2. "Jesus" from Grosseteste's translation of *Suidas* — 91
3. *The Childhood of Jesus Christ (Les Enfaunces Jesu Crist)* — 97
4. *The Vengeance of Our Lord (La Vengeance Nostre Seigneur)* — 125
5. *Little St. Hugh of Lincoln (Hugues de Lincoln)* — 135
6. *Passion Meditations and Prayers*
    a. *Seven-Part Meditation on the Passion* (Dublin, Trinity Coll. MS 374) — 141
    b. *Meditation on the Cross, in verse* (Dublin, Trinity Coll. MS 374) — 157
    c. *Meditation on the Wounds of Christ* (Lambeth Palace MS 522) — 163
    d. *Prayer by the Wounds, in verse* (Lambeth Palace MS 522) — 165
    e. *Three Prayers by the Crucifixion, in prose* (Lambeth Palace MS 522) — 167
    f. *Contemplation on the Passion* (London, BL, Harley MS 2253) — 169

Appendix I: Texts of Unpublished Passion Meditations and Prayers — 175

Appendix II: Original Text Extracts — 203

Index of Proper Names — 215

Series Editors' Preface

The theological and devotional writings which flourished in French in England from the twelfth century through to the fifteenth have yet to receive full attention, but scholars and students are beginning to appreciate the interest of this literature and its many ramifications for the literature and history of medieval England and to some extent of medieval France. The literary rewards for readers of these texts can be great, as, for example, in the first text here, where Grosseteste's narrative allegories articulate salvation history in his great lay *'summa'*, *The Castle of Love* (*Chasteau d'Amour*). But, given the intimacy with which Christian identity has so often been predicated on the identification of Jewish people as Christianity's 'other', piety and persecution can also be closely entwined in medieval devotional texts, often and even especially in those focussed on the Virgin Mary. Several of the texts translated here for the first time can be both dismaying and challenging. They reveal the persecutory impulses sometimes couched at the heart of asserted or practiced piety, or found in the kind of God such texts represent (such as the vicious little boy Jesus of the *Childhood of Christ* translated here). The varied selections in *Piety and Persecution* exemplify how much medieval people, lay and cleric alike, could value precise doctrinal articulation and sensuously and intellectually memorable representation, but they also remind us that religious literature is not without its cultural and social politics. The dismaying, the glorious, and their interrelations deserve fuller exploration for any adequate account of medieval English literature and culture.

All scholars and students of medieval French and English literature owe Professor Maureen Boulton a debt both for her own scholarship and for her years of selfless labor on the indispensable reference work that has put the field of French in England on a new basis (published as Ruth J. Dean with Maureen B. M. Boulton, *Anglo-Norman Literature: A Guide to Texts and Manuscripts*, ANTS OPS 3, London: ANTS, 1999). In the present volume Professor Boulton, a specialist in medieval religious literature and an editor of medieval French religious texts from both France and England, offers translations of texts both well known and less studied in the French of England. She also, in her introductions, makes a point of relating these texts to the Middle English works of which they are often relatives or equivalents. We are very pleased that she has agreed to make this thought-provoking selection of works more widely available by translating them for the FRETS series.

Thelma Fenster
Jocelyn Wogan-Browne

Acknowledgments

I take this opportunity to acknowledge the University of Notre Dame's Institute for Scholarship in the Liberal Arts for supporting travel to examine many of the manuscripts that underlie this volume. The project could not have been completed without the gracious help of many libraries and librarians, but I am particularly grateful to Lambeth Palace Library and to the Board of Trinity College Dublin, whose manuscripts are the basis of the editions.

I acknowledge the cooperation of the Bodleian Library in granting permission to reproduce on the cover the miniature from MS Selden Supra 38, f. 24r; it shows the child Jesus sitting on a sunbeam, and below a child who has fallen off, while at the right another child reports the disaster to his father.

My debt to the Series editors, Thelma Fenster and Jocelyn Wogan-Browne, is immense. They have been unstintingly generous in their scholarly dialogue, as well as meticulous in their editorial oversight. As always, my husband Jonathan has proved himself a *preux chevalier* with his unfailing support.

Abbreviations

A-N	Anglo-Norman
AND	*Anglo-Norman Dictionary,* ed. Louise W. Stone, William Rothwell, et al. (London: Modern Humanities Research Association, 1977–92); 2nd ed., ed. Stewart Gregory, William Rothwell, and David Trotter. London: Modern Humanities Research association, 2005; online at: www.anglo-norman.net
ANTS	Anglo-Norman Text Society
BL	British Library
CCCM	Corpus Christianorum Continuatio Medievalis
CPPM	Corpus Patristica Pseudoepigraphorum Medii Aevi
Dean with Boulton	*Anglo-Norman Literature: A Guide To Texts and Manuscripts*, ed. Ruth J. Dean, with the collaboration of Maureen B. M. Boulton, ANTS Occasional Publications Series 3 (London: Anglo-Norman Text Society, 1999)
EETS	Early English Text Society
FRETS	French of England Translation Series
ME	Middle English
MRTS	Medieval and Renaissance Texts and Studies
ODB	*Oxford Dictionary of the Bible,* ed. W. R. F. Browning (Oxford: Oxford University Press, 1996)
ODCC	*The Oxford Dictionary of the Christian Church*, 2nd ed., ed. F. L. Cross and E. A. Livingstone (Oxford: Oxford University Press, 1974)
ODMA	*Oxford Dictionary of the Middle Ages*, ed. R. Bjork, 4 vols. (Oxford: Oxford University Press, 2010)
OED	*Oxford English Dictionary*
PL	*Patrologiae cursus completus ... series Latina*, ed. J.-P. Migne (Paris: Garnier, 1844–65)

Ps.-Matt.	*Libri de Nativitate Mariae, Pseudo-Matthei Evangelium*, ed. J. Gijsel, Corpus Christianorum Series Apocryphorum 9 (Turnhout: Brepols, 1997)
Ps.-Matt. "pars altera"	a Latin version of the *Infancy Gospel of Thomas*, ed. Constantin von Tischendorf, *Evangelia apocrypha* (Leipzig: Mendelsohn, 1876; repr. Hildesheim: Georg Olms, 1966), 93–111

Introduction

Religious texts composed in Anglo-Norman—the French of England—constitute a rich instructional and devotional tradition, including biblical translations and paraphrases, saints' lives, sermons, hymns, prayers, and meditations. In fact, significantly more than half of the texts catalogued in *Anglo-Norman Literature: A Guide to Texts and Manuscripts* fall under the heading of religious literature.[1] Although the earliest French religious texts of England date to the twelfth century, the flow of original compositions, translations, and popularizations increased hugely in the thirteenth and fourteenth centuries and continued well into the fifteenth. Thus, Insular devotional and doctrinal texts in French continued to be written and copied alongside those in English in the later Middle Ages. The production of Anglo-Norman religious literature also parallels developments in France: one finds the same generic range and a similar wealth of manuscripts. While some texts circulated only in one area or the other, many others were known on both sides of the Channel. The Latin Psalter, for instance, was first translated into French in England in the mid-twelfth century, but later translations were made into the Picard and Lorraine dialects. Similarly, French translations of the Sunday gospels appear in the thirteenth century independently in both England and France. Adgar's *Miracles of the Virgin*, composed around the middle of the twelfth century, antedate Gautier de Coinci's Continental collection by some three-quarters of a century.[2] Some texts of Continental origin survive in so many Insular copies that they must be seen as part of the cultural life of England.[3] In England, as on the Continent, the production of religious literature was spurred by the pastoral concerns of the Fourth Lateran Council (1215), which intensified clerical attention to the European laity.

---

[1] Dean with Boulton, nos. 442–986.

[2] On biblical texts, see "Bible française" in *Dictionnaire des lettres françaises: Le Moyen Age*, ed. Geneviève Hasenohr and Michel Zink, 2nd ed. (Paris: Fayard, 1992), 179–96 (184 on psalters). See "Évangiles des domnées" and "Robert de Gretham" in *Dictionnaire des lettres,* 433 and 1287; on the latter, see also Dean with Boulton, no. 589. On A-N miracles of the Virgin, see Dean with Boulton, nos. 558–65.

[3] For example, eighteen of the thirty-six manuscripts of the *Bible* (or *Roman de Dieu et de sa mère*) of Herman de Valenciennes (Dean with Boulton, no. 485) were copied in England.

Although medieval French religious literature in general has long suffered from neglect, scholars have begun to devote serious attention to Anglo-Norman religious texts and to make them available in translation. The anthology *Anglo-Norman Lyric* includes a large selection of religious poems and hymns.[4] A number of saints' lives have been translated and others are in progress: there is work forthcoming on Henry of Lancaster, Nicole Bozon, and other writers and texts of Anglo-Norman piety.[5]

The selection of texts in this volume is meant to provide an entrée to this tradition, and includes examples of several different genres in verse and prose, loosely centered on the life of Christ. They range from the theologically sophisticated *The Castle of Love* (*Chasteau d'Amour*) to the popular tale of *Little St. Hugh of Lincoln*. In between are prayers and meditations on the Passion, the folkloric *Childhood of Jesus Christ* (*Les Enfaunces Jesu Crist*), and the *Vengeance of our Lord*.

The Castle of Love is a fundamental manual of Christian doctrine composed by Robert Grosseteste, a noted theologian and bishop.[6] In contrast, the other works in the volume occupy a different intellectual space: even if most were probably written by clerics, they are theologically more simple and often express

---

[4] David L. Jeffrey and Brian Levy, *Anglo-Norman Lyric: An Anthology. Edited from the Manuscripts with Translations and Commentary*, Studies and Texts 93 (Toronto: Pontifical Institute of Mediaeval Studies, 1990).

[5] Brigitte Cazelles translates some Insular lives and extracts in *The Lady as Saint: A Collection of French Hagiographic Romances of the Thirteenth Century* (Philadelphia: University of Pennsylvania Press, 1991); Clemence of Barking's *Life of St. Catherine* and the anonymous *Life of St. Lawrence* are translated by Jocelyn Wogan-Browne and Glyn S. Burgess, *Virgin Lives and Holy Deaths: Two Exemplary Biographies for Anglo-Norman Women* (London: J. M. Dent; Rutland, VT: C. E. Tuttle, 1996); for other lives see Thelma Fenster and Jocelyn Wogan-Browne, *The History of St. Edward the King by Matthew Paris*, FRETS 1 (Tempe, AZ: ACMRS, 2008), eaedem, *The Life of St. Alban by Matthew Paris*, FRETS 2 (Tempe, AZ: ACMRS, 2010); Delbert W. Russell, *Verse Saints' Lives Written in the French of England*, FRETS 5 (Tempe, AZ: ACMRS, 2012). Further texts are translated in Brent A. Pitts, *The Anglo-Norman Gospel Harmony*, FRETS 7 (forthcoming); Catherine Batt, *Henry of Lancaster's Book of Holy Medicines* (FRETS, forthcoming); Laurie Postlewate, *Preaching and Poetry in Medieval England: The Works of Nicholas Bozon* (FRETS, in progress). For a collection of previously unedited texts see Tony Hunt, ed., *"Cher alme": Texts of Anglo-Norman Piety*, FRETS OPS 1 (Tempe, AZ: ACMRS, 2010), with translations by Jane Bliss and an introduction by Henrietta Leyser.

[6] This text has been translated by Evelyn A. Mackie, "Robert Grosseteste's Anglo-Norman Treatise on the Loss and Restoration of Creation, Commonly Known as *Le Château d'Amour:* An English Prose Translation," in *Robert Grosseteste and the Beginnings of a British Theological Tradition*. Papers delivered at the Grosseteste Colloquium held at Greyfriars, Oxford, on 3rd July 2002, ed. Maura O'Carroll, Bibliotheca Seraphico-Cappuccina 69 (Rome: Istituto Storico dei Cappuccini, 2003), 151–79.

virulently anti-Jewish sentiments. To judge by their prologues, the authors conceived of them as religiously wholesome entertainment because they reinforced orthodox beliefs and practice. Repellent as their hostility to the Jews appears today, these texts are nevertheless significant for the light that they shed on the prejudices and beliefs they shared with or attempted to create in medieval English society. As we shall see with the life of Little St. Hugh of Lincoln, these beliefs not only fostered intolerance toward non-believers but could provoke outbreaks of violent persecution of Jewish neighbors. As far away as fifteenth-century Spain, where Little St. Hugh's story was conflated with that of "The miracle of the boy singer" familiar from Chaucer's Prioress's Tale, England was sometimes admired for its anti-Judaism and the English crown taken as a model of "anti-Jewish lordship."[7]

The Castle of Love

Robert Grosseteste, author of the Anglo-Norman poem known as the *Chasteau d'amour*, was one of the great English intellectuals of the thirteenth century. While biographical facts, especially for his early life, are sparse, it seems that he came from a humble but French-speaking family in Stowe (Suffolk) and began his career in the service of the bishop of Hereford.[8] Whether he studied theology at Paris is a contested point, but he was familiar with the work of Parisian masters, and by the 1220s was teaching theology at Oxford, where he was also named Chancellor. He became a deacon in 1225, and teacher to the Franciscans in England 1229/30–1235, before being consecrated as bishop of Lincoln.

Grosseteste's writings form a considerable corpus in several genres: there are scientific works, exegetical works, and writings on philosophical topics. The commentaries on the Gospels, the epistles of Paul, and the Psalms show that he had some knowledge of Hebrew as well as Greek, and his translations from Greek to Latin were important to the history of medieval philosophy. In addition, he did original work on astronomy, cosmology, light, and optics.

A number of texts in Anglo-Norman, attributed more or less certainly to Grosseteste, reveal a similarly broad range of interests. In addition to the *Castle of Love*, we find ascribed to him another allegorical poem (*Le mariage des neuf filles du diable* or the *Marriage of the Devil's Nine Daughters*), a treatise on estate management (*Les Reules Seynt Roberd* or *Rules of St. Robert*) composed for the countess of Lincoln, a treatise on the sacrament of confession (*La Manere de sey*

---

[7] Anthony Bale, *The Jew in the Medieval Book: English Antisemitisms, 1350–1500* (Cambridge: Cambridge University Press, 2006), 60–61.

[8] This paragraph is based on James McEvoy, *Robert Grosseteste* (Oxford: Oxford University Press, 2000), especially "A Life Poorly Known," 19–30.

confesser), another on purgatory (*Les Peines de purgatorie*), and a couple of prayers.[9] One strand that runs through most of his work, however, is a passion for pastoral care. He was dedicated to offering priests and pastors the means to deepen their knowledge of scripture and their understanding of the faith, through his preaching and treatise on confession, as well as through his exegetical writings. The "fullest expression of his pastoral theology,"[10] the nearest that Grosseteste came to a *summa*, is the *Chasteau d'amour* or *Castle of Love*.[11]

Around 1230, Grosseteste extended his pastoral mission to those not literate in Latin. He probably devised his *Castle of Love* for an audience that included laypeople, but also embraced religious who could have used it as a manual of pastoral theology.[12] The work is a manual of Christian doctrine cast in the form of an allegorical poem. It contains a coherent summary of essential scriptural passages together with traditional patristic commentary on them. The main theme of the *Castle of Love*, the redemption of humanity, is elaborated in a variety of ways: narratively, in an account of the creation of Adam and Eve and their fall through sin; allegorically, first in the debate of the Four Daughters of God, then through the image of Mary as the Castle of Love; dramatically, in the debate between Christ and the Devil in the Temptation scene; anagogically, in the imagination of the Last Judgment, the final entry of the saved into heaven (and the condemnation of unrepentant sinners to hell). This projection into the future is the logical conclusion and necessary counterpoise to the account of the fall of man, for it demonstrates the reconciliation of humankind with God. It serves as a useful reminder for the reader of the ultimate rewards and punishments of deeds in this world.[13]

---

[9] McEvoy, "Anglo-Norman Works," in *Robert Grosseteste*, 146–59. See Dean with Boulton, nos. 392, 622, 645, 660, 662, 670, 686, 859, 937.

[10] R. W. Southern, *Robert Grosseteste: The Growth of an English Mind in Medieval Europe* (Oxford: Clarendon Press, 1986), 225.

[11] The *Chasteau* was first edited by Jessie Murray, *Le Château d'amour de Robert Grosseteste évèque de Lincoln* (Paris: Champion, 1918), on the basis of Oxford, Corpus Christi College, MS 232, with selected variants from ten other manuscripts. Evelyn A. Mackie has produced a new edition, "Robert Grosseteste's *Chasteau d'amur*: A Text in Context" (Ph.D. diss., University of Toronto, 2002), using London, Lambeth Palace, MS 522 as a base with significant variants from all the extant manuscripts. Cf. Dean with Boulton, no. 622.

[12] Mackie, "Robert Grosseteste's *Chasteau*," 51–53 argues that Grosseteste composed the work not for the sons of Simon and Eleanor de Montfort, but for the use of the Oxford community of Franciscans, which included several laymen; she proposes 1230–35, when Grosseteste served as lector to the convent of Franciscans in Oxford, as the most likely period of composition (59).

[13] For a detailed examination of the structure and contents of the poem, see Southern, *Robert Grosseteste*, 225–26.

The title *Chasteau d'amour*, which does not appear in any of the manuscripts, singles out only a small part of the whole work. French rubrics in two manuscripts (Oxford, Bodl. Libr., Laud Misc. MS 471 and Brussels, Bibl. royale, MS 9030–37) describe the poem as "The life of sweet Jesus Christ." On the basis of the Latin prologue found in most of the complete copies, scholars have proposed more accurately descriptive titles—"The Loss and Restoration of Creation" or "Carmen de Creatione Mundi."[14] Nevertheless, the French title is the one usually used to designate the poem, and for the sake of clarity, it is retained here.

Although the *Castle of Love* is not a biography of Christ, the events of his life underlie the work. At its heart is the Incarnation—the need for it (Adam's sin), the inspiration for it (God's love and compassion for mankind), its vehicle (the Castle of Love who is the Virgin Mary), and its effect (the entry of human souls into heaven). Other events of Christ's life (his birth and presentation in the temple), his miracles (at Cana, the feeding of the multitude, the raising of Lazarus) are presented allusively as part of his battle against the devil which culminates in his death and descent to break the gates of Hell. The resurrection and ascension conclude the biographical elements of the poem.

Grosseteste did not condescend to an audience he described as ignorant of "Latin and learning" (vv. 27–28), but sought (and the number of manuscripts and translations of the *Castle* suggests that he succeeded) to give them the fruit of his own theological reflections and of his study of philosophy. In practice this means that certain passages of the *Castle* use terminology and make distinctions unfamiliar outside clerical circles. For example, the passage on the nature of Adam's sin asserts that the first man was subject not to a single command but to two laws: the first "natural" (i.e., conscience) and the second "positive" (not to eat from the forbidden tree).[15] In order to explain (vv. 866–72) how the whole universe was embellished by God's entry into his creation through the Incarnation, Grosseteste resorts to philosophical terms. He uses the phrase "nature naturante" to express the concept, derived from Aristotle's *Physics*, of God as creator (or First Cause) of the universe as distinct from "nature naturee" which indicates what was created.[16] These distinctions were quite new in thirteenth-century theological thought even in Latin. Their appearance in the vernacular demonstrates that

---

[14] Mackie uses the first in her translation, "Robert Grosseteste's A-N Treatise" (160), while the second was proposed by Kari Sajavaara, "Château d'Amour," in *Robert Grosseteste: New Perspectives on his Thought and Scholarship*, ed. James McEvoy, Instrumenta Patristica 27 (Turnhout: Brepols, 1995), 394.

[15] Southern's assertion (*Robert Grosseteste*, 224) "that Adam and Eve disobeyed the positive command; but they did not, as the disobedient angels, reject the law of their nature" is contradicted by vv. 135–37 "Kant il la pome manga Ambedeus les leis trespassa, E naturel e positive."

[16] Southern, *Robert Grosseteste*, 228 explains these terms well, but interprets their use negatively: "how difficult he found it to separate the various parts of his mind."

Grosseteste hoped to convey his thought with the same precision that he used in his Latin works, "with undiminished originality."[17]

Another original aspect of the *Castle of Love* lies in its presentation of the devil's role in redemption theory. Grosseteste, in effect, combines two separate strands, and modifies both in his presentation.[18] The language of ransom, based on Matthew 20:28, is sometimes used of Christ's death to redeem humankind. Because Adam sinned voluntarily, his thraldom to the Devil was justified, and he must (at least in early formulations) be ransomed by God, at the price of Christ's death. On the other hand, the killing of an innocent man (Christ) was an injustice for which the Devil was responsible. The evolution of these two ideas in medieval theological thought is subtle and complicated.[19] Grosseteste's use of them reflects the thinking of more recent medieval theologians, but he modifies them and combines them in a new way. One new strand is the argument, formulated by Mercy (vv. 260–70), that the prisoner (Adam) was unjustly held because he had been deceived by his foes (the devil). In the *Castle of Love* this argument is restated by Christ in his debate with the devil during the temptation in the desert (vv. 1040–48). Similarly, the ransom of Christ's death is paid, not to the Devil (who mistakenly thought that he would increase his power through it [vv. 1105–10]), but rather to God. Through his death, Christ reconciles Adam and his descendants with the Creator. In Grosseteste's formulation (vv. 431–56), the king's son agrees to submit to judgment and punishment in place of the prisoner, thereby reconciling the requirements of both Justice and Mercy.

In his presentation of the Incarnation in the *Castle of Love*, Grosseteste makes extensive use of the terminology of common law as a means of adapting and explaining the Incarnation doctrine to a lay audience. Before the Fall, for example, Adam had "seisine" or possession of the joys of Paradise.[20] As we have seen above, his sin consists in disobedience to the two laws placed upon him, but this sin is further defined as "defaute" or default, which has two senses in Anglo-Norman. Its primary meaning—"lack, need, want, shortage, privation, loss"—is consistent with the notion of evil as an absence of good rather than a separate malevolent force in its own right. In common law, however, it denotes the "failure to answer a legal summons," and it is in this sense that it occurs most

---

[17] McEvoy, *Robert Grosseteste*, 153.

[18] For the following, I have relied on C. W. Marx, *The Devil's Rights and the Redemption in the Literature of Medieval England* (Woodbridge: D. S. Brewer, 1995), 65–79.

[19] See Marx, *The Devil's Rights*, 7–25 for a discussion of the themes of abuse of power and ransom in Augustine, Gregory the Great, Anselm, Peter Lombard, Hugh of St. Victor, and Abelard; chapter 2 (26–46) traces the two themes in biblical commentaries and commentaries on Lombard's *Sentences*.

[20] Frederick Pollock and Frederic William Maitland, *The History of English Law Before the Time of Edward I*, 2 vols. (Cambridge: Cambridge University Press, 1895, repr. 1968), 2:29–80.

often in the text. There is one instance (vv. 165–68) where Grosseteste reminds his audience that a second default results in a legal decision ("fine" v. 165) depriving a person of his right of possession ("seisine" v. 166) of a property. Through his sin or default, Adam and his lineage became "serfs." The exact translation of Anglo-Norman "serf" is rather vexed, as it can mean serf, servant, and slave, even though the status of a serf in thirteenth-century England was quite distinct from that of a slave. While a serf had no rights against his lord, and no protection from him in royal courts, with respect to all other persons he was treated as free.[21] In general, I have rendered the word as "serf" rather than servant.[22]

It is worth noting that Grosseteste's use of French legal language reflected the reality of the Anglo-Norman world. French was the language of English royal courts in the twelfth and thirteenth centuries, and thus much pleading was conducted in Anglo-Norman.[23] A thirteenth-century legal code was composed in Anglo-Norman. For all these reasons, the legal metaphors of the *Castle of Love* would have been both comprehensible and unsurprising to its readers.

The second theme of the texts in this volume is the treatment of Jews. In the *Castle of Love* there is no direct mention of Jews, nor any overt sentiment against them; indeed the word "Jew" does not even appear in the poem.[24] In the Passion section, Grosseteste evokes a series of familiar events, associating each one with a particular type of sin. He thus subordinates the biographical elements to his didactic intent and his rhetorical structure. In addition, the alternation of human sin and its consequences in Christ's sufferings stresses human guilt for the Crucifixion. But in contrast to the less theological treatments of this point in the other texts in this volume, this guilt belongs not to a group of Palestinian Jews but to us ("nus"). It is Christians and their repeated falls from grace—our sins, our foolish glances, our cursing and slander, our gluttony, misdeeds, and wicked thoughts—that repeat the fall of Adam and that are responsible for the tortures inflicted during the Passion. Grosseteste's treatment of the Passion is therefore remarkable for the absence of accusatory anti-Jewish comments.

The *Castle of Love* succeeds on several levels. The product of profound theological reflection, it is also a work of great literary artistry that makes its readers see elements of their ordinary lives in another way. Its treatment of theological

---

[21] Pollock and Maitland, *The History*, 1:415.

[22] In other texts, where medieval legal status does not seem to be at issue, I have translated it as "slave."

[23] Pollock and Maitland, *The History*, 1:80–87.

[24] Such restraint, however, was not always typical of Grosseteste's attitude toward the Jews in England. When the Jews of Leicester found refuge in Winchester after being expelled by Simon de Montfort, Grosseteste (then the archdeacon of Leicester) wrote to the countess of Winchester condemning her hospitality; Southern, *Robert Grosseteste*, 244–49 quotes extracts of the letter in translation and comments on it. See also the A-N version of the article "Jesus" from his translation of the Greek *Suidas* (below).

issues may, without exaggeration, be compared to Langland's in *Piers Plowman*. The portrayal of Adam's fall and redemption also brings to mind Julian of Norwich's theology of the servant who falls and is forgiven.[25] This sophisticated approach to the essential elements of Christian theology is brilliantly cast in terms that would have been completely familiar to a lay audience—monarchy, castles, and feudal law, including serfdom, forfeiture, and imprisonment. The first part of the poem, with its elaboration of the metaphor of the heavenly kingdom, is similar to other Anglo-Norman descriptions of God's court.[26]

For both medieval and modern readers of secular literature, Grosseteste's castle metaphor may recall Jealousy's castle in the *Roman de la Rose*.[27] There are obvious similarities of structure between the castles—foundation, wall, corner towers, central tower—but the differences are nonetheless profound. In the *Rose*, Jealousy's castle is a fairly simple structure with a curtain wall enclosing a square courtyard with a central tower, and reinforced with a turret at each corner. Although it is set within a larger allegory, the parts of Jealousy's castle are not allegorized. In contrast to the straightforward description in the *Rose*, each part of Grosseteste's castle has a double meaning. It is simultaneously both the instrument and the plan of the Incarnation as well as an image of the Virgin's body. It features three baileys inside a curtain wall punctuated with seven barbicans, which makes it far more complicated than the *Rose* castle. The resulting image is a highly sophisticated and theologically cogent version of architectural allegory, a "castle of the mind" as Christiania Whitehead has termed this mode of writing.[28]

---

[25] See, e.g., Nicholas Watson, "Visions of Inclusion: Universal Salvation and Vernacular Theology in Pre-Reformation England," *Journal of Medieval and Early Modern Studies* 27 (1997): 145–87.

[26] See, for example, T. Atkinson Jenkins, ed., *Eructavit: An Old French Metrical Paraphrase of Psalms XLIV...*, Gesellschaft für Romanische Literatur 20 (Dresden: Niemeyer, 1909), vv. 1753–1896 (the poem is associated with Marie de Champagne, but wrongly ascribed to Adam de Perseigne by Jenkins): it survives in one A-N copy as well as numerous Continental manuscripts; cf. Dean with Boulton, no. 705, and the newer edition by Walter Meliga, *L'Eructavit antico-francese secondo il ms. Paris B.N. fr. 1747*, Scrittura e scrittori 6 (Alessandria: Edizioni dell'Orso, 1992). For a study see Morgan Powell, "Translating Scripture for *Ma dame de Champagne*: The Old French 'Paraphrase' of Psalm Forty-Four (*Eructavit*)," in *The Vernacular Spirit: Essays on Medieval Religious Literature*, ed. R. Blumenfeld-Kosinski, D. Robertson, and N. Bradley Warren (New York and Houndmills, Basingstoke: Palgrave, 2002), 83–103.

[27] See *Le Roman de la Rose*, ed. Daniel Poirion (Paris: Garnier-Flammarion, 1974), vv. 3797–958; *Le Roman de la Rose*, ed. Félix Lecoy, vol. 1, Classiques français du moyen âge 92 (Paris: Champion, 1968), vv. 3779–930.

[28] Christiania Whitehead, *Castles of the Mind: A Study of Medieval Architectural Allegory* (Cardiff: University of Wales Press, 2003).

Manuscripts

There are nineteen known copies of the Anglo-Norman *Castle of Love*, twelve complete and seven partial. Eighteen of these manuscripts survive.[29] The earliest (Oxford, Corpus Christi Coll., MS 232) dates from the mid-thirteenth century; another nine were made in the second half of the century, and six manuscripts were copied around the turn of the century. Two copies were made in the first half of the fourteenth century and another (Brussels, Bibl. Royale, MS 9030–37) was made in the mid-fifteenth century for Margaret of York, duchess of Burgundy. Several other copies of the *Castle of Love* are associated with women. In Princeton, Univ. Libr., Taylor Medieval MS 1, Joan Tateshall (d. 1310) of Tattershall Castle in Lincolnshire is represented in two initials and the book was presumably prepared for her.[30] Yet another volume, Cambridge, Fitzwilliam Museum, McClean MS 123, belonged in the fourteenth century to the nuns of Nuneaton priory in Warwickshire, and may have been compiled for them. Several copies had ecclesiastical associations: Durham cathedral priory owned London, BL, Harley MS 3860, and the Benedictine abbey of St. Augustine in Canterbury possessed two (London, Lambeth Palace, MS 522 and Oxford, Corpus Christi College, MS 232). Such a pattern of transmission demonstrates the continued appeal of the work, and to audiences beyond those initially targeted.

It is also worth noting that several of the manuscripts of the *Castle of Love* are found in bi-lingual or even tri-lingual volumes. The Cambridge manuscript (Fitzwilliam Museum, McClean MS 123) contains, in addition to several Anglo-Norman items, a Middle English poem as well as prayers and an Office in Latin. Similarly, both the Digby (Oxford, Bodl. Libr., Digby MS 86) and the Vernon manuscripts (Oxford Bodleian Libr., MS Eng. poet. a.1) are tri-lingual compilations: while Digby transmits the Anglo-Norman *Castle of Love*, Vernon contains its Middle English translation.[31] Other volumes are bi-lingual in nature. The two Harley manuscripts (London, BL, Harley MSS 1121 and 3860)

---

[29] For a complete list of manuscripts, see Mackie, "Robert Grosseteste's A-N Treatise," 159–60. Marx, *The Devil's Rights*, Appendix 4, 160–70 describes all of the manuscripts of the French text and of the English versions based on it. The incomplete thirteenth-century copy in Metz, Bibl. mun., MS 1238 (Salis 88) burned in 1944; it was described in *Catalogue générale*, 48 (Paris, 1933), 417.

[30] See Adelaide Bennett, "A Book Designed for a Noblewoman: An Illustrated *Manuel des Péchés* of the Thirteenth Century," in *Medieval Book Production: Assessing the Evidence*, ed. Linda L. Brownrigg (Los Altos Hills, CA, and Oxford: Anderson-Lovelace, 1990), 163–81.

[31] Oxford, Bodl. Libr., Bodley MS 652 also contains texts in three languages, but it is a composite volume composed of three originally separate manuscripts. Oxford, Bodl. Libr., Laud Misc. MS 471 contains works mainly in French and Latin, with one ME religious lyric.

contain works in Latin and French.[32] The manuscript tradition of Grosseteste's poem illustrates vividly the multi-lingual nature of religious writing in England in the thirteenth and fourteenth centuries.

One striking feature of the transmission of the poem is the presence in most of the complete copies of a Latin prologue that indicates the content and structure of the poem, which it calls a *tractatus* or treatise. In two manuscripts (Oxford, Corpus Christi College, MS 232 and Paris, BnF, MS fr. 902) the margins of the text have frequent Latin annotations that either summarize the content of the passage or cite sources, both scriptural and patristic authorities. According to the most recent editor, these notes "demonstrate that the text was closely studied in a scholastic fashion."[33] As a whole, however, the manuscript tradition of the Anglo-Norman *Castle of Love* shows that the serious, if non-scholastic, interest of lay as well as clerical patrons in theological issues stimulated the production of many religious texts. The same serious concern for theological questions among the laity appears in a different form in, for example, the Middle English poem *Pearl*.[34]

Sources

Investigations into the sources of the *Castle of Love* have concentrated on its allegory of the Four Daughters of God because of the interest of this motif for Grosseteste's views on the doctrine of human redemption.[35] The scriptural basis of the allegory is to be found in Psalm 84: 11–12: "Mercy and truth have met each other; justice and peace have kissed."[36] The allegory itself appears in Jewish commentaries (Midrash), and was used in the twelfth century by Hugh of St. Victor and by Bernard of Clairvaux in a sermon on the Annunciation; it also occurs in the Latin sermon *Rex et Famulus*, extant in several versions.[37] Because of the multiplicity of sources and analogues, both for the allegory and for various

---

[32] The Latin poems of Walter of Wimbourne in Oxford, Corpus Christi College, MS 232 were added in a hand later than that of the body of the manuscript.

[33] Mackie, "Robert Grosseteste's *Chasteau*," 50.

[34] On lay spiritual concerns see further Nicole R. Rice, *Lay Piety and Religious Discipline in Middle English Literature* (Cambridge: Cambridge University Press, 2008).

[35] Hope Traver, *The Four Daughters of God*, Bryn Mawr College Monographs 6 (Philadelphia: J.C. Winston, 1907). The earlier work, including an unpublished dissertation by Sr. Mary Immaculate Creek ("The Sources and Influence of Robert Grosseteste's *Le Chasteau d'Amour*," Yale University, 1941) is summarized by Kari Sajavaara, *The Middle English Translations of Robert Grosseteste's Château d'amour*, Mémoires de la Société Néophilologique de Helsinki 32 (Helsinki: Société Néophilologique, 1967), 54–101. For a more recent review of sources, see Marx, *The Devil's Rights*, 66–74.

[36] *The Holy Bible, Douay Version*, Translated from the Latin Vulgate (Douay, A.D. 1608: Rheims, A.D. 1582; London: Catholic Truth Society, 1956).

[37] For details, see Sajavaara, *The Middle English Translations*, 62–85; and Marx, *The Devil's Rights*, 68.

concepts on the nature of redemption, it is clear that Grosseteste relied on no single source. On the contrary, he combined different strands and motifs in an eclectic fashion.[38]

The quest for the source of the Castle of Love, the vivid image that has given the text its traditional title, has proved inconclusive.[39] Although there are many examples of figurative castles of the body, including some in connection with the Blessed Virgin, no direct source for Grosseteste's castle has yet been identified.[40] The most recent editor of the Anglo-Norman *Castle* points out similarities between the architecture of the castle and the description of the New Jerusalem in Apocalypse 21:11–23.[41] This beautiful image, one of the most elaborately developed in medieval literature, may well be the invention of the bishop of Lincoln.

Influence

The popularity of the Anglo-Norman *Castle of Love* is attested not only by the relatively large number (eighteen) of surviving manuscripts, but by the number of translations and paraphrases of the poem.[42] Modern Anglophone audiences are familiar with Grosseteste's work mainly through an anonymous Middle English translation, *The Castle of Love*. Composed around 1300 in rhymed couplets and preserved in three manuscripts, this translation is generally faithful to the original, although it makes numerous small additions and omissions. The French original apparently continued to be of interest, however, as it was copied several times in England, even after the early appearance of this English translation.

In the first half of the fourteenth century, a monk of Sawley abbey (a Cistercian foundation in the West Riding of Yorkshire) wrote a paraphrase entitled the *Myrour of Lewed Men*. This version is an abridgement and a reworking of the original that avoids both its poetical and rhetorical elaboration and

---

[38] On Grosseteste's eclecticism, see Marx, *The Devil's Rights*, 66–70.

[39] Roberta Cornelius, *The Figurative Castle* (Bryn Mawr: Private Edition, 1930), 37–48, esp. 44–47.

[40] Sajavaara, *The Middle English Translations*, 93–94; idem, "Château d'Amour," in McEvoy, *Robert Grosseteste: New Perspectives*, 393–94. See also Christiania Whitehead, "A Fortress and a Shield: The Representation of the Virgin in the *Château d'Amour* of Robert Grosseteste," in *Writing Women Religious: Female Spiritual and Textual Practices in Late Medieval England*, ed. Denis Renevey and eadem (Toronto: University of Toronto Press, 2000), 109–32.

[41] Mackie, "Robert Grosseteste's *Chasteau*," 78–80. For a study of this image in a Middle English context, see Rosalind Field, "The Heavenly Jerusalem in *Pearl*," *Modern Language Review* 81 (1986): 7–17. For Anglo-Norman apocalypses, see Dean with Boulton, nos. 473–478.

[42] For discussions of the Middle English versions, see Sajavaara, *The Middle English Translations*, 101–258; the texts (except the *Cursor Mundi*) are edited with notes, 259–407, and idem, "The Use of Robert Grosseteste's 'Château d'amour' as a Source of the 'Cursor Mundi'," *Neuphilologische Mitteilungen* 68 (1967): 184–93.

detailed philosophical discussions. The Middle English *Cursor Mundi* includes a fragmentary translation of the Anglo-Norman *Castle*: it renders about a thousand lines of the original in four separate passages (*CM* 701–10; 9375–10122, 16949–17100, 18661–750). Of all the Middle English versions, the *Cursor* is the most faithful to the French text, containing only one significant addition in the third passage, which expands the description of Christ's suffering during the Passion. Two other Middle English poems recount only the opening allegory of Grosseteste's poem. *The King and Four Daughters* was written in the first half of the fifteenth century in short rhymed couplets, and is very faithful to the original. The *Foure Doughters*, consisting of thirty-two six-line tail rhymed stanzas written in the second half of the fourteenth century, is a thorough reworking of the French text.[43]

In the fourteenth century, Langland revisits some of the themes of Grosseteste's work in *Piers Plowman*. The C-text passus XX (B passus XVIII), for example, incorporates the debate of the four daughters of God, and at least one part of it may have been influenced by the *Chasteau d'amour*.[44] Similarly, Langland's concept of lordly justice and mercy resembles that found in the *Chasteau d'amour*. At earlier points (passus VII, v. 232 ff.; passus IX, v. 1–59), Langland also exploits the image of the castle, though here the castle is in the first case Truth's, surrounded by the moat of Mercy and walls of wit, and in the second, the castle of Kynde (nature) called Caro (flesh) in which Anima (soul) dwells under the constableship of Sir Inwit (conscience).

2) "Jesus" from the *Lexicon* of Suidas, from Grosseteste's Latin translation

The second piece associated with Grosseteste is much less well known, but reveals fascinating aspects of his intellectual life. It was through his translations from Greek that Grosseteste acquired a reputation on the Continent.[45] Among these is a text that was eventually rendered into French, an article on Jesus from the so-called *Lexicon* of Suidas (var. Souidas, Soudas, Suda). The *Lexicon* is an important Greek encyclopedia written by a Byzantine Christian in the mid-tenth century, with articles on figures from classical mythology and history as well as on biblical subjects arranged in more or less alphabetical order.[46] Grosseteste is known

---

[43] For further information on the Middle English Castle of Love texts see Robert R. Raymo, "Works of Religious and Philosophical Instruction," in *A Manual of the Writings in Middle English 1050–1500*, gen. ed. Albert E. Hartung (New Haven: Connecticut Academy of Arts and Sciences, 1986), 2:2255–2378, 2467–2582.

[44] Marx, *The Devil's Rights*, 104.

[45] See McEvoy, "Greek Scholarship," in *Robert Grosseteste*, 113–21.

[46] A. Kazhdan, "Souda," in *Oxford Dictionary of Byzantium*, 3 vols. (New York: Oxford University Press, 1991), 3:1930–31.

to have obtained a copy of the *Lexicon*, and translated into Latin some seventy of its articles, including the article on Jesus.[47] In its Latin form, also known as "De probacione virginitatis beate Marie," this article also circulated independently, and is the source of the anonymous Anglo-Norman version translated here.[48]

The text is an elaborate piece of anti-Jewish propaganda.[49] It purports to relate a conversation between a Jew (one Theodosius) and a Christian (Philip), in which the former confesses that Jesus was well known to Jewish leaders, who made him a priest of the synagogue after questioning his mother as to his parentage. In this account, Mary relates the Annunciation, and asserts that Jesus had no human father, but was engendered by the Holy Spirit. According to Theodosius, the Jewish priests, once they verified her claim to virginity, accepted her statement and duly recorded it in the "book" of the synagogue. After the Crucifixion, however, they removed the book and hid it in the city of Tiberias. The narrator adds that when the existence of this evidence leaked out, it resulted in the destruction of Jerusalem "with great bloodshed"—a clear reference to the events recounted in the *Vengeance of Our Lord* (see text no. 4 below).

According to this narrative, Jewish leaders knew and acknowledged that Jesus was the Son of God, but deliberately withheld this information from their people so that it could not be used to persuade ordinary Jews to convert to Christianity. The conclusion of the conversation between the Jew and the Christian, where the former refers to the consequences of an attack on the Jews and concludes "we would have wasted our pains," suggests that it might have been intended for such an apologetic end. On the other hand, the text could also serve

---

[47] For an English translation of the Greek original, see Pieter W. van der Horst, "Jesus and the Jews according to the *Suda*," *Zeitschrift für die neutestamentliche Wissenschaft und die Kunde der älteren Kirche* 84 (1993): 268–77. A translation is also available at the site "Suda on Line": <www.stoa.org/solbin/search.pl?db=REAL&search_method=QUERY&login=guest&enlogin=guest&user_list=LIST&page_num=1&searchstr=iota,229&field=adlerhw_gr&num_per_page=1>

On Grosseteste's Latin version, see S. Harrison Thomson, *The Writings of Robert Grosseteste, Bishop of Lincoln 1235–53* (Cambridge, MA: Harvard University Press, 1940), 63–65.

[48] Grossteteste gave a copy of the article on Jesus and his version of the *Twelve Patriarchs* to Matthew Paris: see A. C. Dionisotti, "Robert Grosseteste and the Greek Encyclopedia," in *Rencontres de cultures dans la philosophie médiévale: traductions et traducteurs de l'Antiquité tardive au XIVe siècle*, ed. Jacqueline Hamesse and Marta Fattori (Louvain-la-Neuve: Institut d'Etudes Médiévales de l'Université Catholique de Louvain, 1990), 337–53, 377.

For the A-N text, see Ruth J. Dean, "An Anglo-Norman Version of Grosseteste: Part of His *Suidas* and *Testamenta XII Patriarcharum*," *PMLA* 51 (1936): 607–20; Dean with Boulton, no. 487.

[49] On the *Lexicon*'s lack of historicity, see van der Horst, "Jesus and the Jews," 274–77.

a polemical purpose, for a Jewish refusal to convert could, in light of the text, be construed as willful obstinacy in the face of incontrovertible evidence.

A single manuscript (Paris, BnF, MS nouv. acq. fr. 10176) preserves the Anglo-Norman translation, in combination with another text based on Grosseteste's translations from Greek, an incomplete Anglo-Norman translation of the *Testament of the Twelve Patriarchs*. The Paris manuscript contains only five folios, written by two different English scribes of the thirteenth century. The *Lexicon* of Suidas appears on ff. 1^r-2^r and is followed without any break by the second text.

The anonymous Anglo-Norman translator prefaced his work with a short prologue in verse in which he declared his intention of abandoning rhyme, the demands of which would entail too much departure from his source. Even in prose, however, he had difficulty rendering the Latin, and left a number of phrases untranslated. Ruth Dean compared the Anglo-Norman version with one of the Latin manuscripts of the article, and found it generally faithful, although somewhat looser in structure.[50] No English equivalent text is known.[51]

3) The Childhood of Jesus Christ

The Childhood of Jesus Christ (*Les Enfaunces Jesu Crist*) is an imaginative, colorful, and sometimes shocking account of the childhood of Christ, in the form of a poem of slightly more than 2,000 verses, organized into quatrains.[52] Its immediate source is probably a thirteenth-century Continental French poem, the Old French *Évangile de l'Enfance*, but the serially organized miracle stories that comprise the narrative of both the *Enfaunces* and its Continental source come ultimately from Latin apocryphal sources.[53]

In the prologue (vv. 1–32), the narrator addresses an inscribed audience of romance readers, asserting that his poem will be as pleasing, but much more profitable, because its subject is Jesus Christ. He goes on to insist on its veracity, citing written sources that he has followed exactly, without additional glosses. To strengthen his truth claims, the infancy miracles are framed by retellings of gospel events (the visit of the Three Kings, the marriage feast of Cana), but most of the tales are obviously fanciful and are clearly included for their perceived entertainment value and potential for polemic. The religious lessons illustrated by

---

[50] Dean, "An A-N Version of Grosseteste," 608.

[51] The Middle English *Parliament of Devils* is loosely analogous for its representation of devils as seeking to discover Christ's paternity: see on this text Marx, *The Devil's Rights*, 126–39, esp. stanza A2–6.

[52] See Dean with Boulton, no. 495; Maureen Boulton, ed., *Les Enfaunces de Jesu Crist*, ANTS 43 (London: ANTS, 1986).

[53] Maureen Boulton, ed., *The Old French* Évangile de l'Enfance: *An Edition with Introduction and Notes*, Studies and Texts 70 (Toronto: Pontifical Institute of Mediaeval Studies, 1984).

the miracles are rudimentary but forceful demonstrations of the divine omnipotence of Jesus; those who humbly recognize his power are praised while all who try to exert ordinary human authority over him are punished; only his mother's intercession is capable of influencing him, a point reiterated in the epilogue (vv. 1917–72).

The only complete Insular manuscript of the poem (Oxford, Bodl. Libr., Selden Supra MS 38) adds a second epilogue (vv. 1973–2020) that modifies the poem's lessons significantly. This passage, which has no equivalent in the Continental version, articulates a starkly anti-Jewish message. The narrator names the Jews as wicked people motivated by envy of Jesus and Mary, and he curses them roundly if they fail to repent. Many of the tales support this message, and clearly reflect a current of anti-Jewish sentiment that increased steadily in England throughout the thirteenth century.[54] In several episodes, Jews are portrayed as violent: Jewish boys attack Jesus without provocation as he plays quietly; and schoolmasters strike him for his impertinence. On each occasion, Jesus manifests his power in reactions that range from ignoring a broken water jar and carrying water in his tunic to striking dead an aggressor whom he later restores to life at his mother's request. The repeated point of these stories, however, reinforces the image of a stubborn Jewish refusal to recognize the obvious divinity of the child in their midst. The illustrations reinforce this message, for all the adult Jewish characters are portrayed with large noses, and wear stereotypically Jewish hats (*pileus cornutus*).

Manuscripts

The Oxford manuscript (Bodl. Libr., Selden Supra MS 38), copied c. 1325, is the only complete copy of the Anglo-Norman poem.[55] The *Enfaunces Jesu Crist* occupies the first section of the volume, the rest of which is devoted to a glossed Apocalypse in French prose.[56] Both texts are heavily illustrated, and the Infancy poem is accompanied by a series of sixty miniatures, most divided into two

---

[54] Maureen Boulton, "Anti-Jewish Attitudes in Anglo-Norman Religious Texts: Twelfth and Thirteenth Centuries," in *Christian Attitudes Toward the Jews in the Middle Ages: A Casebook*, ed. Michael Frassetto (New York: Routledge, 2006), 151–65.

[55] For a detailed description, see Boulton, *Les Enfaunces*, 2–7; for the date, see O. Pächt and J. J. G. Alexander, *Illuminated MSS in the Bodleian Library, Oxford* (Oxford: Oxford University Press, 1973), 3:53. On the owners, see also Renana Bartal, "A Note on Bodleian Library MS. Selden Supra 38, Jehan Raynzford and Joanna de Bishopsdon," *Bodleian Library Record* 19.2 (2006): 239–43. For color digitization of the *Enfaunces* images in MS Selden Supra 38 see http://bodley30.bodley.ox.ac.uk:8180/luna/servlet/view/all/what/MS.+Selden+Supra+38,+pt.+1

[56] See L. Delisle and P. Meyer, *L'Apocalypse en français au XIIIe siècle (Bibl. Nat., Fr. 403)* (Paris: Société des Anciens Textes Français, 1901), esp. ccxxiv-ccxxix and cclxviii-cclxix; for the images in the Selden Apocalypse see http://bodley30.bodley.ox.ac.uk:8180/luna/servlet/view/all/what/MS.+Selden+Supra+38,+pt.+2. Lucy F. Sandler, *Gothic Man-*

panels with different scenes, but none is accompanied by a caption or a rubric.[57] The miniatures are stylistically related to those executed by Walter de Milemete in Oxford, Christ Church MS 92.[58]

Cambridge, Univ. Libr., MS Gg.1.1, at more than 600 leaves, is a vast trilingual miscellany written in the first quarter of the fourteenth century (but after 1307). Most of the texts are religious, didactic, or historical in character. Items in French include the *Lumere as lais*, the *Manuel des péchés*, Robert of Gretham's *Évangile des Domnées*, the *Image du monde*, and an illustrated *Apocalypse*, as well as the Edward I section of Peter Langtoft's *Chronicle* and the *Brut d'Angleterre*. In Middle English, there is a poem on the Passion and the *Proverbs of Hending*. Latin items include various methods of prognostication, a compendium for interpreting dreams, and miracles of the Virgin. This manuscript (ff. 479^{v1}–484^{v1}) contains only 646 lines of the Anglo-Norman *Enfaunces*, with each episode introduced by a rubric, but without miniatures, although other texts in the volumes are illustrated.[59]

There was a third copy of the poem, but only a single leaf survives (Cambridge, Univ. Libr., Add. MS 6855 (G)), now folded to form two flyleaves at the beginning of a fifteenth-century English manuscript from the priory of St. Mary Overy (the Southwark Augustinian house of the poet John Gower's later years). The fragment, consisting of forty-six lines (vv. 1107–56), is written in a script of the fourteenth century, probably the second half; the scribe left a blank space on the sheet which was probably meant to accommodate a miniature.

The manuscript tradition of *The Childhood of Jesus Christ* is more complicated than this evidence might initially suggest, because the Middle English translation of the poem survives in a manuscript older (by perhaps a quarter-century) than any of the Anglo-Norman copies. As will be explained in more detail in the discussion of the Middle English poem below, it seems likely that

---

uscripts, *1285–1385*, 2 vols., vol. 5 of *A Survey of Manuscripts Illuminated in the British Isles*, ed. J. J. G. Alexander (London: Harvey Miller, 1975–1996); 1 (1986), 62–63.

[57] Some of the miniatures have been reproduced: Adey Horton, *The Child Jesus* (New York: Dial Press, 1975): color plate 73 shows one miniature from f. 21^v, and plate 89 the three illustrations to the "Miracle of the Dyer" on ff. 25^v, 26^v, and 27^r; f. 32^v is the frontispiece to Boulton, *Les Enfaunces*; eadem, "*The Évangile de l'Enfance*: Text and Illustration in Bodleian Library MS. Selden Supra 38," *Scriptorium* 37 (1983): 54–65 and plate 8. On the artist, see Renana Bartal, "The Illuminator of Bodleian Library, Selden Supra 38 and his Working Methods," *Pecia* 13 (2012): 387–404.

[58] See Boulton, *Les Enfaunces*, 4–6 for a list of the subjects of the illustrations; cf. Pächt and Alexander, *Illuminated MSS in the Bodleian Library*, 3:53.

[59] For the French texts, see Paul Meyer, "Les Manuscrits français de Cambridge, II: Bibliothèque de l'Université," *Romania* 15 (1886): 236–357, esp. 283–340; for a fuller list of contents, see Glynn Hesketh, *Lumere as Lais by Pierre d'Abernon of Fetcham*, vol. 3, ANTS 54 (London: ANTS, 2000), 25–29.

the *Enfaunces Jesu Crist* in quatrains was preceded by a now-lost Anglo-Norman version in couplets.[60]

Style

The *Childhood of Jesus Christ* is a world away from the theological preoccupations and extended allegorical images of Robert Grosseteste. The emphasis of the *Childhood*'s poet is almost entirely narrative. Only the most elementary of lessons are explicitly drawn from the various incidents—that one should honor and obey Jesus Christ, and request the intercession of his mother. In the incident where Jesus strikes dead the boy who ruins the pools of water he has made (vv. 397–456), the boy is explicitly restored to life at Mary's request. This lesson is reiterated at the end of the poem: "Indeed, when his mother requested anything of her Son, sweet Jesus Christ, he did it immediately, as soon as she asked it" (vv. 1921–24).

Stylistically the poem is fairly simple. Sentences are completed within the quatrain, and often within a pair of lines. Although the syntax of the sentences themselves is not very complex, there is sometimes a surprising number of nouns in apposition, such as "En la terre cel tiraunt / Herode, ke fu reis e sire / E governur de tut l'empire" (in the land of that tyrant, Herod, who was king and lord and governor of the whole realm, vv. 64–66). Many lines are only minimally connected—fully 286 lines of the total or some 14 percent begin simply "and" ("e"). On the other hand, the narrative is enlivened with frequent passages of dialogue where Jesus's impertinence is a striking feature.

Because the Anglo-Norman poem is itself a metrical translation—into monorhymed quatrains from couplets—the redactor's need of additional rhymes required much alteration of his source. Frequently he was able to modify the word order of his source without much distortion of the syntax. For example, v. 81 "Vus [me] trespassez, ben le vei" (I see clearly you are wronging me) is clearly related to the Old French line "Bien voi que vous me trespasséz" (I see well that you are wronging me) and presents no difficulties. On other occasions, the insertion of a line solely for its rhyme makes the syntax less clear, as in "Si nus pussum par nuil afere" (If we can by any means, v. 75), which lacks any expected verbal complement after *poeir* (*aler* is implied). The pursuit of rhyme also led the reviser to pad his lines, which explains the profusion of adverbs in sentences such as "Jesu dunc, ke tut savoit, / A cel arbre dunc parloit" (Then Jesus, who knew everything, spoke to the tree, vv. 221–22). In this case, I have suppressed the repeated *dunc* (then or therefore), but in general I have tried to stay as close as possible to the structure of the Anglo-Norman. In other cases, the need for rhyme in the Anglo-Norman text has led to contradictions that are often preserved in the translation. For example, after the Jewish boys have broken Jesus's water pot, we read: "Then Jesus became very angry that his pot was smashed and for that reason he threatened all the children there" (vv. 705–08). The last two phrases were added to

---

[60] See Boulton, *Les Enfaunces*, 28–30 for a discussion and a hypothetical stemma.

complete the quatrain, but contradict the next lines: "Jesus remained calm, for he did not want to sow disorder" (vv. 709–10). These features of style have increased the difficulty of translation, but I have generally kept close to the text in order to convey its flavor, although at the price of some loss of fluidity of style.

In the account of Jesus hanging his water jar on a sunbeam, there is an interesting discrepancy between the text and its illustration that suggests that the artist was instructed in English, and had not read the French text, for whatever reason. The word for sunbeam ("rai") occurs at vv. 728 and 740, but the illustration shows a wooden beam with handles on it and broken jars below. The artist seems to have been misled by the two meanings of "beam" in English, though the Middle English poem clearly specifies "sonne beme" (v. 641; "sonne bem" v. 653).[61]

As noted above, the Anglo-Norman *The Childhood of Jesus Christ* depends immediately on a Continental French poem on the same subject written in octosyllabic couplets. Aside from the change of form and small alterations of detail, the Anglo-Norman poem differs from the Old French in adding three episodes (vv. 501–64, 1537–92, 1761–84) that are doublets of incidents already related.

Both French poems derive ultimately from the Latin *Gospel of Pseudo-Matthew* and the older *Infancy Gospel of Thomas*, although it is not known whether the poets writing in French worked directly from these texts or used an intermediary Latin text composed later but now lost.[62] The first group of miracles—those that occur during the flight to Egypt—all come from the *Gospel of Pseudo-Matthew*.[63] Most of the remaining miracles of Jesus's childhood depend on the *Infancy Gospel*

---

[61] According to the *Oxford English Dictionary*, vol. 2, 16, "beam" meaning a ray of light is attested as early as 885 [the *Old English Chronicle*], but is less common than the meaning "a plank of wood."

[62] While admitting the existence of these "apparent sources," Evelyn Birge-Vitz argues for the essentially oral character of the *Enfaunces* in "The Apocryphal and the Biblical, the Oral and the Written, in Medieval Legends of the Life of Christ: The Old French *Évangile de l'Enfance*," in *Satura: Studies in Medieval Literature in Honour of Robert R. Raymo*, ed. Nancy M. Reale and Ruth E. Sternglantz (Donington, UK: Shaun Tyas, 2001), 129–55, at 134–41.

[63] The *Pseudo-Matthew* is also known as the *Liber de ortu Beatae Mariae et infantia salvatoris* or the *Liber de Infantia Mariae et Christi*; for a modern edition with a facing French translation, see J. Gijsel (ed.), *Libri de Nativitate Mariae. Pseudo-Matthaei Evangelium*, Corpus Christianorum Series Apocryphorum 9 (Turnhout: Brepols, 1997). For an English translation, see A. Roberts and J. Donaldson, *The Ante-Nicene Fathers*, vol. 8 (New York: Scribner's, 1890; repr. Grand Rapids: Eerdmans, 1951), 368–77; J. K. Elliott, *New Testament Apocrypha: A Collection of Apocryphal Christian Literature in an English Translation* (Oxford: Clarendon Press, 1993; rev. repr. 1999), 84–99, has a good introduction and translations of extracts. There is an A-N translation of the *Pseudo-Matthew* in the fourteenth-century MS. Oxford, Bodl. Libr., Bodl. MS 82 (Dean with Boulton, no. 645r); see "Young Mary," in Hunt et al., "*Cher alme*," 129–47.

of Thomas, composed in Greek before the sixth century, and known also in Latin translation.[64] In at least some Latin manuscripts, the *Infancy Gospel of Thomas* is combined with the *Pseudo-Matthew*.[65] These miracles are self-contained episodes linked by indications to the age of Jesus, and portray him as a child wonder-worker. A couple of episodes are modeled on incidents from the canonical gospels: the conclusion to Jesus's encounter with the teacher Zacharias (v. 565–640) is close to John 8:55–58. Similarly, the Wedding of Architeclin (vv. 1813–1940) is a reworking of the Marriage Feast of Cana (John 2:1–10). Three miracles common to all the French poems have no counterpart in the Latin versions of the *Infancy Gospel of Thomas.* An incident similar to the "Children in the Oven" (vv. 1101–56) is found in the *Arabic Infancy,* while there are analogues of "Jesus Sitting on a Sunbeam" and the "Miracle of the Dyer" in an Armenian version.[66] Since recent research shows that Armenia was important to Franco-English diplomacy in the fourteenth century, it is possible that this miracle is based on the *Armenian Infancy,* although perhaps through an as yet unidentified Latin intermediary.[67]

---

[64] Edited by Constantin von Tischendorf, *Evangelia apocrypha* (Leipzig: Mendelsohn, 1876; repr. Hildesheim: Georg Olms, 1966): the *Tractatus de pueritia Iesu secundum Thomam,* 164–80; the English translations in Elliott, *New Testament Apocrypha* and Roberts and Donaldson, *Ante-Nicene Fathers* are based on the Greek text. On this apocryphon, see Stephen Gero, "The Infancy Gospel of Thomas: A Study of the Textual and Literary Problems," *Novum Testamentum* 13 (1971): 46–80; and Ronald F. Hock, *The Infancy Gospels of James and Thomas,* The Scholar's Bible (Santa Rosa, CA: Pollbridge, 1995), 84–101.

[65] The second part ("pars altera," i.e., chapters 25–42) of the *Pseudo-Matthew,* as edited by Tischendorf, *Evangelia apocrypha,* 93–111 are in fact a Latin version of the *Infancy Gospel of Thomas.* An English translation is found in Roberts and Donaldson, *Ante-Nicene Fathers,* 378–83. For this clarification, see Gijsel, *Pseudo-Matthaei Evangelium,* 39–40. Consequently, the indications of sources in my edition should be corrected: where chapters 26–42 of the *Pseudo-Matthew* are indicated (referring to Tischendorf's edition), the actual source is the "pars altera," a version of the *Infancy Gospel of Thomas.* On illustrated Latin infancy gospels, see Pamela Sheingorn, "Reshapings of the Childhood Miracles of Jesus," in *The Christ Child in Medieval Culture: Alpha es et O!,* ed. Mary Dzon and Theresa M. Kenney (Toronto, Buffalo, and London: University of Toronto Press, 2012), 254–92.

[66] For an English translation of the Arabic Infancy Gospel, see Roberts and Donaldson, *Ante-Nicene Fathers,* 405–15 and Elliott, *New Testament Apocrypha,* 100–7 On the Armenian text see Paul Peeters, *Évangiles Apocryphes, 2: Évangile de l'Enfance,* Textes et Documents pour l'étude historique du Christianisme 18 (Paris: Picard, 1914), xxix-l, 69–286; cf. Elliott, *New Testament Apocrypha,* 118–19; Abraham Terian, *The Armenian Gospel of the Infancy* (Oxford: Oxford University Press, 2008).

[67] On Armenian influence, see Carolyn P. Collette and Vincent J. DiMarco, "The Matter of Armenia in the Age of Chaucer," *Studies in the Age of Chaucer* 23 (2001): 317–58.

By definition, apocryphal texts were not part of the "canon," that is, the texts officially accepted as part of the Bible, and thus have no authority. The attitude of the Church toward such texts ranged from condemnation to toleration and even acceptance. Vincent of Beauvais is representative; he transcribed the judgment of the Pseudo-Gelasian decree denouncing such texts,[68] but also observed:

> like pagan books, they have no authority for the Christian Church, but nevertheless, even sacred authors have sometimes made use of them (Paul and Jude, for instance). One may read them and believe what they say as long as they do not disagree with Catholic faith . . .[69]

Some apocryphal texts gained acceptance as useful pious readings. Narratives dealing with the conception and birth of the Virgin, for example, could be included in the readings for the office on those feasts.[70] Many books of hours include Christ's childhood miracles among their illustrations,[71] and such scenes could be included in the decoration of churches.[72]

Influence

The Middle English *Childhood of the Savior*, a poem in 1854 verses of rhymed couplets, was copied into the oldest manuscript (Oxford, Bodl. Libr., MS Laud 108) of the *South English Legendary*.[73] The Laud manuscript is actually older than any of the surviving French manuscripts, dating to the last quarter of the thirteenth century, which might suggest that it is the source of the Anglo-Norman poem, rather than the reverse, or else that it was an independent translation

---

[68] The *Decretum Gelasianum*; see *ODCC*, 385.

[69] *Liber apologeticus*, chap. 9, "Apologia de apocryphis," cited by Monique Paulmier-Foucart and Alain Nadeau, "The History of Christ in Vincent of Beauvais' *Speculum historiale*," in *Christ among the Dominicans*, ed. Kent Emery, Jr. and Joseph Wawrykow (Notre Dame: University of Notre Dame Press, 1998), 113–26, at 121.

[70] Solange Corbin, "Miracula beatae Mariae semper virginis," *Cahiers de Civilisation médiévale* 10 (1967): 409–33.

[71] E.g., the Neville of Hornby Hours (London, BL, Egerton MS 2781); cf. Kathryn A. Smith, *Art, Identity and Devotion in Fourteenth-Century England: Three Women and their Books of Hours* (London: British Library and Toronto: University of Toronto Press, 2003).

[72] See below, n. 75 on the Tring tiles.

[73] The rubric announcing the poem is in French: "Ici comence le enfaunce Jhesu Crist"; see the edition by Carl Horstmann, *Altenglische Legenden* (Paderborn: Schöningh, 1875), 3–61; F. Holthausen, "Zum mittelenglischen Gedicht 'Kindheit Jesu' (Ms. Laud 108)," *Archiv für das Studium der neueren Sprachen* 127 (1911): 318–22. On the manuscript see Thomas Richard Liszka, "Manuscript Laud Misc. 108 and the Early History of the South English Legendary," *Manuscripta* 33.2 (1989): 75–91, and Kimberley K. Bell and Julie N. Crouch, eds., *The Texts and Contexts of Oxford, Bodleian Library MS Laud misc. 108: The Shaping of English Vernacular Narrative* (Leiden: Brill, 2011).

from a Latin source. A closer examination of the *Childhood of the Savior*, however, reveals a significant number of French words and phrases, probably carried over from its source. Although composed in rhymed couplets, the English poem includes the three redundant episodes found in the Anglo-Norman quatrain version but omitted from the Continental couplet version. The Middle English poem is also divided into episodes by prose rubrics, which bear a close resemblance to those found in the Cambridge copy of the Anglo-Norman text.

In addition to the poem in couplets, there is a Middle English stanzaic poem on the *Childhood of Christ* preserved in three copies from the fourteenth and fifteenth centuries that contains quite different versions of the infancy miracles.[74] Among the many episodes that correspond to those in the Laud and Selden texts—including the miracles of the fruit tree, the journey shortened, the clay sparrows, the pigs in the oven, the dyer, the boy in the tower—none is told in the same way. The accounts are often much shorter, the three episodes at school are conflated into a single incident, and details differ. Additionally, the three copies display considerable variation in length and order of episodes, and also in wording. These later versions attest to the enduring popularity of these infancy legends in England.

One unusual form of influence is to be found in a set of medieval tiles now preserved in the British Museum.[75] Originally part of the decoration of the parish church at Tring, these eight tiles have the same oblong format as the miniatures in the Selden manuscript, with the same division of the background into two panels (although they are a monochrome brown), and they reproduce several of the same scenes, including the boy who jumps on Jesus's back, the boy in the tower, and the feast at Cana, as well as parts of the miraculous harvest and the pigs in the oven. The tiles differ from the miniatures in their lateral compression: in the manuscript, a scene is usually spread across the double panel covering the whole width of the written space; each tile, by contrast, contains a separate scene in each half of the panel. In one case, where Jesus assists Joseph in his carpenter's

---

[74] Carl Horstmann, ed., *Sammlung altenglischer Legenden* (Heilbronn: Henniger, 1878; repr. Hildesheim and New York: Georg Olms, 1969), 101–10 (Harley MS 3954, 14C; 694 vv.); 111–23 (Harley MS 2399, 15C; 892 vv.); and idem, "Nachträge zu den Legenden, 1: Kindheit Jesu aus MS. Addit. 31043," *Archiv für das Studium der neueren Sprachen* 74 (1885): 327–39 (925 vv.).

[75] M. R. James (with a note by R. L. Hobson), "Rare Mediaeval Tiles and Their Story," *The Burlington Magazine* 42 (1923): 32–37. See also Elizabeth S. Eames, *Medieval Tiles: A Handbook* (London: British Museum, 1968); and Boulton, "The *Évangile de l'Enfance*." The tiles may be seen in color at the website of the British Museum (www.britishmuseum.org/explore/highlights/highlight_objects/pe_mla/t/the_tring_tiles.aspx). See also Mary Casey, "Conversion as Depicted on the Fourteenth-century Tring Tiles," in *Christianizing Peoples and Converting Individuals*, ed. Guyda Armstrong and Ian N. Wood, International Medieval Research 7 (Turnhout: Brepols, 2000), 339–46.

work, the tiles represent the incident on three panels, while there is only one miniature in the manuscript. Both visual representations show a crooked piece of wood that must be straightened, whereas the account in the text (vv. 1465–1536) specifies that Joseph's assistant fails to cut the wood into two equal pieces, as he had been instructed.[76] Compared with the miniatures in the manuscript, the representation of the Jews in the tiles is significantly more negative. The stereotypical representation of a large nose to signal "Jew" is, for instance, taken to an extreme caricature here.

4) The Vengeance of Our Lord

The anti-Jewish sentiment apparent in varying degrees in most of the other texts translated here is the dominant theme of the *Vengeance of Our Lord*. The historical core of all of the medieval versions of the Vengeance story is the Roman suppression of the Jewish rebellion of 66 CE that ended with the destruction of the Temple four years later.[77] In the many medieval retellings of this history, the Romans are portrayed as the legitimate instruments of divine retribution for the crucifixion of Christ. As the legend developed, it merged with the legends of Veronica (the possessor of a portrait of Jesus) and of Pilate.[78] The Vengeance tradition in French is the most extensive in Europe, with versions in both verse and prose, and the earliest was written as a *chanson de geste* in the thirteenth century,

---

[76] Several of the miracles in the *Enfaunces* are also represented in the *Holkham Bible Picture Book*, ff. 14ᵛ-16ʳ; see Michelle Brown, *The Holkham Bible: A Facsimile* (London: British Library, 2007); and Kathryn Smith, "Accident, Play, and Invention: Three Infancy Miracles in the Holkham Bible Picture Book," in *Tributes to Jonathan J. G. Alexander: The Making and Meaning of Illuminated Medieval and Renaissance Manuscripts, Art, and Architecture*, ed. Susan L'Engle and Gerald B. Guest (London: Harvey Miller, 2006), 357–69.

[77] For a concise summary of the historical background with references to historical sources, see Stephen K. Wright, *The Vengeance of Our Lord: Medieval Dramatizations of the Destruction of Jerusalem*, Studies and Texts 89 (Toronto: Pontifical Institute of Mediaeval Studies, 1989), 2–6. For an excellent discussion of literary aspects of the legends surrounding the destruction of Jerusalem, see David Hook, *The Destruction of Jerusalem: Catalan and Castilian Texts* (London: King's College London Centre of Late Antique & Medieval Studies, 2000), 115–44.

[78] Veronica's portrait of Christ is supposed to have been formed by the permanent imprint of Christ's face on a cloth she offered him en route to Calvary: see Ewa Kuryluk, *Veronica and her Cloth: History, Symbolism, and the Structure of a 'True' Image* (Oxford: Blackwell, 1991). For an example of a thirteenth-century devotional 'Veronica' image of Christ, see the well-known representation by Matthew Paris reproduced in N. J. Morgan, *Early Gothic Manuscripts*, 2 vols., A Survey of Manuscripts Illuminated in the British Isles 4 (London: Harvey Miller, 1982–1988), 1: *1190–1250*, no. 24.

perhaps as early as 1200.[79] These texts normally treat (in varying detail) the cure of the emperor, revenge for the killing of Christ, and punishment of those responsible for it.

Later in the thirteenth century, the Vengeance legend was cast in French prose; fifty-four known manuscripts contain nine distinct versions.[80] Of these, two versions in the French of England are preserved in five manuscripts and in a fragment of a sixth.[81] One Anglo-Norman *Vengeance* is transmitted in four copies along with a version of the *Gospel of Nicodemus* in prose that concludes with an account of the events of the Crucifixion and Resurrection purportedly written by Pilate to the emperor Claudius.[82] This version of the text is concerned exclusively with Veronica's portrait of Jesus and the cure of the emperor Tiberius through the portrait's power. There is no account of the destruction of Jerusalem, so the conventional denomination of this version as the "Vengeance" is somewhat misleading.

The *Venjance del Mort Nostre Seignur* ("The Vengeance for the Death of Our Lord") translated here is preserved in British Library, Egerton MS 613 (possibly, as we shall see, a nunnery manuscript) and is quite distinct from the other Anglo-Norman version of the legend. It opens with the appearance of Nathan, a Christian convert, before Titus, king of Aquitaine under the emperor Tiberius. Both king and emperor suffer from cancer-like maladies. Titus is inspired to belief by Nathan's reports of Jesus Christ, and is cured of his wound. In gratitude for his cure, he enlists his brother Vespasian to join him in punishing the enemies of Christ. During their sojourn in Judea, they hear of a portrait of Christ in the possession of a certain Veronica. Tiberius dispatches his emissary Volusianus to find and bring back the portrait which eventually effects the emperor's cure. There is no elaborate account of the destruction of Jerusalem as revenge for the

---

[79] Loyal A. T. Gryting, *The Oldest Version of the Twelfth Century Poem, 'La Venjance Nostre Seigneur,'* University of Michigan Contributions in Modern Philology 19 (Ann Arbor: University of Michigan Press, 1952), dates the poem c. 1200 on linguistic grounds (31); but see corrections in the review by Raphael Levy, *Symposium* 8 (1954): 175–79. The unpublished edition by Melitta S. G. Buzzard, " 'C'est li romanz de la Vanjance que Vaspasiens et Tytus ses fiz firent de la mort Jhesucrist': Édition du ms. 5201 Bibliothèque de l'Arsenal, Paris" (Ph.D. diss., University of Colorado, 1970), is an essential complement to Gryting's edition.

[80] Alvin E. Ford, ed., *La Vengeance de Nostre-Seigneur: The Old and Middle French Prose Versions, The Version of Japheth*, Texts and Studies 63 (Toronto: Pontifical Institute of Mediaeval Studies, 1984).

[81] Dean with Boulton, no. 502; this entry should be revised to show two distinct versions: London, BL, Egerton MS 613 (Family I) and the remaining manuscripts (Family D). The Egerton text has been edited by Alvin E. Ford, *The Vengeance de Nostre-Seigneur: The Old and Middle French Prose Versions*, Studies and Texts 115 (Toronto: Pontifical Institute of Mediaeval Studies, 1993), 195–205; for the edition of Family D text, see 52–64.

[82] Dean with Boulton, nos. 497–498.

crucifixion: there is punishment, but it is limited to the populace, to Pilate, and to the members of the Sanhedrin.

The life and passion of Christ are narrated in an abbreviated form twice in the text. Nathan's account (ll. 16–31) concentrates on Christ's miracles (particularly his cures and raisings from the dead), and on the evidence of his own resurrection. This information is later repeated by Volusianus in his report to Tiberius, with considerably more detail about the Passion (ll. 158–173). In each case, the emphasis on Christ's wonder-working highlights the willful malice of his persecution by the Jews and reinforces the anti-Jewish theme that is central to the text. As reported by Volusianus, the Jews are the sole architects of the crucifixion, and Volusianus presents himself and his fellow Romans as victims of Jewish malice. The Romans (with the notable exception of Pilate) are exculpated from any involvement in the event and associated rather with the followers of Christ.

The anti-Jewish theme inherent in any narrative entitled "The Vengeance for the Death of Our Lord" is further heightened in this manuscript version by its treatment of the actions of the Jews. After Titus and Vespasian first invade Palestine, Archelaus (described as the king of the region and the father of Pilate) commits suicide in despair. The survivors of seven years of siege finally surrender while admitting their guilt and thus justifying the actions of their attackers. Through the technique of inversion, the punishment that Titus and Vespasian mete out to the survivors explicitly mirrors the details of Christ's passion. For example, as Christ was sold for thirty pieces of silver, thirty Jews are sold for one piece of silver.[83] The punishment of their leaders follows the same pattern, as Titus asks "What shall we do with them" (l. 178) and Vespasian responds with punishments drawn from the crucifixion narratives. While the description of the Passion in the *Vengeance* has elements similar to those in the Passion meditations that we will examine below, the effect, rather than inspiring compassion, is used to arouse indignation, and then serve as a blueprint for retaliatory violence. The Romans, including the newly baptized Titus, are shown behaving in a completely un-Christian manner. The narrative conspicuously omits Christ's request in the Bible that his executioners be pardoned and concentrates on justifying ruthless retribution.[84] Rather more disturbingly, the final lines step outside the narration itself and call for a blessing on Christ's avengers, implying that, just as Christ continues to live and reign in the present, so does vengeance against his enemies.

The only copy of this version of the *Vengeance of Our Lord* is British Library, Egerton MS 613, a tri-lingual compilation of mainly edifying texts, probably for the use of nuns; the volume is a composite, but most of it (ff. 7–58) had been

---

[83] On this motif, see F. de Mely, "Les Deniers de Judas dans la tradition du moyen âge," *Revue Numismatique* 4 (1899): 500–9.

[84] See Wright, *The Vengeance*, 15–17 on the ethical dimensions of this point.

assembled by the mid-fourteenth century.[85] The dialect of the longer English texts suggests that the volume may have been compiled in the South West Midlands. There are two texts addressed to female religious: the English "Conduct of Life" and the Anglo-Norman "Les Quatre Titres d'une Nonne," indicating the compiler's interest in literature for professed nuns, but it is not clear whether the book belonged to a convent or was used by male clergy responsible for a female congregation. The *Venjance* is copied into the fourth quire which also includes the end of the *Gospel of Nicodemus* in prose (devoted to the Passion) and two others related to the Cross—the *Finding of the Cross* (by St. Helena) and the *Exaltation of the Cross*. The group of texts makes a coherent set of prose narratives in French related to the Passion and its aftermath.

Sources

The general versions of the *Vengeance,* including the more common Anglo-Norman one, derive ultimately from Latin apocryphal sources that recount the miraculous cure of the emperor Tiberius by means of Veronica's portrait of Christ, the destruction of Jerusalem, and the punishment of Christ's executioners—the *Cura Sanitatis Tiberii,* the *Vindicta Salvatoris,* and the *Mors Pilati*.[86] The thirteenth-century Continental *Venjance* relates the cure and the destruction of Jerusalem, but alters the cast of characters: the emperor there is Vespasian and Titus is his son. The alternative text in Egerton 613 appears to rely more closely on the first part of the *Vindicta*: it begins in the reign of the emperor Tiberius with the arrival of Nathan in Aquitaine, where Titus is king, and Vespasian is Titus's ally.[87]

---

[85] For a full description, see Betty Hill, "British Library MS. Egerton 613," *Notes and Queries* 223 (1978): 395–409, 492–501. For the *Quatre Titres*, see Dean with Boulton, no. 620. In the first section of the volume there is a trilingual prose treatise for nuns on the "Sufferings of Christ" (Dean with Boulton, no. 619).

[86] On the sources, see Ford, *Vengeance* (1993), 4–34 and 207–8. See also Dom Etienne Darley, OSB, *Les Actes du Sauveur, la Lettre de Pilate, les Mission de Volusien, de Nathan, la Vindicta, leurs origines et leurs transformations* (Paris: Picard, 1919). For editions, see Ernst von Dobschütz, *Christusbilder,* Texte und Untersuchungen zur Geschichte der altchristlichen Literatur 3 (Leipzig: Hinrichs, 1899), 163**–89** (*Cura sanitatis Tiberii*); Tischendorf, *Evangelia Apocrypha,* 471–86 (*Vindicta Salvatoris*). For a discussion of the diffusion of the Latin apocrypha in England, see the survey by Thomas N. Hall, "The *Euangelium Nichodemi* and *Vindicta saluatoris* in Anglo-Saxon England," in *Two Old English Apocrypha and their Manuscript Source: 'The Gospel of Nichodemus' and 'The Avenging of the Saviour,'* Cambridge Studies in Anglo-Saxon England 19 (Cambridge: Cambridge University Press, 1996), 36–81.

[87] The mission of Nathan is also recounted in *Nathanis Judaei Legati*: see Etienne Darley, *Les Acta Salvatoris: une Évangile de la Passion et de la Résurrection et une Mission apostolique en Aquitaine* (Paris: Picard, 1913), 38–46; and Ford, *Vengeance* (1984), 14–15.

Influence

In Middle English, the siege and destruction of Jerusalem were the most popular elements of the Vengeance legend, which is retold in at least three versions in verse and prose, none of which stems from the Anglo-Norman prose texts. *Titus and Vespasian*, composed near London in the late fourteenth century, survives in two versions (long and short) in twelve manuscripts.[88] The poem is written in romance form, in four-stressed couplets, and was based on a form of the Old French *Vengeance Nostre Seigneur*, probably one of the epic versions, rather than either of the Anglo-Norman prose accounts.[89] The anonymous author omitted much of the detail of the siege, but added passages expounding the Christian faith, as well as a life of Judas. *Titus and Vespasian* is itself the source of a prose abridgement, the *Sege of Jerusaleme*, which survives in a single manuscript from the second half of the fifteenth century.[90]

The alliterative *Siege of Jerusalem*, composed toward the end of the fourteenth century and preserved in nine manuscripts, relies on three principal sources: the Latin *Vindicta Salvatoris*, Ranulf Higden's *Polychronicon*, and Roger d'Argenteuil's *Bible en français*.[91] Its genre—history or romance or epic—has vexed modern critics, but this very diversity doubtless contributed to its appeal for various medieval audiences. Modern readers, however, are often appalled by its violence even as they admire its elaborate structure.[92]

---

[88] The long version: J. A. Herbert, ed., *Titus and Vespasian, or the Destruction of Jerusalem in Rhymed Couplets* (London: Roxburghe Club, 1905); the short version: Rudolf Fischer, "*Vindicta Salvatoris*," *Archiv* 111 (1903): 285–98 and 112 (1904): 24–45. On the source, see Phyllis Moe, "Titus and Vespasian: A Study of Two Manuscripts" (Ph.D. diss., New York University, 1963), 54. For a study and comparison with the alliterative poem, see Bonnie Millar, *The Siege of Jerusalem in its Physical, Literary and Historical Contexts* (Dublin: Four Courts Press, 2000), 106–22; on its manuscripts, 127–37.

[89] For a discussion of sources including a summary earlier research, see Millar, *The Siege of Jerusalem*, 112–16.

[90] Auvo Kurvinen, *The Siege of Jerusalem in Prose*, Mémoires de la Société Néophilologique de Helsinki 34 (Helsinki: Société Néophilologique, 1969), 9, 27.

[91] Ralph Hanna and David Lawton, eds., *The Siege of Jerusalem*, EETS 320 (Oxford: Oxford University Press, 2003); Michael Livingston, ed., *Siege of Jerusalem* (Kalamazoo: Medieval Institute Publications, 2004). On sources, see Livingston, *Siege*, 21–30 and Millar, *Siege*, 42–75. For the French source, see Ford, *Vengeance* (1993), Family F, *Bible en français* of Roger of Argenteuil, 74–138; for a ME version, see Phyllis Moe, ed., *The ME Prose Translation of Roger d'Argenteuil's Bible en français* (Heidelberg: Winter, 1977); see also eadem, "The French Source of the Alliterative *Siege of Jerusalem*," *Medium Aevum* 39 (1970): 147–54. For a study, in addition to Millar, see Roger Nicholson, "Haunted Itineraries: Reading the *Siege of Jerusalem*," *Exemplaria* 14 (2002): 447–84.

[92] Livingston, *Siege of Jerusalem*, 13–21, 30–36.

5) Little St. Hugh of Lincoln

The next text in the volume suggests, unhappily, that there were not only medieval audiences for stories such as the *Vengeance of Our Lord*, but enactments of their implicit message. With the ballad of *Hugues de Lincoln* we move from the realm of fiction to that of history. In 1255 in the city of Lincoln, the body of a child who had been missing for a month was found in a well in the city, and was then buried in a shrine in the cathedral. One of the city's Jews confessed to the crime and named his accomplices; on the strength of that testimony, nineteen of Lincoln's Jewish inhabitants were executed.[93] Contemporary witnesses to the incident include a chronicle account by Matthew Paris[94] and the poem in the French of England, *Hugues de Lincoln*, translated here as *Little St. Hugh*. Several English and Scottish ballads also deal with the matter.[95]

Little St. Hugh presents a lurid tale of child-murder and ritual desecration that both reflected and inflamed anti-Jewish sentiment in thirteenth-century Lincoln. Since it refers to King Henry III as living (v. 52), it was presumably written before 1272, hence within two decades of the event. Not only is it the earliest witness to the incident, but it contains more local detail than any other account.[96] It is alone in naming as the abductor a certain "Peitevin" who was actually a prominent Jew in Lincoln.[97] Similarly, the Jewish quarter of Lincoln is identified as "Dernestal" (v. 6), and the execution site, "Canevic" (v. 366), refers to a hill outside the city.[98] Given these specific references, the poem probably reflects the version of the story current in Lincoln itself. It is also striking that Matthew Paris' account is very close to it.

---

[93] On the event and associated texts, see Gavin Langmuir, "The Knight's Tale and Young Hugh of Lincoln," *Speculum* 47 (1972): 459–82. On the A-N poem, see Dean with Boulton, no. 531.

[94] This account is cited in Latin in Francisque Michel, *Hugues de Lincoln: recueil de ballades anglo-normandes et écossoises. . .* (Paris: Silvestre, 1834), 28–30; there is an English translation in Joseph Jacobs, "Little St. Hugh of Lincoln: Researches in History, Archaeology, and Legend," first publ. 1896, repr. in *The Blood Libel Legend: A Casebook in Anti-Semitic Folklore*, ed. Alan Dundes (Madison: University of Wisconsin Press, 1991), 41–71, at 43–46.

[95] Although these ballads may represent older traditions, none was collected before the early nineteenth century: see Francis James Child, *The English and Scottish Popular Ballads*, vol. 3 (New York: Cooper Square, 1962), 233–54.

[96] Michel, *Hugues de Lincoln*; Ferdinand Wolf, *Ueber die Lais Sequenzen und Leiche* (Heidelberg: Winter, 1841), 443–53. An examination of the MS. shows that the edition is generally reliable; the errors that I have found are noted in the translation. Prof. Roger Dahood at the University of Arizona is preparing an edition forthcoming in *Chaucer Review* 49 (2014); I am grateful to him for sharing his material before publication.

[97] See Langmuir, "The Knight's Tale," 466.

[98] Michel, *Hugues de Lincoln*, 60–63, notes 2 and 27.

Whether a case of accidental child death provided an occasion for the accusation of ritual murder dealt with in the ballad, and however historical the existence of a particular child called Hugh may be, the poem presents a martyrdom at once highly localized and simultaneously modeled on the Passion of Christ.[99] Hugh is kidnapped, condemned to death by an assembly of English Jews, and sold for thirty pennies to one of their number, who nails him to a cross before piercing his heart with a knife (v. 125). Lest anyone miss the similarities, the text insists that Hugh's execution was a conscious imitation of that meted out to Jesus (v. 76).[100] In a burlesque form of Eucharist, the assembled Jews eat the dead child's heart before trying to hide the corpse. The repeated reappearances of the body, after it has been buried (v. 141), hidden in a privy (v. 159), and finally placed in a well (v. 183), are a macabre echo of Christ's appearances to his disciples, but they also illustrate the proverb "murder will out." The second half of the poem is devoted to the aftermath of the crime: first Hugh's sainthood is established by a miracle and his body buried in the cathedral; then one of the perpetrators confesses to the crime and is condemned by a council of the Jews of Lincoln.

The emotional tone of the poem is heightened by repeated insistence on the child's youth and innocence as well as on his fear—the boy trembles, is afraid, and calls for his mother. This pathetic quality is balanced by assertions of Hugh's sanctity: he prays to Jesus as he is killed, his soul is escorted to heaven by angels, and a blind woman who touches his body is miraculously cured. As if the attribution of the gratuitous murder of an innocent child to a group of Jews were not serious enough, the text further inflames anti-Jewish sentiment. The act is portrayed not as the work of an evil individual, but as the result of collective decision and action by "the Jews of Lincoln." In the confession at the end of the text (vv. 318–24), the guilt is spread further to implicate all of English Jewry.

In this short poem's admixture of piety and virulent propaganda, elements of the life of Christ are luridly exploited to focus hostile attention on a minority group: the Jews of both Lincoln and all of England. They are portrayed not only as the descendants of the enemies of Jesus Christ, but also as their eager imitators. In such a text, the anti-Jewish current latent in some of the gospel accounts is modernized and appropriated to a new time and place, showing a new Jewish population to be guilty of the same crimes, and thus worthy of the same persecutions as their ancestors who lived more than a millennium earlier.

In its versification, *St. Hugh* is similar to the *Childhood of Jesus*. The poem is written in monorhymed quatrains, with some irregularities: one stanza (vv. 53–55) has only three lines, while another (vv. 344–48) has five. The meter exhibits to a greater than usual degree the flexibility typical of Anglo-Norman verse.

---

[99] For a fifteenth-century analogue, see S. Bowd and J. D. Cullington, *"On Everyone's Lips": Humanists, Jews, and the Tale of Simon of Trent*, MRTS 418 (Tempe: ACMRS, 2012).

[100] The references to Christ are repeated at vv. 84, 108, 324, 328.

Although the poet perhaps aimed at octosyllables, the syllable count varies (by Continental rules) from as few as six (in one instance) to as many as twelve. Variation may derive from the influence of English and Latin prosody.[101] Similarly, the need for four rhymes in a row leads to a certain license in spelling, often in the service of providing eye-rhymes. Examples include final –e: the scribe drops it at the end of *vie, mie* (vv. 46, 48), and *vue* (v. 262) to match the other rhyme words, but adds it to *Henri* and *merci* (vv. 49, 52). (In another instance, however, correctly spelled *esglise* (v. 272) rhymes with words lacking a final *e*.)

Manuscript

The poem is preserved in a single manuscript (Paris, MS BnF, fr. 902) made in England in the second half of the thirteenth century. The script is a neat *textura*, and the decoration is confined to simple red initials and paraph marks. Other than the orthographical evidence of its country of origin, the manuscript contains little to suggest its provenance, although the addition in a later hand of a Latin prose account of a vision that occurred in a Cistercian convent in 1347 suggests that it might have belonged to such a house in the fourteenth century, and indeed the austerity of its decoration is consistent with the hypothesis of Cistercian origin. The volume is a collection of religious texts in the French of England, most of English origin, including a poem on the Old Testament, the play *La Seinte Resureccion*, Grosseteste's *Chasteau d'amour*, *Le Petit sermon*, a group of saints' lives (George, Nicholas, Thomas Becket, Hugh of Lincoln), Guillaume le Clerc's *Bestiaire divin*, and a paraphrase of Psalm 45 (44) *Eructavit*. It is worth noting that *Little St. Hugh*'s ballad style is not typical of the rest of the anthology. Indeed, as we saw above (p. 10), BnF, fr. 902's copy of the *Castle of Love* is provided with extensive marginalia in Latin indicating the content and sources of the poem; such apparatus suggests that one part of the book was prepared for study, while the other texts may have served as pious reading for people of some cultivation. The fact that texts of such different tone and style were compiled into a single anthology illustrates vividly the wide range of piety in medieval England.

Influence

This gruesome story survives in various ballad versions in both England and Scotland, where it is known as "Sir Hugh," "Hugh of Lincoln," or "The Jew's Daughter." Some eighteen different versions were collected in the nineteenth century, although they may be much older.[102] These songs are all much shorter than the Anglo-Norman poem, and they abandon the realm of historical event

---

[101] For a helpful discussion of A-N versification, see Jeffrey and Levy, *The Anglo-Norman Lyric*, 17–27; also Fenster and Wogan-Browne, *Edward*, 32–33 and Fenster and Wogan-Browne, *Alban*, 44–48.

[102] Several of these are printed by Michel, *Hugues de Lincoln*, 18–20, 22–24, 34–37, 39–42, 43–48. The fullest collection is in Child's *English and Scottish Ballads*, no. 155.

for that of folklore. While some versions name the city as "Linkin", in others it is deformed to "Mirry-land toune." The victim has risen in social class: instead of simply "Huchon," a child of the city, as he is in French, the English ballads sing of "Sir Hugh" and his formerly nameless mother is variously called "Lady Helen" or "Lady Maisry." The ballad tradition also transforms the crime. Instead of a ritual murder by a group of important Jews, the gratuitous murder is performed by the "Jew's daughter" who stabs the child and covers him in lead before casting his body in a well. The martyrdom with its allusions to the Passion is gone; all that remains is the conviction of wanton and unmotivated Jewish malice.[103]

6) Passion Meditations and Prayers

The final group of texts, all related to Christ's Passion, represents a major current in Anglo-Norman religious literature. Christians in the later Middle Ages expressed their engagement with the Passion in painting, in the celebration of the feast of Corpus Christi, and in Eucharistic devotion, as well as in a wealth of written texts including sermons, prayers, poems, hymns, meditations, and devotional readings. In all of these forms, there is a striking insistence on stimulating an intense emotional response to the sufferings of Christ, a type of devotion usually characterized as "affective."[104] This emotional response seeks "to create a very direct and personal relationship with the crucified Christ, in appreciation of the intensity of the suffering he had endured, and of the value of the redemption bought with his blood."[105] As Eamon Duffy observes, "Emphasis on the suffering humanity of Jesus gave medieval men and women confidence to see in him a

---

[103] For a study of the ballads, see Brian Bebbington, "Little Sir Hugh: An Analysis," *UNISA English Studies* (Journal of the Department of English, University of South Africa) 9.3 (Sept. 1971): 30–36; repr. in *The Blood Libel Legend: A Casebook in Anti-Semitic Folklore*, ed. Dundes, 72–90.

[104] For a concise introduction to the characteristics and the major texts of affective devotion, see James Marrow, *Passion Iconography in Northern European Art in the Late Middle Ages and Early Renaissance: A Study of the Transformation of Sacred Metaphor into Descriptive Narrative* (Kortrijk: Van Ghemmert, 1979), 1–27. See also Thomas H. Bestul, *Texts of the Passion: Latin Devotional Literature and Medieval Society* (Philadelphia: University of Pennsylvania Press, 1996), 65–67 on English texts; and Sarah McNamer, *Affective Meditation and the Invention of Medieval Compassion* (Philadelphia: University of Pennsylvania Press, 2010).

[105] R. N. Swanson, "Passion and Practice: The Social and Ecclesiastical Implications of Passion Devotion in the Late Middle Ages," in *The Broken Body: Passion Devotion in Late Medieval Culture*, ed. A. A. MacDonald, H. N. B. Ridderbos, and R. M. Schlusemann (Groningen: Egbert Forsten, 1998), 1–30, at 14.

loving brother, and to claim from him the rights of kin."[106] The small sample included here, drawn from three manuscripts, is intended to exemplify a devotion also evident in many other Anglo-Norman texts.[107] The texts translated here had a fairly restricted circulation, some surviving in single copies, others in two or four. But the large number of such texts suggests that common traditions of devotional meditation were often customized for particular individuals or groups. These examples illustrate a major current in Insular (as well as Continental) piety, and there are many similar texts in Middle English even if it is often difficult to trace precise influences.[108]

6a) Seven-Part Meditation on the Passion, in prose (Dublin, Trinity College, MS 374)

A manuscript from Dublin (Trinity College, MS 374) provides two very different meditations on the Passion: a set of seven meditations in prose (henceforth *Seven-Part Meditation*) and a verse meditation (*Meditation on the Cross*).[109] The Dublin manuscript, copied in the second half of the thirteenth century, is the oldest of those extant for any of the meditations presented in this section. The long *Seven-Part Meditation* in prose (untitled in all copies) treats various aspects of the Passion and related themes in seven relatively independent parts, and is apparently designed for people in religious orders. The *Meditation on the Cross* is a much shorter text in verse that gives instructions to lay people for meditating before a crucifix, very different from the treatment of the same subject in the longer prose meditation.

The opening sections of the *Seven-Part Meditation* deal explicitly with the Passion. The person praying addresses Jesus in recognition that his sufferings were done for "me," before turning to God the Father, drawing attention to the dreadful wounds suffered by his Son: then the devotee reflects on the gravity of his own sins which required such reparation. In the second section, the devotee responds to Jesus's listing of the steps necessary for forgiveness. While the reader is made to feel guilty for Christ's sufferings, he is also reassured that forgiveness is eminently possible. In contrast to other meditative texts, there is more appeal to reasoned argument than to the emotions. The third section introduces a new theme, the power of the name of Jesus, and then considers Christ's Agony in the

---

[106] Eamon Duffy, *The Stripping of the Altars: Traditional Religion in England 1400–1580* (New Haven and London: Yale University Press, 1992), 236.

[107] E.g., Dean with Boulton, nos. 861, 888, 889, 915, 916, 942, 947, 955, 956, 958, 961, 963, 966, 971, 972, 976, 980, 981, 984.

[108] For Middle English examples see *A New Index of Middle English Verse*, ed. Julia Boffey and A.S.G. Edwards (London: British Library, 2005); Linne R. Mooney, ed., *The Digital Index of Middle English Verse* (DIMEV): http://www.cddc.vt.edu/host/imev/

[109] Dean with Boulton, nos. 942, 981.

Garden before his arrest. The Passion theme is treated through a meditation on the five wounds in the fourth section, and another on the crucifix in the fifth. Christ's wounds are portrayed as resulting from the devotee's five senses and the sins committed with them. As in Grosseteste's *Chasteau d'amour*, there is a reminder of the human as slave and rightful property of God. The meditation on the crucifix assumes a material or visual crucifix before which the devotee meditates—whether three-dimensional in a church (*a muster*) or an image in a prayer book (*en vostre livere peint*, f. 41[r1])—evoking the figures of St. John, Mary, and the crucified Christ. It then arranges them in hierarchical order and entreats each one's intercession with the next, with Christ finally pleading with his Father on the sinner's behalf. At the end of the fifth meditation there is a section on the power of the name of Mary, and her importance as an example and guide, the "Star of the Sea." The sixth meditation examines the role of the two guardians—fear of hell and love of God—in achieving salvation. The entire meditation closes, in the final section, with an invocation of the Holy Spirit, and a plea for mercy cast in rhyming couplets.

There are four surviving copies of the *Seven-Part Meditation*, of which the Dublin manuscript is the fullest,[110] and, as noted above, the earliest extant, with its dating to the second half of the thirteenth century. In this manuscript, the *Seven-Part Meditation* and the verse *Meditation on the Cross* (see 6b below) are part of a larger religious anthology comprising the New Testament section of Herman de Valenciennes' *Bible*, a mystical poem, a prose version of the *Our Father*, treatises on the Pains of Hell and on Penance, two other verse meditations on the Passion and Crucifix, a sermon, and a lament of the Virgin.[111] One of the striking features of this collection is the incorporation of the extract from Herman's versified *Bible*, which occupies nearly the whole of the first half of the volume. The Dublin manuscript is unique in selecting such a long portion of Herman's text: other anthologies either extract the Passion section alone, or choose the Assumption (which the Dublin scribe did not include).[112] Given the devotional character of most of the other texts, the extract from the *Bible* seems to complement them by supplying a narrative account of the life of Christ. The opening piece provides, as it were, a vernacular substitute for one or more gospels.

---

[110] The Dublin manuscript lacks the Prologue, which I have supplied from London, BL, Arundel MS 288.

[111] Dean with Boulton, nos. 485, 618, 845, 672, 961, 981, 651, 955. Three of these, "On Penance," "Three Vows," and "Mary's Lament," are included in Hunt et al., "*Cher alme*"; see 74 for a description of the manuscript.

[112] London, BL, MS Harley MS 2253, for example, inserts Herman's Passion between the *Vies des Pères* and the *Évangile de Nicodème*. On the transmission of Herman's poem, see M. Boulton, "La 'Bible' d'Herman de Valenciennes: texte inconstant, texte perméable," in *Mouvance et jointures: Du manuscrit au texte médiéval* (Orléans: Paradigme, 2005), 87–98.

In its Dublin form, sections of the *Seven-Part Meditation* seem originally intended for a male reader, who is invoked as "brother" and invited to supply his own name to personalize the prayers. That this male reader was a member of a religious order is suggested by a couple of references to the "rule" of religious life. At other points, however, a much broader (or vaguer) readership is suggested by the phrase "whether you may be man or woman, religious or lay" (*quelkeunkes seez home ou femme ou en religion ou hors de religion...*, f. 42^{r2}). There are occasional references in the text to "ordinary people" (*simple gent*), from whom the reader is distinguished at these points. Similarly the presence of Latin quotations, some untranslated, suggests that the intended readership was masculine and in a religious order.[113] But once again, the final meditation, which recommends the recitation of a Latin prayer to the Holy Spirit, also allows those who do not know it to substitute *Pater Noster*s and *Ave*s.[114] The accumulation of contradictory evidence opens the possibility that the meditation was originally intended for monks, but that at least some of the meditations were adapted for nuns or laypeople. The inclusion of the verse *Bible* might have been intended for people without the ability to read the gospels in Latin elsewhere.

The remaining copies of the *Seven-Part Meditation on the Passion* are all fragmentary. The context provided for it in the early fourteenth-century Cotton manuscript (London, BL, Cotton Vitellius MS F.VII) is quite different. This extremely important volume contains the only extant copy of one of the two Anglo-Norman versions of *Ancrene Wisse (Guide for Anchoresses)*, a treatise on Purgatory, Heaven, and Hell, Rolle's *De XII utilitatibus tribulationis,* and the *Pasturel Gregoire* (a partial translation of Gregory the Great's *Cura Pastoralis*).[115] In its current, damaged condition, the manuscript transmits only the first four sections of the Meditation, but its table of contents (in a contemporary hand) states that it contains seven chapters, like the Dublin copy. The Cotton scribe added a prologue with an indication of sources and instructions for using the meditations, explaining that it is not necessary to read the entire set each time, but that the reader should choose what appeals most.[116] Like the Dublin version, the Cotton text was initially directed toward a male reader, and the pronouns of its prologue

---

[113] Other parts of the anthology support this interpretation, for the Sermon on Romans 12:1 is also addressed to male religious: ed. Hunt, "*Cher alme*," 345.

[114] Cf. J. A. Herbert, ed., *The French Text of the Ancrene Riwle* (London: EETS, 1944), 32, ll. 31–34.

[115] Dean with Boulton, nos. 643, 646, 648, 674; for a description, see Herbert, *Ancrene Riwle*, ix-xiii; it is very difficult to read because much of the parchment has become transparent, and the ink shows through from the other side of the leaf.

[116] The prologue derives from the Preface to Anselm of Canterbury's *Prayers and Meditations*, ed. F. S. Schmitt, *Anselmi opera omnia*, 6 vols. (Edinburgh: Nelson, 1946–61), 3:3; for the Middle English version see Jocelyn Wogan-Browne et al., *The Idea of the Vernacular: An Anthology of Middle English Literary Theory, 1280–1520* (University Park,

are masculine. Nevertheless, the presence of the *Ancrene Wisse*, in its early versions a work clearly aimed at female recluses, suggests that the meditation was used by women as well as men. London, Lambeth Palace MS 182, from the middle of the fourteenth century, transmits only the final third of the work (from the end of part IV), and contains no information as to intended readership.[117] The fourth manuscript (London, BL, Arundel MS 288), although the shortest, contributes its own evidence as to the audiences of the *Seven-Part Meditation*. The fragment, consisting of the Prologue and the first prayer, was added in the second half of the fourteenth century in a separate gathering at the beginning of a book written nearly a century earlier.[118] In contrast to the Cotton manuscript, the Arundel prologue uses feminine pronouns to indicate the reader. Although the evidence here is slight, it does suggest that the readership for meditations of this kind was varied and shifting.

The Cotton Prologue cites as authorities Augustine, Anselm of Canterbury, and Bernard of Clairvaux—among the most popular, not to say ubiquitous, Latin authors of the Middle Ages. Alexandra Barratt, the only scholar to have examined this text, has identified some of the Meditation's sources, which are, indeed, the very ones identified in the Cotton manuscript.[119] In addition to the Anselmian prologue, it is possible to identify if not sources then analogues of other sections of the *Seven-Part Meditation*. Much of the meditation on the name of Jesus relies on Bernard of Clairvaux's Sermon 15 on the *Song of Songs*, "How the Name of Jesus is Medicine in All Adversities."[120] The meditation on the crucifix in the fifth part, with its invocation of Mary and John as witnesses of the Crucifixion, echoes parts of the "O Intemerata," a prayer dating from Carolingian times and later included in most books of hours.[121]

PA: Pennsylvania State University Press, 1999), 212–13; see 224–26 for a similar prologue used to introduce the Middle English version of the *Pseudo-Augustinian Soliloquies*.

[117] It contains the Pater Noster in prose, the "Pains of Hell," a Passion meditation, and "On Penance": see Dean with Boulton, nos. 845, 647, 961 and 672; cf. Hunt, "*Cher alme*," 294–319.

[118] The manuscript also contains the *Manuel des péchés* and *Mirur de sainte eglise*, the "Pains of Purgatory," and four sermons (including a version of *Admonicio valde salubris de alimosina*, attributed to Rolle): Dean with Boulton, nos. 635, 629, 645, 636, 617, 715, 691, 616. Hunt, "*Cher alme*", 393–421 has edited the "Pains of Purgatory," attributed to Grosseteste.

[119] Alexandra Barratt, "Dame Eleanor of Hull: The Translator at Work," *Medium Aevum* 72 (2003): 277–96, at 281–83. Specific references are indicated in the translation itself.

[120] Ed. *PL* 183, cols. 843–848 (esp. 846).

[121] For an English translation, see Roger Wieck, *The Book of Hours in Medieval Art and Life* (London: Sotheby's, 1988), 164; for a discussion and Latin versions see André Wilmart, *Auteurs spirituels et textes dévots du moyen âge latin: Etudes d'histoire littéraire* (Paris: Etudes Augustiniennes, 1932; repr. 1971), 474–504.

While it is usually difficult to trace specific influences among such hugely popular subjects as Passion meditations, Eleanor Hull made a partial translation into English of the *Seven-Part Meditation* in the fifteenth century.[122] She translated the Prologue, parts I-III, and the portion on the name of Mary from part V, incorporating them into a much larger whole. In the sections where she relied on the Anglo-Norman text, Eleanor was generally faithful to her source, even as she adapted it to a new context.[123]

The *Seven-Part Meditation* participates in the devotional tradition dependent ultimately on Latin texts like the *Libellus de scripturis et verbis patrum collectus* of John of Fécamp (long attributed to Augustine), the *Soliloquia* also attributed to Augustine,[124] and the *Meditationes piissimae de cognitione humanae conditionis* attributed to Bernard of Clairvaux.[125] Scholars have traced the evolution of this affective tradition and its vernacular (particularly English and German) offshoots.[126] Several Middle English devotional texts share the preoccupations of the *Seven-Part Meditation*, even if they are unlikely to have been directly influenced by it. For example, Richard Rolle's *Meditation A*, although it includes much gruesome detail absent from the French text, promotes examination of conscience, repentance, and confession in similar ways.[127] Certain of the Dublin meditation's descriptive details of the dying body of Christ, such as his flesh drying on the Cross, also appear in the Short Text of Julian of Norwich's *Revelations*, and especially in the long version.[128] Although I have not identified exact parallels with the meditation on the crucifix, images of the Passion, whether

---

[122] The text has been edited by Sheila Cornard, "Dame Eleanor Hull's 'Meditacyons upon the VII Dayes of the Woke': The First Edition of the Middle English Translation in Cambridge University Library MS. Kk.i.6" (Ph.D. diss., University of Dayton, 1995). For extracts see *Women's Writing in Middle English*, ed. Alexandra Barratt (London: Longman, 1992), 223–31.

[123] Barratt, "Dame Eleanor" discusses the translation in some detail.

[124] *PL* 40, cols. 898–942 and cols. 863–98.

[125] *PL* 184, cols. 485–508. For Continental vernacular versions of the *Soliloquia*, see Geneviève Hasenohr-Esnos, "Les Traductions médiévales françaises et italiennes des *Soliloques* attribués à saint Augustin," *Mélanges d'archéologie et d'histoire* 79 (1967): 299–370.

[126] See Rachel Fulton, *From Judgment to Passion: Devotion to Christ and the Virgin, 800–1200* (New York: Columbia University Press, 2002); also McNamer, *Affective Meditation*.

[127] Alexandra Barratt, "*Stabant matres dolorosae*: Women as Readers and Writers of Passion Prayers, Meditations and Visions," in *The Broken Body: Passion Devotion in Late-Medieval Culture*, ed. MacDonald et al., 55–71, at 57.

[128] See *A Book of Showings to the Anchoress Julian of Norwich*, ed. Edmund Colledge and James Walsh, 2 vols. (Toronto: Pontifical Institute of Mediaeval Studies, 1978), chapter 16 Revelation 8: "The Short Text," ll. 9–14 (1:233–34) and especially "The Long Text," ll. 9–14 (2:357–59).

material crucifixes or images in books, were an important theme in Middle English devotion.[129] Both Julian of Norwich and Margery Kemp attribute some of their visions to the impetus provided by the sight of the crucifix.[130]

The Dublin manuscript also contains, as noted above, a *Meditation on the Cross* (no. 6b here), a poem of 308 lines in octosyllabic couplets. It opens with an invitation to the reader to pay careful attention to the crucifix. The next section (vv. 17–120) addresses the reader in the voice of Jesus Christ, encouraging examination of the image of his Passion. In the remainder of the poem, the preacher offers further reflections and draws lessons from the meditation before commenting in the final lines that this form of meditation is effective in reaching ordinary people. The Dublin version includes a passage (omitted in the Cambridge copy) in which Christ addresses in turn "brother," "sister," "wife," suggesting that the poem was intended for a very broad audience. In contrast to the prose meditation, there are no Latin references. On the contrary the preacher-narrator resorts to explaining fairly basic allusions—listing the four elements, for example—and allegorizing the shape of the cross.

Although the *Meditation on the Cross* is more dramatic than the crucifix section of the *Seven-Part Meditation*, especially in its use of the voice of the crucified Christ to instruct the reader or listener, many of its lessons are similar. The text emphasizes that the Passion was necessary for the sinner's redemption, and caused by his or her sins. It also stresses God's love for sinners, urging them to love Him in return and to "bind your body by obedience, crucify it by patience, persevere to the end" so as to win personal salvation and heavenly reward. In his commentary, the preacher allegorizes the cross, whose upright shaft links both heaven and earth, while its cross-piece extends to embrace everyone. The arms of the cross offer a hiding place that shelters the penitent from the devil and his snares.

In addition to the Dublin manuscript, there is a partial copy of the poem in Cambridge, Emmanuel College, MS 106, a devotional and didactic anthology with texts in Latin and English as well as French. Compiled in the middle of the fourteenth century, this small volume has been described as "a friar's handbook,"[131] with a variety of liturgical texts, prayers, and narratives. Its version

---

[129] See the useful survey by Vincent Gillespie, "Strange Images of Death: The Passion in Later Medieval English Devotional and Mystical Writing," in *Zeit, Tod und Ewigkeit in der Renaissance Literatur*, Analecta Carthusiana 117 (Salzburg: Institut für Anglistik und Amerikanistik, Universität Salzburg, 1986), 111–59; he characterizes this type of meditation as a *lectio domini*, rather than a *lectio divina* or meditation on a sacred text.

[130] See William F. Hodapp, "Sacred Time and Space Within: Drama and Ritual in Late Medieval Affective Passion Meditations," *Downside Review* 115 (1997): 235–48, at 241–42.

[131] Felicity Riddy, "Mother Knows Best: Reading Social Change in a Courtesy Text," *Speculum* 71 (1996): 66–86, at 70.

of the *Meditation on the Cross* omits the preacher's parts, preserving only the section spoken by Jesus himself. As it stands, the extract is a devotional aid rather than a sermon.

6c-e The Lambeth Meditation and Prayer on the Wounds of Christ and Three Prayers by the Crucifixion (Lambeth Palace Libr., MS 522)

Devotion to the wounds inflicted on Jesus is a specialized form of Passion meditation, and was extremely popular in England in the later Middle Ages.[132] Although disconcerting, even repugnant, to modern sensibility, the vivid and sensual aspects of this devotion were nonetheless quite traditional. This kind of devotion is firmly within the tradition of St. Bernard,[133] and indeed recalls Christ's words to Thomas after the resurrection: "Put in thy finger hither and see my hands; and bring hither thy hand and put it into my side; and be not faithless but believing."[134]

The *Meditation on the Wounds of Christ* (no. 6c) is a brief spiritual exercise designed for a member of a religious order.[135] The meditation proper opens with the recitation of a verse from a psalm (unspecified) before a crucifix, and continues with additional verses for the wound, the wood of the cross, the nail, and the blood; beginning with one hand, the exercise continues with the other wounds.[136] The text then evokes the wounds again, beginning with the feet, but here the instructions are considerably more vivid. The cleric is to recreate in his imagination the body of the crucified Christ, then to kiss—even to lick—each wound, smearing himself with the blood of the Savior. The text concludes with a short examination of conscience, reminding the reader that a member of a religious order is held to a higher standard than others. He is urged to imagine Christ as his companion in the activities of the day.

In addition to the *Meditation on the Wounds* and other religious texts (such as the *Castle of Love*), the Lambeth 522 manuscript includes a number of prayers. Four of these are related to Christ's Passion and are also translated here as texts 6d

---

[132] Duffy, *Stripping of the Altars*, 238.

[133] Cf. R. N. Swanson, *Religion and Devotion in Europe, c. 1215-c. 1515* (Cambridge: Cambridge University Press, 1995), 181; and idem, *Catholic England: Faith, Religion and Observance Before the Reformation* (Manchester: Manchester University Press, 1993), 130.

[134] John 20:27.

[135] Dean with Boulton, no. 962.

[136] On devotion to the crucifix, see Louis Gougaud, *Devotional and Ascetic Practices in the Middle Ages* (London: Burns, Oates and Washbourne, 1927), 78–80.

and 6e. The short verse *Prayer by the Wounds of Christ* (6d)[137] evokes the wounds in Christ's body, but uses them to organize a series of petitions for the speaker to be preserved from the sins associated with them. Elsewhere in the manuscript is a group of three prose prayers related to the Crucifixion (6e).[138] The first of these differs from the other texts presented here, in both content and theology. It is to be said during Mass, and mentions Jesus's death before requesting forgiveness for sins and protection from enemies and ill-fortune (including sudden death). The association this prayer makes between the Mass and the Crucifixion serves as a useful reminder that according to Catholic doctrine, Christ's sacrifice and death are repeated in every Mass, so as to transmit the benefits of that death.[139] The prayer also reminds us that the recipient of Holy Communion consumes Christ's body and blood. In the manuscript, the prayer is followed immediately by a simple petition to Christ on behalf of all one's friends and benefactors whose names can be inserted; in this way the reader is encouraged to broaden his concern to the welfare of others (although not, apparently, to his enemies). The last prayer of the group professes adoration of Jesus Christ while mentioning specific moments in the act of salvation and interspersing *Pater noster*s and *Ave Maria*s: as he was crucified and wounded, when he died, descended into Hell, and rose again, and finally when he will come for the Last Judgment.

The Lambeth 522 manuscript contains the only copy of each of 6c (the *Meditation on the Wounds of Christ*), 6d (the *Prayer by the Wounds*), and 6e (the *Prayers by the Crucifixion*). The manuscript, which dates to about 1300, is a large collection of religious literature in French that came originally from the Benedictine abbey of St. Augustine's in Canterbury, although it seems to have been intended for an audience beyond the abbey.[140] Each major text is preceded by an

---

[137] Dean with Boulton, no. 904. The prayer is copied twice in the MS: f. 83^{r-v}, repeated at ff. 200^v-201^r with only minor spelling variants.

[138] Dean with Boulton, no. 980, ff. 196^v-199^r. Several poems from the Lambeth MS are published in Jeffrey and Levy, *The Anglo-Norman Lyric*, including three further pieces related to the Passion or the Cross (nos. 10 [Dean with Boulton, no. 973], 12 [no. 914], 14 [no. 969], 35 [no. 967].

[139] Joseph Pohle, "Sacrifice of the Mass," in *The Catholic Encyclopedia*, Vol. 10 (New York: Robert Appleton Company, 1911), accessed 6 Jun. 2012, www.newadvent.org/cathen/10006a.htm, especially the section "The Physical Character of the Mass." See E. M. Willingham and D. J. Kennedy, "Eucharist," *ODMA* 2:593–94.

[140] John Frankis, "The Social Context of Vernacular Writing in Thirteenth Century England: The Evidence of the Manuscripts," *Thirteenth Century England* 1 (1986): 175–84; he observes (177): "use of French for religious literature is a long-recognized aspect of English monasticism." On writing in A-N in English religious houses, see M. Dominica Legge, *Anglo-Norman in the Cloisters* (Edinburgh: Edinburgh University Press, 1950), 48: "Latin and French were not rivals but partners." For recent work on the French texts of English monasteries see Jean-Pascal Pouzet, "Augustinian Canons and their Insular French Books in Medieval England: Towards an Assessment," *in Language and Culture*

illustration depicting an aspect of religious life: figures thus shown in contemplation (often prostrate before the cross) are usually Benedictine monks, but several illustrations show preachers, either friars (two Dominicans and two Franciscans) or a bishop, addressing a group of listeners.[141]

As we saw above (p. 9), the Lambeth manuscript opens with Grosseteste's *Castle of Love*. The next section contains a series of meditations, an extract from St. Edmund of Abingdon's *Mirror of the Holy Church* (*Mirour de sainte eglise*), the *Meditation on the Wounds* given here (6c), and a short verse "Hours of the Cross."[142] The other long pieces—a verse translation of the *Gospel of Nicodemus*, sermons on the transitory nature of life, on sin, the last judgment, a sermon by Nicholas Bozon, a treatise on confession as well as a formula for confession—are punctuated by groups of prayers in verse and prose to the Blessed Virgin and to Jesus Christ.[143] One puzzling aspect of the book is that most of these prayers were copied twice by the scribe, who seems to have worked alone: the repetitions are too frequent to have been oversights. Yet the placement of the prayers in the volume may suggest an explanation. The prayers occur in five groups, each following one or more longer didactic, narrative, or homiletic texts. In this way they divide the contents of the book into five parts, each consisting of a pious reading to be followed by prayers to the Virgin and Christ. The reader of the book could thus move effortlessly from instruction or edification to a personal pious response.

The *Meditation on the Wounds of Christ* represents a particular type of Passion devotion.[144] Obviously related to meditations on the Passion, the text directs the reader's thoughts in turn to the five major wounds inflicted on Christ's body, those in his hands and feet from being nailed to the cross, and the one in his side from the soldier's lance. Here again it is difficult to identify a specific source, although the practice of meditating on the wounds probably derives from Bernard of Clairvaux, particularly *Sermon lxi on Canticles*, which urges the listener to meditate continually on the wounds of Christ, and indeed to enter into them.[145]

---

in *Medieval Britain: The French of England c. 1100-c. 1500*, ed. Jocelyn Wogan-Browne et al. (York and Woodbridge: York Medieval Press, 2009), 266–77.

[141] Frankis, "Social Context," 177; for a list of the illustrations, see the description by M. R. James and Claude Jenkins, *A Descriptive Catalogue of Manuscripts in the Library of Lambeth Palace: The Medieval Manuscripts*, vol. 2, part 5 (Cambridge: Cambridge University Press, 1932), 715–23.

[142] Dean with Boulton, nos. 629 (also 959) and 967.

[143] Dean with Boulton, nos. 501, 659, 639, 637, 655, 592, 667. The only exception (no. 935) is one prayer to St. Margaret, ff. 283^r-284^v.

[144] Gougaud, *Devotional and Ascetic Practices*, 80–104.

[145] See Douglas Gray, "The Five Wounds of Our Lord," *Notes and Queries* 208 (1963): 50–51, 82–89, 127–34, 163–68, at 85, 86. Cf. Swanson, *Religion and Devotion*, 181, who cites the fifteenth-century *Book of the Craft of Dying*, which quotes Bernard's exhortation to "Take note and see his head bowed to greet you, his mouth to kiss you, his

The devotion was also popular among Franciscans, influenced by the stigmata (marks of the wounds of the Passion) that St. Francis of Assisi received during a vision in 1224.[146]

Devotion to the wounds of Christ is exemplified in Middle English as well as Anglo-Norman. There are several Middle English lyrics about Christ's wounds,[147] some of which invite the reader/listener to observe the Savior's bloodied body, while others are effectively prayers.[148] Several others differ from the Lambeth meditation and prayers in being spoken by Christ himself, who reminds the reader of the grace and forgiveness that he offers.[149] There is an English prose meditation on the Wounds in Oxford, University College, MS 97.[150] The text allegorizes each wound as a "welle-sprynge" of different qualities: wisdom, mercy, grace, "goostly comfort," and everlasting life, each of which is then examined in detail. The verse meditation on the Passion in Rolle's treatise *Ego Dormio* also concentrates on all of Christ's wounds, including those inflicted by the scourging and the crown of thorns as well as the "Five Wounds."[151] From the fifteenth century, there is William Billyng's stanzaic poem "The Five Wounds of Christ."[152] One of the most famous devotees of the Five Wounds of Christ is

---

arms spread to clasp you, his hands trembling to hold you, his side open to love you, his body stretched taut to give himself wholly to you."

[146] Louis Bouyer, Jean Leclercq, and François Vandenbroucke, *A History of Christian Spirituality, II: The Spirituality of the Middle Ages* (first published in French, Paris, 1961; New York: Seabury Press, 1968), 293: "it was a sign that Francis, by his humility and his suffering, had united himself to the Redeemer." St. Francis was the first known stigmatic.

[147] Carleton Brown and Rossell Hope Robbins, *Index of Middle English Verse* (New York: Columbia University Press, 1943), 784–85. Cf. Gray, "The Five Wounds," 127–34; idem, *Themes and Images in the Medieval Religious Lyric* (London: Routledge and Kegan Paul, 1972), 122–46. For a discussion of the wounds in English prose texts, see Sarah Beckwith, *Christ's Body: Identity, Culture and Society in Late Medieval Writings* (London and New York: Routledge, 1993), esp. 55–63.

[148] Carleton Brown, ed. *Religious Lyrics of the XIVth Century*, rev. ed. (Oxford: Clarendon Press, 1956), nos. 1, 2, 52.

[149] Brown, *Religious Lyrics*, nos. 3, 4, 46, 51, and 127.

[150] C. Horstmann, ed., *Yorkshire Writers: Richard Rolle of Hampole and his Followers*, 2 vols. (London: Sonnenschein, 1895–96; repr. Cambridge: D.S. Brewer, 1989), 2: 440–41, where it is wrongly ascribed to Rolle.

[151] *Yorkshire Writers*, 1:50–61 (esp. 57–59). On this text, see Marion Glasscoe, "Time of Passion: Latent Relationships between Liturgy and Meditation in Two Middle English Mystics," in *Langland, the Mystics, and the Medieval English Religious Tradition: Essays in Honour of S. S. Hussey*, ed. Helen Philips (Cambridge: D. S. Brewer, 1990), 141–60, at 151–54.

[152] William Bateman, ed. [William Billyng], *The Five Wounds of Christ: A Poem: from an Ancient Parchment Roll* (Manchester: R. and W. Dean, 1814); cf. Gray, "The Five Wounds," 164–65.

of course Gawain, of whom the *Pearl* poet says (642–43): "And alle his afyaunce upon folde warz in the fyve woundez Þat Cryst kast on the croys, as the crede tellez."[153] The English meditations, although they are broadly similar in spirit and approach to those in Anglo-Norman, do not depend on French originals and emerge perhaps a half-century later.

6f. The Contemplation of the Passion of Jesus Christ (London, BL, Harley MS 2253)

The *Contemplation on the Passion* (*Contemplacioun de la Passion Jhesu Crist*) is a brief meditation on the Passion organized according to the canonical hours, beginning with Compline and continuing through to Vespers of the following day.[154] Its structure thus follows the chronological sequence of events from Holy Thursday through to the Deposition on Good Friday evening. For each of the hours, the reader is enjoined to thank Jesus Christ for the sufferings undergone at that point in his Passion. In this way, the reader recounts the events of the Passion and his (or her) interlocutor is Christ himself. By giving thanks repeatedly, the reader acknowledges the immense debt owed to the Savior, while the use of the second person supplies the means of establishing a close relationship with Christ. The division of the meditation into seven parts fosters the practice of brief, pious interruptions in the secular day.[155]

The text puts the reader into a dialogue with Christ, thus personalizing the otherwise spare narrative of the events of the Passion and creating an intimate relationship between speaker and listener. Characteristic of the style of the meditation is its intensification of the emotional impact through the accumulation of verbs (*lyé, despoillé, batu, buffeté, escharny*; "bound," "stripped," "struck," "buffeted," "mocked"), and the use of adverbs (*vilement, crueument*; "vilely," "cruelly"). The descriptive details of the narrative (like *tot soul lessé*, "left all alone") that stress the psychological isolation of Christ, as well as the narrative voice and the stylistic features of the meditation, are all designed to provoke an emotional response from the devout reader.[156] In this way, the Harley *Contemplation* reveals itself to be an early example in England of the vogue for affective devotion that becomes increasingly important in the later fourteenth and fifteenth centuries.

In contrast to the *Childhood of Jesus Christ* (no. 3, above), the references to Jews in the Harley *Contemplation* are fairly restrained, particularly given that it deals with the Passion. There are two references to "felouns Gyus," "wicked Jews"

---

[153] *Sir Gawain and the Green Knight*, ed. J. R. R. Tolkien and E. V. Gordon (Oxford: Clarendon Press, 1925; 2nd ed. rev. by Norman Davis, Oxford: Clarendon Press, 1967).

[154] The text has been edited and translated by Hunt et al., "*Cher alme*," 254–61.

[155] For this phenomenon in England, see Glasscoe, "Time of Passion."

[156] Maureen Boulton, "Le Langage de la dévotion affective en moyen français," *Le Moyen Français* 39–41 (1996–97): 53–63.

(f. 139ʳ, Terce and Midday), but no vicious denunciations are added. Nevertheless, the act of crucifixion itself (f. 140ʳ, Nones) is ascribed to the Jews rather than to the Roman soldiers who actually carried it out. In contrast to Grosseteste's presentation of the Passion, which stressed his listener's implication in the event, the *Contemplation* urges the reader to feel Christ's suffering, but implicitly absolves him of responsibility for it.

The *Contemplation of the Passion* is preserved in a single manuscript, Harley 2253, now housed in the British Library in London, and best known for its important collection of Middle English lyrics.[157] The volume as a whole is a trilingual anthology including both religious and secular works in prose and verse composed in two major sections. To a set of religious texts in French copied toward the end of the thirteenth century a later Herefordshire compiler added (c. 1330–40) a miscellany with texts in French, English, and Latin, ranging from Bible stories to racy *fabliaux*.[158] Despite this diversity of content, recent scholars have identified coherent groups of texts, organized by genre or content.[159] Many of the religious texts have a clearly Franciscan character.[160] The *Contemplation* is found near the end of the volume, in a section composed of seven singletons (ff. 134ʳ-140ᵛ) devoted mainly to religious texts in prose in both Latin and French, including a saint's life (St. Wistan, in Latin) as well as prayers. There are also two quite extraneous pieces, though the one that immediately precedes the *Contemplation*—the poem "Against the King's Taxes"—may have been included as a religious piece, since its opening ("Dieu, roy de magesté," "God, king of majesty") sounds like the beginning of a prayer.[161]

---

[157] N. R. Ker, *Facsimile of British Museum MS. Harley 2253*, EETS 255 (London, New York, and Toronto: Oxford University Press, 1965); see also the review by R. J. Dean, *Speculum* 41 (1966): 739–41; and Susanna Fein, ed., *Studies in the Harley Manuscript: The Scribes, Contents and Social Contexts of British Library MS Harley 2253* (Kalamazoo: Medieval Institute Publications, 2000).

[158] On the dating and localization of the manuscript see Carter Revard, "Scribe of MS Harley 2253," *Notes and Queries* 227 (1982): 62–63; and idem, "Scribe and Provenance," in Fein, *Studies in the Harley Manuscript*, 21–109.

[159] Theo Stemmler, "Miscellany or Anthology? The Structure of Medieval Manuscripts: MS Harley 2253, For Example," *Zeitschrift für Anglistik und Amerikanistik* 39 (1991): 231–37; repr. in Fein, *Studies in the Harley Manuscript*, 111–21. Thorlac Turville-Petre, *England the Nation: Language, Literature, and National Identity 1290–1340* (Oxford: Clarendon Press, 1996), 192–217 (esp. 198–203) argues that the scribe paired a number of English and French secular pieces.

[160] David L. Jeffrey, "Authors, Anthologists, and Franciscan Spirituality," in Fein, *Studies in the Harley Manuscript*, 261–70.

[161] Cf. Stemmler, "Miscellany or Anthology," 114; the one verse piece in this section, the translation of the Gloria, is written as prose. The Latin description of the magical properties of heliotrope and celandine that occurs in this otherwise religious context reflects the mingling of practical and literary texts that is also found in commonplace

The final segment of the manuscript contains several sets of instructions encouraging regular prayer before daily activities.[162] On the page preceding this section of the manuscript (f. 133ᵛ), a Latin prayer is prefaced with an explanation that its daily use will assure the remission of one's sins. According to the passage on the next page (f. 134ʳ), thinking of different angels on various occasions (rising, hearing thunder, eating, traveling, and so on) will ensure appropriate good fortune. The same page (f. 134ʳ) also contains a set of fifteen psalms recommended for protection in various situations; while the instructions to recite each one three times are in French, the *incipit*s of the psalms are given in Latin. There are two sets of recommendations in French for having masses said—weekly masses in time of trouble (f. 135), and seven masses in honor of St. Giles (f. 135ᵛ); and two lists (f. 136ᵛ), one in Latin and one in French, of psalms to be said on special occasions. The *Contemplation*, with its instructions for prayers at different times during the day, is thus perfectly consistent with its context.

Although I have not established a precise source for the Harley *Contemplation of the Passion*, it may be noted that there was a long tradition in England of Passion meditation according to the canonical hours, beginning with the *Liber Confortarius* written by Goscelin of Canterbury c. 1080 for a recluse named Eve. Goscelin recommended that each hour be consecrated to the sufferings of Christ, which were greatest between Sext and Nones, when he recommends reciting five psalms in honor of the five wounds.[163] Roughly a century later, the *Ancrene Wisse* gives similar but more specific advice to a female recluse who is advised to say at noon an office consisting of versicles, responses, antiphon, and prayers repeated with each of five short psalms (nos. 99, 122, 124, 130, and 116 of the Vulgate), and five short prayers.[164] Since there are no lessons, only the references to "crux sancta" and the instructions to "think of the cross as much as you can and of his grievous sufferings" associate the liturgical texts with the Passion. In the first half of the thirteenth century, Edmund of Abingdon's *Mirour de seint eglise* recommended a double meditation on the life and passion of Christ, to be conducted

---

books: see Marilyn Corrie, "Harley 2253, Digby 86, and the Circulation of Literature in Pre-Chaucerian England," in Fein, *Studies in the Harley Manuscript*, 427–43, esp. 438.

[162] Edited and translated by Hunt et al., "*Cher alme*," 237–61.

[163] A. Wilmart, "Eve et Goscelin, II," *Revue Bénédictine* 50 (1938): 42–83, esp. 72, 82–83. Cf. Elizabeth Salter, *Nicholas Love's "Myrrour of the Blessed Lyf of Jesu Christ*," Analecta Cartusiana 10 (Salzburg: Institut für englische Sprache und Literatur, 1974), 135–36.

[164] *Ancrene Wisse*, ed. Robert Hasenfratz (Kalamazoo: Medieval Institute Publications, 2000), Part I, ll. 212–231. For the A-N translation, in a manuscript of the early fourteenth century, see Dean with Boulton, no. 643; and Herbert, *Ancrene Riwle*, 23–24.

during the liturgical hours.[165] Similar guidance is given pictorially c. 1240 in the de Brailes Hours (London, B.L., Add. MS 49999), where the Hours of the Virgin (f. 1r) open with a composite miniature of four scenes of the Passion: the Betrayal, the Scourging (with Peter's first denial), the Mocking of Christ (with Peter's second denial), and the Spitting at Christ (with the third denial).[166] Although there is no text (except for explanatory rubrics in the margins), the miniature directs the reader's thoughts toward the Passion at each Hour.

The starting point of the *Contemplation*, however, distinguishes it from other Passion meditations, for it opens with Compline, while the earlier texts all begin with Matins or Lauds, as do the *Hours of the Cross* and other Offices included in Books of Hours.[167] The Pseudo-Bonaventuran *Meditationes Vitae Christi* is often associated with the *Contemplation*,[168] but it too follows the standard organization from Matins to Compline on a single day. As we have seen, the Anglo-Norman meditation adopts a chronological organization, beginning at Compline on Holy Thursday, a structure found in a Latin text known as the *Libellus de Meditatione Passionis Christi per septem diei horas*, attributed to Pseudo-Bede.[169] Aside from a certain similarity of organization, however, the *Contemplation* is otherwise quite different from the *Libellus*. Not only is it much shorter, but it uses a different

---

[165] Alan D. Wilshere, ed., *Mirour de Seinte Eglise (St Edmund of Abingdon's Speculum Ecclesiae)*, ANTS 40 (London: ANTS, 1982): the texts of the two recensions, that for religious based on the Oxford, St. John's College MS 190, and the "lay" form based on the BL, Arundel MS 288; see the introduction for the dates of the original Latin (1213–14) and the French translation (1235–50), the different versions, and the manuscripts (23 French). In chapters 21–27, the successive events of the Passion (beginning with Judas's betrayal) are linked to an unchronological series of moments from the rest of Christ's life: the Nativity, the Resurrection, Pentecost, the Annunciation, the Ascension, the Last Supper, and the Agony in the Garden.

[166] Claire Donovan, *The de Brailes Hours: Shaping the Book of Hours in Thirteenth-Century Oxford* (Toronto: University of Toronto Press, 1991), 24, 25.

[167] See, for example, the edition of Bonaventure's *Officium de Passione Domini*, ed. A. Lauer, *S. Bonaventurae Opera Omnia* 8 (Quaracci: Typographia Collegii S. Bonaventurae, 1908), 152–58. For some relationships between Books of Hours and other forms of devotion see Bella Millett, "*Ancrene Wisse* and the Book of Hours," in *Writing Women Religious: Female Spiritual and Textual Practices in Late Medieval England*, ed. Renevey and Whitehead, 21–40.

[168] Michael P. Kuczynski, "An 'Electric Stream': The Religious Contents," in Fein, *Studies in the Harley Manuscript*, 123–61, at 146; Jeffrey, "Authors, Anthologists, and Franciscan Spirituality," 263, describes the *Contemplacioun* as "an Anglo-Norman paraphrase of a pseudo-Bonaventuran meditation on the passion."

[169] The Latin text is found in *PL* 94, cols. 561–68; J. Machielsen, ed., *Clavis patristica pseudepigraphorum Medii Aevi*, 5 vols. (Turnhout: Brepols, 1990–2003), 2:710–11 (no. 3089) (hereafter CPPM); see Bestul, *Texts of the Passion*, 190 (no. 25). Christine de Pizan's *Heures de la Contemplacion de la Passion* adopts the same structure.

narrative voice. An Anglo-Norman text with an organization similar to that of the *Libellus* is the Passion section of the *Gospel Harmony* contained in the "Black Book" of Christ Church Cathedral, Dublin.[170] This text divides the life of Christ according to the days of the week, and, like the *Contemplation*, the Passion section begins with Compline; its narrative of the events, however, is very spare, with no affective elements.

The *Holkham Bible Picture Book* is a contemporary visual witness to a similar sensibility. Compiled at the same period as the Harley anthology, the Passion section (ff. 29^r-33^r) consists of a series of vivid emotional scenes accompanied by short Anglo-Norman texts that serve as captions to the illustrations.

While I know of no direct Middle English translations of the Harley *Contemplation*, there are a number of pieces in prose and verse that bear some resemblance to it, although all begin with Matins or Prime rather than Compline. Among these are at least four Passion poems,[171] as well as a number of Middle English prose meditations organized by the hours. The prose *Mirror of St. Edmund*, which may have been translated by Richard Rolle, resembles its Anglo-Norman source (*Mirour de sainte eglise*) in providing parallel meditations on the life of Christ and his Passion for each of the hours beginning with matins.[172] The *Privity of the Passion* is a much longer series of hourly meditations, beginning with Prime and based loosely on the Pseudo-Bonaventuran *Meditationes Vitae Christi*.[173] The two forms of Rolle's *Devoute Meditaciouns of the Passioun of Crist* lack references to the canonical hours, but begin the account of each event in the Passion with the phrase "Swete Ihesu, I thanke thee . . ."[174] It is also possible to relate the "Showings" of Julian of Norwich to the liturgical hours.[175]

---

[170] Ed. Brent Pitts, *Estoire de l'Évangile (Dublin, Christ Church Cathedral, MS. 6.1.1)*, Medium Aevum Monographs 28 (Oxford: Society for the Study of Medieval Languages and Literature, 2011); a translation by Brent Pitts for FRETS is forthcoming. On the manuscript, see Colmán Ó'Clabaigh OSB, "The *Liber niger* of Christ Church Cathedral, Dublin," in *The Medieval Manuscripts of Christ Church Cathedral, Dublin*, ed. Raymond Gillespie and Raymond Refaussé (Dublin: Four Courts Press, 2006), 60–80; he erroneously (66) identifies the *Estoire des evangeiles nostre doux seignur* as a poem.

[171] See Brown, *Religious Lyrics*, nos. 30, 34, and 69. Glasscoe, "Time of Passion," 158–60 edits another.

[172] *Yorkshire Writers*, 1:219–40 (esp. 235–37) and 240–61 (esp. 254–58).

[173] *Yorkshire Writers*, 1:198–218.

[174] *Yorkshire Writers*, 1:83–91 and 92–103.

[175] Glasscoe, "Time of Passion," 154–58.

Conclusion

This anthology provides an introduction both to a range of pious texts and to the issues they raise. The texts appear in a group of thirty-one manuscripts (the nineteen known for the *Castle of Love*; three for the *Childhood of Jesus Christ*; the four known for the *Seven-Part Meditation*; two for the *Meditation on the Cross*; and three *unica*).[176] Since the present volume includes texts ranging from theological treatises to popular ballads, it is important to note that some of the manuscripts reveal an equivalent range of taste and intellectual level. One manuscript (Paris, BnF, MS fr. 902) contains two of our texts, Grosseteste's *Castle of Love* as well as *Little St. Hugh of Lincoln*. Two manuscripts of the *Childhood of Jesus Christ* (Oxford, Selden Supra 28 and Cambridge, Univ. Libr., MS Gg.1.1) illustrate the combination of high and low in another way, for they both contain a French translation of the Apocalypse as well as the poem on the childhood pranks of Jesus. In two other books (Oxford, Bodl. Libr., Digby MS 86 and London, BL, Harley MS 2253), serious works like an extract from the *Castle of Love* or a Passion meditation rub elbows with lyric poems and even racy *fabliaux*.

It is difficult to generalize about the owners of these books, because the evidence is fragmentary. Of the thirteen volumes where ownership has been studied, three (Princeton, Univ. Libr., Taylor MS. 1; London, BL, Hatton MS 99; and Brussels, Bibl. Royale, MS 9030–37) were written for or were later owned by women. (Additionally, two books—Cambridge, Emmanuel College, MS 106 and London, BL, Arundel 288—contain texts with inscribed female readers.) Three other manuscripts (Cambridge, Fitzwilliam, McClean MS 123; London, BL, Egerton MS 613;and London, BL, Cotton Vitellius MS F.VII) belonged to or seem to be intended for nuns. The remaining seven volumes can be associated with male readers, either clerical (London, Lambeth Palace, MS 522; London, BL, Harley MS 3860; Oxford, Corpus Christi Coll., MS 232) or lay (Oxford, Bodl. Libr., Selden Supra MS 38 and Digby MS 86; London, BL, Harley MS 2253 and Royal MS 20 B.XIV), though in the case of large collections such as Digby 86 and Harley 2253 the readers and hearers of the manuscripts are likely to have constituted a variety of audiences.

The linguistic range of the books is also significant. Four of them (London, BL, Harley MSS 1121 and 3860; Oxford, Corpus Christi Coll., MS 232; and Bodl. Libr., Laud Misc. MS 471) contain texts in both Latin and French, while another six (London, BL, Harley 2253 and Egerton MS 613; Cambridge, Fitzwilliam Museum, McClean MS 123; Emmanuel Coll., MS 106; and Univ. Libr., MS Gg.1.1; and Oxford, Bodl. Libr., Digby MS 86) are tri-lingual anthologies. Interestingly, two of the latter were owned by laymen. The manuscripts

---

[176] The Dublin, Trinity College, MS 374 contains both meditations, while the meditation on the Cross is found also in Cambridge, Emmanuel College, MS 106.

preserving the texts of this anthology thus illustrate in their diversity the social and linguistic realities of medieval England and its literature.

The collection of texts offered in the volume (among many that could be chosen from this large corpus) illustrates strikingly different responses to the passion and redemption in the multi-lingual environment of post-conquest England. There are examples of high-level theological reflection, folkloric tales, and ardent piety juxtaposed with what we now consider an unChristian thirst for vengeance, particularly against the Jews. As will be evident from the related texts in Middle English (and sometimes in Continental French), this variety is typical not only of Anglo-Norman circles, but also of the larger culture, in which the continuing vitality of Francophone religious writing both Insular and Continental plays so significant a part.

Further Reading

1. Editions, Translations and Related Texts

(1) Grosseteste, *Le Chasteau d'amour*

Murray, Jessie, ed. *Le Château d'amour de Robert Grosseteste évêque de Lincoln.* Paris: Champion, 1918.

Mackie, Evelyn A., ed. "Robert Grosseteste's *Chasteau d'amur*: A Text in Context." Ph.D. diss., University of Toronto, 2002.

———, trans. "Robert Grosseteste's Anglo-Norman Treatise on the Loss and Restoration of Creation, Commonly Known as *Le Château d'Amour:* An English Prose Translation." In Maura O'Carroll, ed., *Robert Grosseteste and the Beginnings of a British Theological Tradition*, 151–79. Bibliotheca Seraphico-Cappuccina 69. Rome: Istituto Storico dei Cappuccini, 2003.

Sajavaara, Kari. *The Middle English Translations of Robert Grosseteste's Château d'amour.* Mémoires de la Société Néophilologique de Helsinki 32. Helsinki: Société Néophilologique, 1967.

(2) "Jesus" from the *Lexicon* of Suidas

Dean, Ruth J. "An Anglo-Norman Version of Grosseteste: Part of His *Suidas* and *Testamenta XII Patriarcharum*." *PMLA* 51 (1936): 607–20.

(3) *Les Enfaunces de Jesu Crist*

Boulton, Maureen, ed. *Les Enfaunces de Jesu Crist.* ANTS 43. London: ANTS, 1986.

Holthausen, F. "Zum mittelenglischen Gedicht 'Kindheit Jesu' (Ms. Laud 108)." *Archiv für das Studium der neueren Sprachen* 127 (1911): 318–22.

Horstmann, Carl, ed. *Altenglische Legenden*, 3–61. Paderborn: Schöningh, 1875.

———, ed. *Sammlung altenglischer Legenden*, 101–10. Heilbronn: Henniger, 1878; repr. Hildesheim and New York: Georg Olms, 1969.

———, ed. "Nachträge zu den Legenden, I: Kindheit Jesu aus MS. Addit. 31043." *Archiv für das Studium der neueren Sprachen* 74 (1885): 327–39.

(4) *La Vengeance de Jesu Crist*

Fischer, Rudolf. "*Vindicta Salvatoris.*" *Archiv für das Studium der neueren Sprachen* 111 (1903): 285–98; 112 (1904): 24–45.
Ford, Alvin E., ed. *La Vengeance de Nostre-Seigneur: The Old and Middle French Prose Versions: The Version of Japheth.* Studies and Texts 63. Toronto: Pontifical Institute of Mediaeval Studies, 1984.
———. *The Vengeance de Nostre-Seigneur. The Old and Middle French Prose Versions.* Studies and Texts 115. Toronto: Pontifical Institute of Mediaeval Studies, 1993.
Gryting, L. A. T. *The Oldest Version of the Twelfth Century Poem, 'La Venjance Nostre Seigneur.'* University of Michigan Contributions in Modern Philology 19. Ann Arbor: University of Michigan Press, 1952.
Hanna, Ralph, and David Lawton, eds. *The Siege of Jerusalem.* EETS 320. Oxford: Oxford University Press, 2003.
Herbert, J. A., ed. *Titus and Vespasian, or the Destruction of Jerusalem in Rhymed Couplets.* London: Roxburghe Club, 1905.
Kurvinen, Auvo. *The Siege of Jerusalem in Prose.* Mémoires de la Société Néophilologique de Helsinki 34. Helsinki: Société Néophilologique, 1969.
Levy, Raphael. Review of Gryting, *Oldest Version. Symposium* 8 (1954): 175–79.
Livingston, Michael, ed. *Siege of Jerusalem.* Kalamazoo: Medieval Institute Publications, 2004.

(5) *Little Saint Hugh of Lincoln*

Child, Francis James. *The English and Scottish Popular Ballads*, 3:233–54. New York: Cooper Square, 1962.
Dahood, Roger. "The Anglo-Norman 'Hugo de Lincolnia,' Edited and Translated from the Unique Text in Bibliothèque nationale de France ms. fonds français 902." *Chaucer Review* 49 (2014).
Michel, Francisque, ed. *Hugues de Lincoln: recueil de ballades anglo-normandes et ecossoises relatives au meutre de cet enfant...* Paris: Silvestre, 1834.
Wolf, Ferdinand. *Ueber die Lais Sequenzen und Leiche*, 443–53. Heidelberg: Winter, 1841.

(6) *Passion Meditations*

Barratt, Alexandra, ed. [Eleanor Hull], *Women's Writing in Middle English*, 223–31. London: Longman, 1992.

Bateman, William, ed. [William Billyng], *The Five Wounds of Christ: A Poem from an Ancient Parchment Roll*. Manchester: R. and W. Dean, 1814.

Cornard, Sheila. "Dame Eleanor Hull's 'Meditacyons upon the VII Dayes of the Woke': The First Edition of the Middle English Translation in Cambridge University Library MS. Kk.i.6." Ph.D. diss., University of Dayton, 1995.

Gray, Douglas. "The Five Wounds of Our Lord." *Notes and Queries* 108 (1963): 50–51, 82–89, 127–34, 163–68.

Horstmann, Carl, ed. *Yorkshire Writers: Richard Rolle of Hampole and his Followers*. 2 vols. London: Sonnenschein, 1895–96; repr. Cambridge: D.S. Brewer, 1999.

Hunt, Tony, ed. "Harley *Contemplacioun*." In *"Cher alme": Texts of Anglo-Norman Piety*, trans. Jane Bliss, intro. Henrietta Leyser, 254–61. FRETS OPS 1. Tempe: ACMRS, 2010.

2. Studies

(1) Grosseteste, *Castle of Love*

Cornelius, Roberta. "The Figurative Castle: A Study in the Mediaeval Allegory of the Edifice with Especial Reference to Religious Writings." Ph.D. diss., Bryn Mawr College, 1930.

Mackie, Evelyn. "Scribal Intervention and the Question of Audience: Editing *Le Château d'amour*." In *Editing Robert Grosseteste: Papers Given at the Thirty-sixth Annual Conference on Editorial Problems*, ed. eadem and Joseph Goering, 61–77. Toronto, Buffalo, and London: University of Toronto Press, 2003.

Marx, C. W. *The Devil's Rights and the Redemption in the Literature of Medieval England*. Woodbridge: D. S. Brewer, 1995.

McEvoy, James. *Robert Grosseteste*. Oxford: Oxford University Press, 2000.

———. "Robert Grosseteste: The Man and His Legacy." In *Editing Robert Grosseteste*, 3–30.

———, ed. *Robert Grosseteste: New Perspectives on his Thought and Scholarship*. Instrumenta Patristica 27. Turnhout: Brepols, 1995.

Sajavaara, Kari. "The Use of Robert Grosseteste's 'Château d'amour' as a Source of the 'Cursor Mundi'." *Neuphilologische Mitteilungen* 68 (1967): 184–93.

Southern, R. W. *Robert Grosseteste: The Growth of an English Mind in Medieval Europe*. Oxford: Clarendon Press, 1986.

Traver, Hope. *Four Daughters of God: A Study of the Versions of this Allegory with Especial Reference to those in Latin, French and English*. Bryn Mawr College Monographs 6. Philadelphia: J. C. Winston, 1907.

Whitehead, Christiania. *Castles of the Mind: A Study Of Medieval Architectural Allegory*. Cardiff: University of Wales Press, 2003.

———. "A Fortress and a Shield: The Representation of the Virgin in the *Château d'amour* of Robert Grosseteste." In *Writing Religious Women: Female Spiritual and Textual Practices in Late Medieval England*, ed. C. Whitehead and Denis Renevey, 109–32. Cardiff: University of Wales Press and Toronto: University of Toronto Press, 2000.

(2) "Jesus," from Grosseteste's translation of *'Suidas'*

Dionisotti, A. C. "Robert Grosseteste and the Greek Encyclopaedia." In *Rencontres de cultures dans la philosophie médiévale: traductions et traducteurs de l'Antiquité tardive au XIVe siècle*, ed. Jacqueline Hamesse and Marta Fattori, 337–53. Louvain-la-Neuve: Institut d'Etudes Médiévales de l'Université Catholique de Louvain, 1990.

———. "On the Greek Studies of Robert Grosseteste." In *The Uses of Greek and Latin: Historical Essays*, ed. A.C. Dionisotti, A. Grafton, and J. Kraye, 19–39. London: The Warburg Institute, University of London, 1988.

McEvoy, James. "Robert Grosseteste's Greek Scholarship: A Survey of Present Knowledge." *Franciscan Studies* 56 (1998): 255–64.

Thomson, S. Harrison. *The Writings of Robert Grosseteste, Bishop of Lincoln 1235–53*. Cambridge: Cambridge University Press, 1940.

(3) *The Childhood of Jesus Christ*

For illustrations of the Tring Tiles see: www.britishmuseum.org/explore/highlights/highlight_objects/pe_mla/t/the_tring_tiles.aspx

Casey, Mary. "Conversion as Depicted on the Fourteenth-century Tring Tiles." In *Christianizing Peoples and Converting Individuals*, ed. Guyda Armstrong and Ian N. Wood, 339–346. International Medieval Research 7. Turnhout: Brepols, 2000.

Couch, Julie Nelson. "Misbehaving God: The Case of the Christ Child in MS Laud Misc. 108 'Infancy of Jesus Christ'." In *Mindful Spirit in Late Medieval Literature: Essays in Honor of Elizabeth D. Kirk*, ed. Bonnie Wheeler, 31–43. The New Middle Ages. New York: Palgrave Macmillan, 2006.

Dzon, Mary, and Theresa M. Kenney, eds. *The Christ Child in Medieval Culture: Alpha es et O!*. Toronto, Buffalo, and London: University of Toronto Press, 2012.

James, M. R. (with a note by R. L. Hobson). "Rare Mediaeval Tiles and Their Story." *The Burlington Magazine* 42 (1923): 32–37.

Vitz, Evelyn Birge. "The Apocryphal and the Biblical, the Oral and the Written, in Medieval Legends of the Life of Christ: The Old French *Évangile de l'Enfance*." In *Satura: Studies in Medieval Literature in Honour of Robert*

R. Raymo, ed. Nancy M. Reale and Ruth E. Sternglantz, 129–55. Donington, UK: Shaun Tyas, 2001.

(4) *The Vengeance of the Death of Our Lord*

Birenbaum, Maija. "Affective Vengeance in *Titus and Vespasian*." *The Chaucer Review* 43.3 (2009): 330–44.

Marx, C. W. *The Devil's Parlament [sic]; and, The Harrowing of Hell and Destruction of Jerusalem*. Heidelberg: C. Winter, 1993.

Millar, Bonnie. *The Siege of Jerusalem in its Physical, Literary and Historical Contexts*. Dublin: Four Courts Press, 2000.

Wright, Stephen K. *The Vengeance of Our Lord: Medieval Dramatizations of the Destruction of Jerusalem*. Studies and Texts 89. Toronto: Pontifical Institute of Mediaeval Studies, 1989.

(5) Little Saint Hugh of Lincoln

Bebbington, Brian. "Little Sir Hugh: An Analysis." *UNISA English Studies* (Journal of the Department of English, University of South Africa) 9.3 (Sept. 1971): 30–36. Repr. in *The Blood Libel Legend: A Casebook in Anti-Semitic Folklore*, ed. Alan Dundes, 72–90. Madison: University of Wisconsin Press, 1991.

Jacobs, Joseph. "Little St. Hugh of Lincoln: Researches in History, Archaeology, and Legend." In idem, *Jewish Ideals and Other Essays*, 192–224. New York: Macmillan, 1896; repr. in *The Blood Libel Legend*, ed. Dundes, 41–71.

Langmuir, Gavin. "The Knight's Tale of Young Hugh of Lincoln." *Speculum* 47 (1972): 459–82.

(6) Passion Meditation and Prayers

Barratt, Alexandra. "Dame Eleanor of Hull: The Translator at Work." *Medium Aevum* 72 (2003): 277–96.

———. "*Stabant matres dolorosae*: Women as Readers and Writers of Passion Prayers, Meditations and Visions." In *The Broken Body: Passion Devotion in Late-Medieval Culture*, ed. A. A. MacDonald, H. N. B. Ridderbos, and R. M. Schlusemann, 55–71. Mediaevalia Groningana 21. Groningen: Egbert Forsten, 1998.

Beckwith, Sarah. *Christ's Body: Identity, Culture and Society in Late Medieval Writings*. London and New York: Routledge, 1993.

Glasscoe, Marion. "Time of Passion: Latent Relationships between Liturgy and Meditation in Two Middle English Mystics." In *Langland, the Mystics and the Medieval English Religious Tradition: Essays in Honour of S. S. Hussey*, ed. Helen Phillips, 141–60. Cambridge: D.S. Brewer, 1990.

Gray, Douglas. *Themes and Images in the Medieval Religious Lyric.* London: Routledge and Kegan Paul, 1972.

Hodapp, William F. "Richard Rolle's Passion Meditations in the Context of his English Epistles: *Imitatio Christi* and the Three Degrees of Love." *Mystics Quarterly* 20.3 (1994): 96–104.

———. "Ritual and Performance in Richard Rolle's Passion Meditation B." In *Performance and Transformation: New Approaches to Late Medieval Spirituality*, ed. Mary A. Suydam and Joanna E. Ziegler, 241–72. London: Macmillan, 1999.

Renevey, Denis. "Richard Rolle." In *Approaching Medieval English Anchoritic and Mystical Texts*, ed. Dee Dyas, Valerie Edden, and Roger Ellis, 63–74. Christianity and Culture 2. Cambridge: D. S. Brewer, 2005.

3. Manuscripts

Bartal, Renana. "A Note on Bodleian Library MS. Selden Supra 38, Jehan Raynzford and Joanna de Bishopsdon." *Bodleian Library Record* 19 (2006): 239–43.

———. "The Illuminator of Bodleian Library, Selden Supra 38 and his Working Methods." *Pecia* 13 (2012): 387–404.

Bennett, Adelaide. "A Book Designed for a Noblewoman: An Illustrated *Manuel des Péchés* of the Thirteenth Century." In *Medieval Book Production: Assessing the Evidence*, ed. Linda L. Brownrigg, 163–81. Los Altos Hills, CA and Oxford: Anderson-Lovelace, 1990.

Boulton, Maureen. "The *Évangile de l'Enfance*: Text and Illustration in Oxford, Bodleian Library MS. Selden Supra 38." *Scriptorium* 37 (1983): 54–65.

Corrie, Marilyn. "Harley 2253, Digby 86, and the Circulation of Literature in Pre-Chaucerian England." In Fein, *Studies in the Harley Manuscript*, 427–43.

Dean, Ruth J. Review of Ker, *Facsimile of British Museum MS. Harley 2253*. *Speculum* 41 (1966): 739–41.

Fein, Susanna, ed. *Studies in the Harley Manuscript: The Scribes, Contents and Social Contexts of British Library MS Harley 2253*. Kalamazoo: Medieval Institute Publications, 2000.

Frankis, John. "The Social Context of Vernacular Writing in Thirteenth-Century England: The Evidence of the Manuscripts." *Thirteenth Century England* 1 (1986): 175–84.

Hill, Betty. "British Library MS. Egerton 613." *Notes and Queries* 223 (1978): 395–409, 492–501.

Horton, Adey. *The Child Jesus.* New York: Dial Press, 1975.

Jeffrey, David L. "Authors, Anthologists, and Franciscan Spirituality." In Fein, *Studies in the Harley Manuscript*, 261–70.

Ker, N. R. *Facsimile of British Museum MS. Harley 2253*. EETS 255. London, New York, and Toronto: Oxford University Press, 1965.
Liszka, Thomas Richard. "Manuscript Laud Misc. 108 and the Early History of the South English Legendary." *Manuscripta* 33.2 (1989): 75–91.
Meyer, Paul. "Les Manuscrits français de Cambridge, II: Bibliothèque de l'Université." *Romania* 15 (1886): 236–357.
Revard, Carter. "Scribe of MS Harley 2253." *Notes and Queries* 227 (1982): 62–63.
———. "Scribe and Provenance." In Fein, *Studies in the Harley Manuscript*, 21–109.
Stemmler, Theo. "Miscellany or Anthology? The Structure of Medieval Manuscripts: MS Harley 2253, for Example." *Zeitschrift für Anglistik und Amerikanistik* 39 (1991): 231–37; repr. in Fein, *Studies in the Harley Manuscript*, 111–21.
Thomson, S. Harrison. "Two Early Portraits of Robert Grosseteste." *Medievalia et Humanistica* 8 (1954): 21–22.
Turville-Petre, Thorlac. *England the Nation: Language, Literature, and National Identity 1290–1340*. Oxford: Clarendon Press, 1996.

4. Anti-Jewish Attitudes

Bale, Anthony. "Fictions of Judaism in England before 1290." In *Jews in Medieval Britain: Historical, Literary and Archaeological Perspectives*, ed. Patricia Skinner, 129–44. Woodbridge: Boydell Press, 2003.
———. *Feeling Persecuted: Christians, Jews and Images of Violence in the Middle Ages*. London: Reaktion, 2010.
———. *The Jew in the Medieval Book: English Antisemitisms, 1350–1500*. Cambridge: Cambridge University Press, 2006.
Boulton, Maureen. "Anti-Jewish Attitudes in Anglo-Norman Religious Texts, Twelfth and Thirteenth Centuries." In *Christian Attitudes Toward the Jews in the Middle Ages: A Casebook*, ed. Michael Frassetto, 151–65. New York: Routledge, 2006.
Fabre-Vassas, Claudine. *The Singular Beast: Jews, Christians and the Pig*. New York: Columbia University Press, 1997. Trans. of *La Bête Singulière: les Juifs, les chrétiens et le cochon*, trans. Casal Volk: Paris: Gallimard, 1994.
Langmuir, Gavin. "Historiographic Crucifixion." In *Approaches to Judaism in Medieval Times*, ed. David R. Blumenthal, 1:1–26. 2 vols. Chico, CA: Scholars Press, 1984.
———. "The Jews and Archives of Angevin England: Reflections on Medieval Anti-semitism." *Traditio* 19 (1963): 183–244.
———. "The Knight's Tale and Young Hugh of Lincoln." *Speculum* 47 (1972): 459–82.

Rubin, Miri. *Gentile Tales: The Narrative Assault on Late Medieval Jews*. New Haven: Yale University Press, 1999.

5. Religious Background

Bestul, Thomas H. *Texts of the Passion: Latin Devotional Literature and Medieval Society*. Philadelphia: University of Pennsylvania Press, 1996.

Donovan, Claire. *The de Brailes Hours: Shaping the Book of Hours in Thirteenth-Century Oxford*. Toronto: University of Toronto Press, 1991.

Duffy, Eamon. *Marking the Hours: English People and their Prayers 1240–1570*. New Haven and London: Yale University Press, 2006.

———. *The Stripping of the Altars: Traditional Religion in England 1400–1580*. New Haven and London: Yale University Press, 1992.

Gougaud, Louis. *Devotional and Ascetic Practices in the Middle Ages*. London: Burns, Oates and Washbourne, 1927.

Hall, Thomas N. "The *Euangelium Nichodemi* and *Vindicta saluatoris* in Anglo-Saxon England." In *Two Old English Apocrypha and their Manuscript Sources: 'The Gospel of Nichodemus' and 'The Avenging of the Saviour'*, ed. J. E. Cross, 36–81. Cambridge Studies in Anglo-Saxon England 19. Cambridge: Cambridge University Press, 1996.

Kuczynski, Michael P. "An 'Electric Stream': The Religious Contents." In Fein, *Studies in the Harley Manuscript*, 123–61.

Legge, M. Dominica. *Anglo-Norman in the Cloisters*. Edinburgh: Edinburgh University Press, 1950.

MacNamer, Sarah. *Affective Meditation and the Invention of Medieval Compassion*. University Park, PA: Penn State University Press, 2009.

Marrow, James. *Passion Iconography in Northern European Art in the Late Middle Ages and Early Renaissance: A Study of the Transformation of Sacred Metaphor into Descriptive Narrative*. Kortrijk: Van Ghemmert, 1979.

Rubin, Miri. *Corpus Christi: The Eucharist in Late Medieval Culture*. 2nd ed. Cambridge: Cambridge University Press, 2002.

Swanson, R. N. "Passion and Practice: The Social and Ecclesiastical Implications of Passion Devotion in the Late Middle Ages." In *The Broken Body: Passion Devotion in Late Medieval Culture*, ed. A. A. MacDonald, H. N. B. Ridderbos, and R. M. Schlusemann, 1–30. Groningen: Egbert Forsten, 1998.

———. *Catholic England: Faith, Religion and Observance before the Reformation*. Manchester: Manchester University Press, 1993.

Villalobos-Hennessy, Marlene. "Passion Devotion, Penitential Reading, and the Manuscript Page: 'The Hours of the Cross' in London, British Library Additional 37049." *Mediaeval Studies* 66 (2004): 213–52.

6. Reference

Dean, Ruth J., with the collaboration of Maureen Boulton. *Anglo-Norman Literature: A Guide to Texts and Manuscripts*. OPS 3. London: ANTS, 1999.

Elliott, J. K. *New Testament Apocrypha: A Collection of Apocryphal Christian Literature in an English Translation*. Oxford: Clarendon Press, 1993; rev. repr. 1999.

Hartung, Albert E., gen. ed. *A Manual of the Writings in Middle English 1050–1500*. 11 vols. New Haven: Connecticut Academy of the Arts and Sciences, 1986–.

Hasenohr, Geneviève, and Michel Zink, eds. *Dictionnaire des lettres françaises: Le Moyen Age*. 2nd ed. Paris: Fayard, 1992.

Raymo, Robert R. "Works of Religious and Philosophical Instruction." In Hartung, gen. ed., *Manual of the Writings in Middle English*, 2 (1986), 2255–2378, 2467–2582.

Roberts, A., and J. Donaldson. *The Ante-Nicene Fathers*, vol. 8. New York: Scribner's, 1890; repr. Grand Rapids: Eerdmans, 1951.

Oxford Dictionary of Byzantium, ed. A. Kazhdan. 3 vols. New York: Oxford University Press, 1991.

Oxford Dictionary of the Christian Church, ed. F. L. Cross and E. A. Livingstone. 2nd ed. Oxford: Oxford University Press, 1974.

7. The French of England: Language and Literature

Calin, William. *The French Tradition and the Literature of Medieval England*. Toronto and Buffalo: University of Toronto Press, 1994.

Crane, Susan. "Anglo-Norman Cultures in England 1066–1460." In David Wallace, ed., *The Cambridge History of Medieval English Literature*, 35–60. Cambridge: Cambridge University Press, 1999.

Ingham, Richard, ed. *The Anglo-Norman Language and its Contexts*. Woodbridge and York: York Medieval Press, 2010.

Jeffrey, David L., and Brian J. Levy, eds. and trans. *The Anglo-Norman Lyric*. Studies and Texts 93. Toronto: Pontifical Institute of Mediaeval Studies, 1990.

Legge, Mary Dominica. *Anglo-Norman in the Cloisters: The Influence of the Orders upon Anglo-Norman Literature*. Edinburgh: Edinburgh University Press, 1950.

———. *Anglo-Norman Literature and Its Background*. Oxford: Clarendon Press, 1963; repr. Westport, CT: Greenwood Press, 1978.

Lusignan, Serge. *La Langue des rois au Moyen Age: Le français en France et en Angleterre*. Paris: Presses Universitaires de France, 2004.

Pensom, Roger. "Pour la versification anglo-normande." *Romania* 124 (2006): 50–65.
Rothwell, William. "The 'Faus franceis d'Angleterre': Later Anglo-Norman." In *Anglo-Norman Anniversary Essays*, ed. Ian Short, 309–26. ANTS OPS 2. London: ANTS, 1993.
———. "The Role of French in Thirteenth-Century England." *Bulletin of the John Rylands Library* 58 (1975): 445–66.
———. "The Tri-lingual England of Geoffrey Chaucer." *Studies in the Age of Chaucer* 16 (1994): 45–67.
Short, Ian. *Manual of Anglo-Norman*. ANTS OPS 7. London: ANTS, 2007.
———. "Patrons and Polyglots: French Literature in Twelfth-Century England." In *Proceedings of the Battle Conference, 1991*, ed. Marjorie Chibnall, 229–49. =*Anglo-Norman Studies* 14. Woodbridge, Suffolk, and Rochester, NY: Boydell Press, 1992.
———. "*Tam Angli Quam Franci*: Self-Definition in Anglo-Norman England." *Anglo-Norman Studies* 18 (1995): 153–75.
Trotter, David. "L'Anglo-Normand: variété insulaire, ou variété isolée?" *Médiévales* 45 (2003): 43–54.
———. "Language Contact and Lexicography: The Case of Anglo-Norman." In *The Origins and Development of Emigrant Languages: Proceedings from the Second Rasmus Rask Colloquium, Odense University, November 1994*, ed. Hans R. Nielsen and Lene Schøsler, 21–39. Odense: Odense University Press, 1996.
———, ed. *Multilingualism in Later Medieval Britain*. Cambridge: D. S. Brewer, 2000.
———. "Not as Eccentric as It Looks: Anglo-French and French French." *Forum for Modern Language Studies* 39 (2003): 427–38.
Tyler, Elizabeth M., ed. *Conceptualizing Multilingualism in Medieval Britain to 1220*. Studies in Early Medieval Europe. Turnhout: Brepols, 2011.
Wogan-Browne, Jocelyn, ed., with Carolyn Collette, Maryanne Kowaleski, Linne Mooney, Ad Putter, and David Trotter. *Language and Culture in Medieval Britain: The French of England c. 1100–c. 1500*. York: York Medieval Press, 2009.

Note on the Treatment of the Text and Translations

The aim of this volume is to provide translations into modern English of a group of Anglo-Norman religious texts, thus making them available to a wider audience than would otherwise be possible. The texts themselves illustrate the variety of Anglo-Norman religious literature that deals more or less directly with the life of Christ, and they range from theological treatise to anti-Jewish tract. In keeping with the FRETS series protocols, I have tried to produce clear and fluent modern English, while respecting the style of the originals. Poetic texts are translated into prose. Medieval French texts tend to omit the subject or to use only pronouns: in cases of potential confusion I have supplied proper names. Although the verb tenses of medieval French narrative can shift rapidly between past and present, I have consistently used the past as the standard narrative tense in English. Each text presented a different set of problems. Robert Grosseteste, expressing new philosophical approaches to complicated theological doctrines in the vernacular, often forged new vocabulary for his purposes. The anonymous translator of the article on Jesus from Grosseteste's Latin version of '*Suidas*' frequently found himself at a loss for French equivalents to Latin forms, even for relatively common French words. The *Childhood of Jesus Christ* is a reworking into monorhymed quatrains of a Continental poem in couplets. In order to keep the flavor of the text, I have kept as close as possible to this version, even at the cost of some fluency in the translation. The style of *Little St. Hugh of Lincoln*, on the other hand, approaches that of the ballad.

The translations are based on the best and most recent editions available, and this volume includes in the Appendix editions of five previously unedited texts. In the case of *Little St. Hugh of Lincoln,* where the only edition was published more than 150 years ago, I verified its readings against the only extant manuscript. I also gratefully acknowledge the generosity of Roger Dahood, who has shared with me his edition-in-progress of *St. Hugh*. The edition of Grosseteste's *Castle of Love* appeared almost a century ago, and more manuscripts have come to light since. Here again, I have compared the edition with two manuscripts, and have also consulted the edition in Evelyn Mackie's excellent dissertation, which she is preparing for publication. In the texts newly edited here, the text of the base manuscript has been conservatively corrected on the basis of other witnesses (when available), or reasonable conjecture. All emendations are clearly indicated in the editions.

1. Robert Grosseteste
The Castle of Love
(Chasteau d'Amour)

[Latin Prose Prologue][1]
This is a treatise in the French tongue by lord Robert Grosseteste, bishop of Lincoln. The first part is about the creation of the world; the middle deals with the death of the world through sin and its restoration through mercy, with the king and the only Son of the Father, his equal, and with his four daughters, namely Mercy and Truth, Justice and Peace. It also treats the coming of Jesus Christ: how he entered into that Castle which was the body of the inviolate Virgin Mary, the properties of the Castle, and the prophecy of Isaiah that speaks about the Child born to us, the Son given to us, who shall be called Marvelous, Counselor, Mighty God, Father of future ages, Prince of Peace.[2] It will explain how he was Marvelous, how he was Counselor, how he was God, how he was Mighty, how he was Father of the future ages and how he was Prince of Peace. The last part covers the end of time and the day of judgment, the pains of hell and the joys of heaven. And although the romance tongue does not sound elegant to the ears of clerics, this little work is nevertheless appropriate for lay people, who know less; because he is prudent who knows how to draw sweetness from stone and oil from the hardest rock,[3] may he find the written text, which contains every article of faith, both of divinity and of humanity, full of heavenly sweetness.

The Castle of Love

He who thinks well speaks well; without thinking one cannot undertake any good work;[4] may God grant that we think of him, by whom and through whom and in whom are all the good things in the world. God the Father, God the Son,

---

[1] **Latin prologue:** eight of the twelve complete manuscripts (and one partial copy) begin with a version of the Latin prologue; London, BL, MS Harley 1121 substitutes an A-N prologue.

[2] **Isaiah ... peace** Isa. 9:6.

[3] **draw sweetness ... hardest rock** *suggere mel ... saxo durissimo*: Deut. 32:13.

[4] **2–3 without thinking ... undertake good work** *Sanz penser ... bien fet comencer*: the sentence resembles a proverb, but I have not been able to identify it. Geoffrey of Vinsauf's *Poetria Nova*, vv. 126–40, recommends several methods of beginning with a

and God the Holy Spirit, three persons in Trinity and a single God in unity, without end and without beginning, to whom belong honor and glory. May he give us his work to do and defend us from harm. We all need his help, but not everyone will know the languages of Hebrew, Greek, and Latin well enough to praise his Creator.[5] So that the mouth of the singer may not be stopped from praising God or announcing his holy name, and so that each one may come to know his God and how his redemption is achieved, in his own language, in all seriousness, I begin my work in French for those who do not have any Latin or learning. I will speak about why the world was made, and then how it was given, as it was, to Adam, our first father, along with the Garden of Eden, with such joy and such honor, then finally about paradise and how it was lost, then restored and afterwards returned. (vv. 1–36)

You have heard often enough how the world was created; for that reason I will not describe it, except for what pertains to my subject—that God created everything in six days—and on the seventh he rested.[6] Listen all together, lords: in the beginning, when God, who knows and sees every good thing, had made heaven and earth and everything in them, the sun at that time was seven times brighter than it is now and the moon shone then as brightly at night as the sun shines now. Do not consider this foolishness, for Isaiah said it.[7] All the things of the world—on earth and in the sea, above and below—were of greater virtue before Eve and Adam had sinned through wickedness. O God! what sorrow and what harm! Everyone in Adam's lineage is handed over to death, this for good reason. Afterwards I will tell you why, because it is good to remember it so as to love God more dearly. (vv. 37–65)

When God had made the world so that it lacked nothing—animals, trees, plants and fruit, each according to what it was: fish in the water, birds in the air, as we ought to know very well—when he had done all this, he finally created Adam, in the valley of Hebron.[8] He made him from earth, in his image; afterwards, the Holy Trinity truly created his soul. Greater love he could not show,

---

proverb; see Edmond Faral, *Les Arts poétiques du XIIe et du XIIIe siècle* (Paris: Champion, 1924), 58, 201.

[5] 16–19 **but not everyone ... Creator** *Mes trestuz ... creatur*: these three languages were desirable for biblical scholarship: Grosseteste himself studied Greek; there is evidence for some knowledge of Hebrew, but it has been treated with scepticism. See D. Wasserstein, "Grosseteste, the Jews, and Medieval Christian Hebraism," in McEvoy, *Robert Grosseteste: New Perspectives*, 357–76.

[6] 41–42 **that God created everything in six days ... rested** *Ke en sis jurs Deus tut cria ... reposa*: Exod. 20:11; for the full account of creation, see Gen. 1:1–2:2.

[7] 48–54 **the sun at that time ... Isaiah said it** *Li solail fu a icel tens ... Cume li solail ore luit / Luisait adonke de nuit ... le dit Ysaïe*: cf. Isa. 30:26.

[8] 74–75 **Adam ... Hebron** *Adam ... Hebron*: cf. A. Hilhorst, "Ager Damascenus: Views on the Place of Adam's Creation," *Warszawskie Studia Teologiczne* 20 (2007): 131–44.

for after forming him himself, he led Adam to paradise, thrust sleep upon him, and from him took a rib from which he made his companion; and then God led her before Adam and gave her to him as a helpmeet. He gave him intelligence and knowledge, beauty, power and free will, lordship over all the world, and everlasting life without death, Paradise as inheritance, and until then, life entirely without pain or sorrow, until that day should come when so many people would have come forth from Adam and Eve as to reach the number of those who had fallen from heaven through folly and pride, and then descended into hell.[9] Do not doubt that they would have been glorified, and been as fair and as bright as the sun was at that time, without dying, without suffering, as I have already told you, and then they would have ascended into heaven. There is no greater joy, no greater lordship or greater glory than having such a heritage, for Adam and all his lineage. (vv. 66–110)

But two laws were imposed on Adam in Paradise, and I will tell you what they were.[10] The first was natural, that he should rightly[11] obey whatever commands God gave him. The law called positive[12] prohibits man: "Do not eat of the apple of the tree that is forbidden to you, for if you do eat it, you will ultimately die, without solace and without comfort. And if you do not transgress this command, you will have all the lordship that there is in paradise and on earth, without trouble or conflict." (vv. 111–28)

Adam had possession[13] of many more joys of paradise than I can enumerate. Alas! how soon his goodness and his power declined! He brought us to great

---

[9] 94–100 **until . . . descended into hell** *Deskes . . . enfern descendirent*: the purpose of the creation of mankind was to make up for the gap in heaven caused by the expulsion of the fallen angels; cf. Anselm, *Cur Deus homo,* ed. F. S. Schmitt, Florilegium Patristicum, fasc. 18 (Bonn: Peter Hanstein, 1929), bk. 1, chap. 16, §18.

[10] 111ff. **But two laws were imposed . . .** *Mes deus leis furent assis . . .*: Grosseteste made a similar point about the types of law imposed on Adam in paradise in his *De cessatione legalium* (bk. 1, chap. 5, § 6), ed. R. C. Dales and E. B. King (London: British Academy, 1986), 23.

[11] 115 **rightly** *nateurement*: a technical philosophical term meaning "in a manner corresponding to the natural order"; cf. Roy J. Deferrari and M. Inviolata Barry, *A Lexicon of St. Thomas Aquinas Based on the Summa Theologica and Selected Passages of his Other Works* (Washington, DC: Catholic University of America Press, 1948–49), 725 s.v. *naturaliter.*

[12] 118–19 **The law called positive . . . man** *La positive est apelé . . . home*: a technical philosophical term translating *ius positivum seu legale* indicating a law that is imposed and that does not arise from the law of nature; cf. Deferrari and Barry, *A Lexicon of Aquinas,* 616.

[13] 131 **possession** *seisine*: a technical legal term, usually denoting a lord's possession of land. Cf. Frederick Pollock and Frederick William Maitland, *The History of English Law Before the Time of Edward I*, 2 vols. (Cambridge: Cambridge University Press, 1895, repr. 1968), 2:592. The existence of a thirteenth-century A-N law code (*Britton*, ed. and

sorrow when he ate the apple, and broke both laws, the natural and the positive, on account of his wretched wife, whom he desired to obey more than he did God himself. Now Adam is disinherited and thrown out of paradise! From joy, he is brought to sorrow in toil and sweat! He will lose his life by dying. Where will he seek[14] any further help since he has lost all his inheritance by this verdict?[15] Through sin and transgression he lost his inheritance. Most grievous was the sin, since all were tainted by it! Because of it, whatever exists under heaven lost part of its virtue.[16] God made nothing that was too exalted to escape abasement through Adam's default.[17] Each thing would have had its rightful nature, were it not for sin, which is so harmful. Sin, in a word, is clearly default; default and sin have the same meaning. By default, he had such a great loss because the default was revealed. Two defaults in succession and a final agreement rightly cause him to lose possession;[18] even now this law is in force in the king's court. (vv. 129–68)

Now, having been previously freer than any living being on earth, they are stained by evil and have become slaves to sin. Is not he who provides service to someone clearly his serf,[19] since he serves him in bondage, without freedom or time limit? But a serf cannot claim his inheritance or any lordship; since he has become a serf, his inheritance is withheld, nor will he be heard in anything or

---

trans. Francis Morgan Nichols [Oxford: Clarendon Press, 1865]) suggests that French legal language was part of the experience of Grosseteste's audience. Hence his metaphor reflects their understanding of the world. For a theologian concerned with the issue of the devil's rights in redemption, feudal terminology was not merely metaphorical, but an expression of the relationship between God and man.

[14] 146 **seek** *guerra*: a scribal error for *querra*, the reading found in Lambeth Palace, MS 522, f. 5ʳ.

[15] 147 **verdict** *jugement*: in law this term may also mean judgment, sentence, or official decree.

[16] 153–54 **Whatever ... virtue** *Kant ke ... vertu*: cf. vv. 48–54 above; here all creation is diminished as a result of Adam's sin.

[17] 161 **Default** *defaute*: the word may mean misdeed, but the sense "lack" is consistent with the Neoplatonist concept of sin or evil as the absence or lack of good, rather than (as the Manicheans held) a negative material force; the word also has a legal meaning of "failure" or "failure to attend." As noted in the introduction (pp. 6–7 above), Grosseteste's use of the word here implies both senses.

[18] 165–66 **Two defaults ... possession** *Defaute apres defaute ... seisine*: according to Pollock and Maitland, *Law*, 2:592, a default in law is a failure to appear before the court; after such a failure a tenant is summoned a second time to explain; on a second failure to appear, the disputed property is adjudged to his opponent. 165 **agreement** *fine*: the legal term refers to a "final agreement." For discussion, see Pollock and Maitland, *Law*, 2:94–105.

[19] 173 **serf** *serf*: cf. Rom. 6:16. English jurists had no way of distinguishing between "serf" and "slave," using *servus* for both; however a serf in England had considerably more rights than a slave (Pollock and Maitland, *Law*, 1:412, 415).

answerable in any court.[20] Therefore, if he wishes to regain his rights, it is fitting for him to seek another who is free-born, who may make his case for him[21] and reclaim his inheritance; and such a one should be of his lineage, and thus a true man who did not eat of the apple.[22] He must come without sin and obey all three laws, both the two of paradise and also that of Mount Sinai which was given to Moses and was never obeyed by anyone who had committed a sin.[23] But who could see so clearly that he could think of such a man and announce such a miracle? Here I will end my account and I will tell a story closely related to my subject, and for that reason I wish to recount it here. (vv. 169–204)

There was once a king of great power, good will, and great knowledge; this king had a son[24] who shared all his wisdom. As the Father is, so the Son is too in his way: of one knowledge, of one substance, of one will, of one power, by which he did everything that pertained to his kingdom. Whatever he began was completed through his son. This king had four daughters;[25] he gave to each one individually her own portion of his wealth, wisdom, and power, but in different ways, according to what belonged to her.[26] Each one partook of his substance, and the

---

[20] 176–82 **But a serf ... answerable in any court** *Mes sers ... en nule court respondu*: Grosseteste's concept of the rightlessness of a serf is closer to that of a slave in Roman law. According to Pollock and Maitland (*Law*, 1:412–19), the serf's person belonged to his lord, with regard to whom he had no rights, though he was technically protected in life and limb; with regard to anyone else, however, serfs in England were treated by the law no differently from free men.

[21] 186 **who may make his case for him** *Ke pur li mustre sa reison*: a serf could not act as an advocate (Pollock and Maitland, *Law*, 1:422).

[22] 188–90 **such a one ... true man ... apple** *E ke il esteit de sun lignage ... pome*: Grosseteste here stresses both the real humanity of Jesus (i.e., that he was not simply God clothed in human form) and his complete freedom from any share in Adam's sin (i.e., the apple).

[23] 195 **that of Mount Sinai** *cele du munt Synaïs*: i.e., the Ten Commandments; see Exod. 20.

[24] 207 **son** *fiz*: Mackie, "Robert Grosseteste's *Chasteau*," notes (73) that this order of introduction places the king's son before the four daughters, thereby indicating Grosseteste's focus on the centrality of Christ in the development of his text.

[25] 217ff. **Four daughters** *Quatre filles*: this passage is based on an exposition of Ps. 84:11; see Sajavaara, *The Middle English Translations*, 65–90; Traver, *The Four Daughters of God*, and eadem, "The Four Daughters of God: A Mirror of Changing Doctrine," *PMLA* 40 (1925): 44–92. For other French versions of the allegory, see T. Hunt, "The Four Daughters of God: A Textual Contribution," *Archives d'histoire doctrinale et littéraire du moyen âge* 48 (1981): 287–316.

[26] 218–22 **to each one ... belonged to her** *A chescune ... li apent*: women in A-N England could and did inherit estates that were often considerable; see Pollock and Maitland, *Law*, 1:482; and John Hudson, *Land, Law and Lordship in Anglo-Norman England* (Oxford: Clarendon Press, 1994), 108, 111–13, 117, 119–21. I. J. Sanders, *English*

substance that belonged to their Father is wholly one; and without it he could not govern his kingdom in peace, nor rule with righteousness. (vv. 205–28)

It is important that I mention their names: the first is Mercy, the first-born of the king; the next is Truth, and Justice is the third; the fourth sister is named Peace. Without these four no king can govern a great domain. The king of whom I speak had a serf who was in a sorry plight; because of a very great offence that he committed against his lord, by legal judgment he was tortured grievously and handed over to his enemies, who put him in a dreadful prison, because they desired nothing except to have him in their power. They put him in the harshest prison, and tormented him immoderately. (vv. 229–48)

Mercy saw this and was so moved by pity that she could no longer restrain herself. She came before the king to present her argument and to free the prisoner:

"Dear Father," she said, "listen to me. I am your daughter, as you know well. I am full of humility, kindness, and pity. I have inherited them from you, dear sweet Father; therefore, hear my prayer on behalf of this sorrowful, miserable prisoner, so that he may be redeemed. For you have put him in prison among his enemies who betrayed him with a promise by which they made him sin.[27] They broke their promise, for they always seek dishonesty, and may falsity be given back to them, and the prisoner surrendered to me. For you are the king of humility, mercy, and pity, and I am your eldest daughter, renowned above all your works. I would not be your daughter if I had no pity on this man! By rights, he deserves mercy. Your mercy must save him and your most sweet pity must put him out of harm's way. I will cry out for mercy for him until I find it." (vv. 249–82)

When Truth heard that Mercy was yielding and wished to save the serf and deliver him from prison, she took her stand before the king:

"Dear Father," said Truth, "I have heard such an outrageous thing from my sister Mercy that I cannot restrain myself from repeating it; through her kindness, in short, she would like to save the prisoner whom Truth condemns. Dear Father, I am your daughter and made of the same substance as you are. Mercy must not be heard unless Truth shows her the way. If my sister could save everyone for whom she pleads, you would no longer be feared, nor any misdeed atoned for. But you are such a trustworthy king and so steadfast of heart that you seek nothing but Truth, while this man asks pity who had no pity for himself;

Baronies: A Study of their Origin and Descent 1086–1327 (Oxford: Clarendon Press, 1960) records scores of examples of women who succeeded to baronial estates.

[27] 263–68 **For you have imprisoned him among his enemies . . . made him sin** *Ke en mi ses enemis Avez en grief prison mis . . . trespasser li firent*: according to Marx, *The Devil's Rights*, 69 the idea that the devil's power over humanity was unjust because it was obtained by deception derives from Anselm and his successors.

The Castle of Love

he can have no other help. He must endure the sentence and be punished for his misdeed." (vv. 283–310)

And then Justice rose and spoke a brief word:

"I am your daughter, dear sweet Father, and you are king and righteous Judge. All your deeds are full of wisdom, and your judgments are just.[28] The serf I hear spoken of deserved judgment; as long as he was free he had Mercy available to him, as well as Truth, Justice, and Peace; but then he left voluntarily and separated himself from us completely and joined discord. For this reason he ought to suffer death, as you promised this before. Now as Justice ordains it, let him be put in prison until the appointed time, when you wish to have him brought out and judged before your court." (vv. 311–32)

Indeed, Justice exempts nothing that Truth tells her; wisely, she gives to each one whatever he ought to have by right.[29] And Truth accuses him[30] of evil, while Justice condemned him, nor was there anyone who spoke well of him since Pity was not heard. Ah! sorrowful and unhappy man, afflicted on all sides. Nor could he save himself no matter where he went, for the enemy assaulted him, and stripped him of his sanity and his virtue. He placed himself and all his lineage in such vile servitude, and made them sin without end. Justice, who followed, sentenced them all, but without Mercy and without Pity. (vv. 333–52)

Peace could not remain. She had to leave the country, because she could not dwell where there was war or hatred, and where Mercy was not mentioned. All four daughters[31] left the country. Nothing could be restored that was destroyed. The waves drowned them all.[32] Only eight souls were saved:[33] these were Noah and his three sons, preserved in the ark with their wives who were with them; nothing more remained from the world. It is a horror to think of such a cruel judgment; and Justice and Truth prevailed but without Peace and without Pity. (vv. 353–70)

Then Peace spoke to the king:

---

[28] 316 **your judgments are just** *dreitureus tes jugemens*: cf. Apoc. 16:7.

[29] 336 **by right** *part dreit*: *part* in Murray's edition is an error for *par*, the reading in London, Lambeth Palace, MS 522, f. 10ʳ. The legal maxim is "suum cuique" (Justinian, *Digest*, 1.1.10).

[30] 337 **accuses him** *l'atice*: a form of *enticer* (whose usual meanings — incite, prompt to, goad — do not suit the context); cf. Mackie, "Robert Grosseteste's A-N Treatise," 164.

[31] 338 **All four** *Tuz*: the text is unclear here, but must refer to the Daughters of God. Mackie, "Robert Grosseteste's A-N Treatise," 164 interprets it to refer only to Peace and Mercy.

[32] 361 **waves** *undes*: the transition to the flood is abrupt, but it is treated as punishment for Adam's sin.

[33] 362 **eight souls . . .** *viii almes*: cf. 1 Peter 3:20. See Gen. 6–7 for the account of Noah and the flood.

"Dear Father, now listen to me. I am certainly your daughter, and have come forth from your substance. I must be heard before you. My two sisters have abandoned me. They make their judgments without me or Mercy. I was never called; that is why no man who lives can ever have refuge, and that is why I have fled from there. I will remain with you until the discord that has broken out[34] among my sisters is at last ended by Peace. But why should Truth or Justice be appointed, if not to keep Peace? Justice has no other duty than to save Peace. Shall I then be refused, when everything good is done and stipulated on my account? But I cannot continue if Mercy is not heard. My speech must carry great weight, for you are the Prince and king of Peace. Peace is the end of all good. Whoever has Peace lacks nothing, and without Peace, wealth and knowledge are worth nothing. (vv. 371–402)

"Whoever strives for Peace will die in Peace, and for that reason, Peace must be heard on behalf of this serf who cries for mercy. I will give you a true account of the four of us. Since four were appointed[35] to deal out lawful justice and must together furnish a single judgment, the judgment will not have the authority of record[36] until they are in agreement. They must reach one agreement and then furnish a judgment. The earlier judgment will be repealed, since the serf must not be judged without us. Without us, he was chastised too much; for this reason he must find pity. Lord, you have done their will; now let ours be laid down, because Mercy always cries out for the serf to have help, and I will flee the country until they are in agreement." (vv. 403–26)

The king's son saw that the dispute which had sprung up would not be ended without him, nor peace made among the sisters. So he said:

"Dear, fair Father, I am your son, of your blood and of your power. I am called your wisdom, and I am so loved by you that through me you made the world;[37] therefore your deeds are my works. We are one in substance, dignity, and power. I will always do your will, O judge and true king. In this quarrel, which causes so much discord, Mercy has so moved me by the arguments that she has

---

[34] 382 **broken out** *hastie*: Murray, *Château*, 181 glosses "hastir" as "commencer, engager."

[35] 409 **four were appointed** *quatre sunt assises*: i.e., the Four Daughters of God.

[36] 413 **have the authority of record** *avra record*: Murray, *Château*, 174 n. 413 notes that this phrase translates the legal term "recordum habere"; in the absence of a "record," a witness who was willing to fight could protest the judgment; cf. Pollock and Maitland, *Law*, 1:536–37.

[37] 431–35 **I am called your wisdom . . . you made the world** *Ta sapïence su clamé . . . fesis le mund*: in the New Testament, Jesus Christ is the incarnation of the wisdom of God; see *ODCC*, 1493, "Wisdom," with a reference to 1 Cor. 1:24. Jesus is also the "Word" of God (John 1:1–4); cf. "Logos," *ODCC*, 833: "In the Prologue of the Gospel the Logos is described as God from eternity, the Creative Word who became incarnate in the man Jesus Christ of Nazareth." Cf. Wisdom 9:1–2.

presented that I feel great pity for the serf. Mercy cries out for mercy and she will be heard first. I will do all her bidding, and I will reconcile her to Truth. I will take on the clothing of the serf,[38] in truth and in righteousness. I will sustain the judgment and whatever befits Justice, and I will cause Peace to be proclaimed on earth, and cause Justice and Peace to kiss.[39] And thus I will end the war and save your people on earth." (vv. 427–56)

Those who hear this exemplum will see clearly that it signifies one power in God. Everything comes from God the Father, all good deeds are done by God the Son, and everything is accomplished in God the Holy Spirit, one God indivisible, one substance and no more.[40] Thus may all those who listen to this text be blessed.[41]

Lords, you have heard why the world was created, why and for what reason everything was made; then how Adam forfeited it, and how he could not recover it through any power of his own, nor could any angel redeem man or bring him back from death. For every reason, therefore, God had to become man, man suffer death, and God come back from death; for otherwise everything in the world would have perished. Now hear about such great kindness, such great pity, such great love, that God came down from heaven for the sheep that he had lost. He left ninety-nine to seek one who strayed;[42] therefore, there is no better shepherd and most merciful Lord. Anyone who thinks about this Lord, who showed him so much love that he formed him in his own image,[43] and then gave himself for him, should rather die or see his heart burst than transgress his command. (vv. 457–96)

Now hear about the great kindness of the Creator's coming. The gift was given to Abraham.[44] The prophets recounted it—that is Moses, and Jonah, Habakkuk and Elijah, Jeremiah and Daniel, Isaiah and Samuel, David and Elisha, who foretold the coming of God. I cannot record everything, but hear Isaiah's message: "A little child is born to us and a son given to us. He will uphold his empire and his name will be called Marvelous and Counselor, and God and the

---

[38] 449 **I will take on the clothing of the serf** *Del serf prendrai la vesteüre*: cf. Phil. 2:7.

[39] 454 **Justice and Peace to kiss** *Justice e Pès baiser*: Ps. 84:11.

[40] 466 **no more** *plus non*: the ME *Castle of Love*, v. 564 reads "no mo" (no more), supporting the reading of the edition (Sajavaara, *Translations*, 278; Murray, *Château*, 174).

[41] 467 **may all . . . be blessed** *La beneiçon a trestuz dunt*: *dunt* is present subjunctive of *donner*.

[42] 487–88 **Ninety-nine . . . strayed** *Nonante e neuf . . . s'en ala*: Luke 15:4.

[43] 493 **formed . . . own image** *apres sei . . . former*: Gen. 1:26.

[44] 505 **To Abraham** *A Abraham*: see Gen. 12:1–3.

Mighty One and Father of the next world. His final name is Prince of Peace."[45] These are the names, in truth, that the prophet gave him. Now listen to me, all of you: His first name is Marvelous. So great a marvel was not heard of, nor will ever be in this life, until the time comes when God becomes man. (vv. 497–524)

If someone saw a child here who had a surfeit—three feet and three hands—or another child with too little, so that he lacked both fist and foot, both having been born like that, would they be marvelous? No! Indeed, I say it straightaway. The latter has a defect of nature, the former is too overburdened. They will never be called marvelous, and should be called monsters.

But it would be a marvel if a man had the whole nature of man, without defect and in the right proportions, and yet, as a true man without blemish, were an actual horse.[46] Such a thing is impossible, but anyone who found such a creature could call him marvelous. (vv. 525–46)

A thousand times more wondrous is the marvel of the Child whom Isaiah foretold, for he is both true man and true God. He lacks no part of humanity, and we surely see that he is fully God,[47] for through him everything was made and without him there is nothing,[48] for he was not created in sin,[49] as I explained to you before.[50] There is no other God but this one. He came down to earth and assumed fully the nature of our humanity beneath our clothing,[51] and truly became man. Since he wished to be man, it was fitting for him to be born of woman in

---

[45] 509–16 **A little child ... Prince of Peace** *Un enfantunet ... Prince de Pès*: Isa. 9:6. These names in the Hebrew Bible are attributes of God; in a Christian interpretation the passage announces the Messiah: e.g., Augustine, *Enarr. in Ps.* 33.2 (*PL* 35.314–15).

[46] 541–43 **so that he was a true man ... true horse** *Issi ke verrai home fust ... verrai cheval*: Murray, *Château*, 174 observes that this example pertaining to the problem of universals is used by Boethius and by John of Salisbury to show the impossibility of uniting two natures in a single being. He comments further that Grosseteste uses the impossibility of the idea to heighten the mystery of the Incarnation. This manner of adapting pagan thought, originating in late antiquity, is characteristic of Grosseteste's borrowings from philosophy.

[47] 551–52 **He lacks ... fully God** *D'humanité ne li faut rien ... plein Dieu*: on becoming incarnate in Jesus Christ, the Son of God lost nothing of his divine nature.

[48] 553–54 **For through him ... there is nothing** *Kar par li ... nule rien ne est*: John 1:3.

[49] 555 **He was not created in sin** *Ke en defaute n'est pas fet*: when he became man, Jesus was free of all sin, unlike all other humans who are born with original sin; on sin as default, see above note 17 to v. 161.

[50] 556 **explained to you before** *avant vus ai retret*: see above vv. 188–190 and note 22 to those lines.

[51] 539 **clothing** *vesteüre*: i.e., skin, or human body; Grosseteste insists that Jesus had a complete human nature as well as the appearance of a man.

order to receive the nature of a human creature. But God would dwell only in a place fair and bright.[52] (vv. 547–68)

It was indeed into a fair place that God descended from heaven, into a large, beautiful castle,[53] well fortified and beautiful, for it is the castle of love, of all solace, of all help. It is located in the border country, but has no fear of its enemies. And I will tell you why: the tower is so well enclosed with deep moats and high ramparts[54] that there is no fear of assault, for it is placed high up on a solid grey rock, and smoothly polished from top to bottom, so that no evil can lodge there, nor a siege machine do it harm. Around it are four small towers — in all the world there are none so beautiful. Then there are three baileys[55] round about, having strong walls and an imposing appearance. As you hear it described, it had much more beauty than tongue could describe, heart imagine, or mouth recount. (vv. 569–94)

The baileys are built on the natural rock, surrounded by very deep moats and provided with smooth, fine and good battlements.[56] There are seven barbicans[57] made with good craftsmanship. Each one has both a door and a tower where rescue will never fail, nor will anyone seeking refuge there encounter obstacles.

The castle is fine and beautiful, painted around the exterior in three different colors. The base adjoining the rock is green. There is no lack of great sweetness, for I say that sweet greenery never loses its color. The color in the middle is indigo, a blue which is a common color and lit with beauty. The third color, finally, covers the circumference of the battlements. It is redder than a rose and

---

[52] 568 **place** *lu*: i.e., the Virgin's body.

[53] 571 **castle** *chastel*: on the image of the castle, see Murray, *Château*, 64–66; Sajavaara, *Translations*, 90–100; Cornelius, *The Figurative Castle*. Mackie, "Robert Grosseteste's *Chasteau*," points out (75–76) that the inspiration for the allegory is the word *castellum* in Luke 10:38, which was interpreted as an allegorical reference to the Virgin and the Incarnation; and (77–80) that many of the architectural details are inspired by the description of the New Jerusalem in Apoc. 21:11–21.

[54] 579 **moats . . . ramparts** *fossez*: because the defenses are described as both deep and high, I have used both senses of *fossé*, rather than substitute the vaguer term "defenses." According to Adrian Pettifer, *English Castles* (Woodbridge: Boydell Press, 1995), 323, most Norman earthwork castles had a rampart or wall (often of earth) with a walkway on top, immediately behind a ditch or moat.

[55] 589 **three baileys** *treis bailles*: courtyards surrounded by the ramparts or curtain walls of a castle; cf. Pettifer, *Castles*, 312.

[56] 597 **battlements** *kerneaus*: battlements consist a platform at the top of a wall or tower surrounded by a low wall (parapet) which is normally crenellated, i.e., with solid portions (merlons) shielding the defenders and gaps (crenels) through which they could fire at the enemy; cf. Pettifer, *Castles*, 314, "Crenellations."

[57] 599 **seven barbicans** *barbecanes i ad set*: fortifications placed outside the moat, before the principal gates of a castle; cf. Pettifer, *Castles*, 312. Mid-thirteenth-century castles had one or two; the number seven here is clearly symbolic.

appears to be a thing afire.[58] It gleams all around, covering the castle keep.[59] No storm ever comes there; rather there is abundant mild weather. Inside, the castle is whiter than freshly fallen snow, and casts a great light far and wide from the tower. From the middle of the highest tower there springs a fountain, and four streams[60] flow from it that rush onto the gravel and fill the moats; there is much joy and delight there. (vv. 595–634)

Whoever can draw this water will be healed; no one who can get this water has to complain of evil.[61] In this fair, good tower there is an ivory throne brighter than a fine midsummer's day. It is cleverly fashioned, with seven steps rising to reach it: there is nothing as beautiful in the world. The rainbow[62] with all its colors extends around the tower. No king or emperor ever had such a beautiful throne. There was abundant beauty where God wished to take rest, and so there has never been so fair a castle. Never before was there one like this, and never will there be another, for the Lord God made it for his use, to take shelter; he loves the place and holds it dear.[63] This is the castle of delight, of solace, of rest, of hope and love, of refuge and kindness: the body of the maiden. (vv. 635–63)

Never was there anyone else who was endowed with as much virtue as the sweet Virgin Mary. She is seated in the border lands for our sake,[64] and for us she is both a shield and buckler[65] for us against all our enemies who always lie in wait for us. The well-polished rock is sweet Mary's heart, which never softened toward evil but resolved to serve God and guarded her holy virginity with humility. (vv. 664–76)

The base described, which is fixed to rock and is painted in color and has such a beautiful shade of green, is the faith of the Virgin that illuminates her blessed heart. Her faith continually renews the green color that is so beautiful,

---

[58] 607–21 **three different colors . . . afire** *De treis colors diversement . . . reflambeie environ*: for medieval color symbolism, cf. F. Boggi, "Color," *ODMA* 2:421–22.

[59] 622 **keep** *dongon*: the keep, donjon, or great tower dominated the rest of the castle, provided the principal accommodation, and was the last refuge of defense in case of siege; cf. Pettifer, *Castles*, 319.

[60] 630–31 **there springs . . . streams** *Est surdant . . . ruissel*: cf. Gen. 2:10.

[61] 637–38 **Never . . . reach this water** *Ja . . . cel ewe puet ateindre*: these two lines appear only in London, BL, MS Harley 1121 and Oxford, Corpus Christi Coll., MS 232.

[62] 647 **rainbow** *arc du ciel*: a symbol of the Holy Spirit, as well as the rainbow that God set before Noah in Gen. 9:13–17, and the rainbow throne in Apoc. 4:3.

[63] 656–58 **for the Lord God . . . dear** *Kar Dampnedeu . . . chier*: cf. Ps. 131:13–14.

[64] 667 **border-lands** *la marche*: it is possible that Grosseteste (who in mid-career held administrative positions in Hereford) is thinking here of the Welsh Marches, a much-contested border zone. But his image of the castle positioned in the border-lands also works as a generic metaphor for the Virgin as a frontline defense for humanity.

[65] 668 **shield and buckler** *escu e targe*: the *ecu* was a flat-topped shield with a pointed bottom carried by heavy cavalrymen (knights) while the *targe* was a round shield carried by infantrymen. Cf. Ps. 90:5.

for faith is clearly the foundation of all virtue. And then it is the common color of beauty and of sweetness. This is the meaning: that she always served her Lord with tenderness, in hope, humility, and kindness. And the uppermost color, which covers all around, is so red that no other is worth more; that is holy Charity, by which she[66] is illuminated and inflamed with the fire of love, to serve God, her Creator. (vv. 677–700)

The four turrets above guard the tower (where nothing wicked may reside) from assault. They are the four cardinal virtues. These are Fortitude and Temperance, Justice and Prudence. At the four doors there are porters,[67] so that only good can enter.[68] The walls of the castle's three baileys[69] are crenellated, so they surround and defend the keep. The bailey wall on the highest level signifies her virginity, which was never violated in any way because she was so full of grace. The central bailey signifies her chastity, that of the outer bailey wall her most holy marriage. They are rightly named baileys since they guard the lady who is unique, without peer, chaste virgin, wife and mother. Anyone in the world who wishes to be saved must pass through one of these doors and through the seven barbicans.[70]

The seven barbicans built outside the walls guard the castle well both from arrows and from crossbow bolts; these are the seven virtues by which the seven vices are confounded. Pride,[71] the root of all evils, which is vanquished and defeated by the Virgin's holy Humility, is clearly there; and Charity confounds Envy, and Abstinence Gluttony, and Lechery is defeated by her holy Chastity; Avarice, who wounds many, is vanquished by her Generosity; while Patience overcomes Anger that tears itself apart; and spiritual Joy[72] confounds wicked Sadness.[73] (vv. 701–46)

---

[66] 698 **she** *ele*: i.e., the Virgin.

[67] 707 **porters** *porter*: i.e., doorkeepers.

[68] 708 **so that ... enter** *Ke ... entrer*: cf. Ps. 117:20.

[69] 709 **walls ... baileys** *bailles*: the text clearly refers here to the wall of the castle, rather than to the courtyard (or ward), which could not be crenellated. The *OED* (1:887B) gives as the first (and older) meaning of "bailey" the external wall enclosing the outer court and forming the first line of defense, but this is no longer its usual meaning.

[70] 672 **seven barbicans** *les barbekanes set*: see note to v. 599.

[71] 733–46 **Pride ... Sadness** *orgoil ... tristesce*: the deadly sins and their opposite virtues are not capitalized in the edition, but I have done so to indicate their status as allegories. The list given here differs slightly from the usual one: *ODCC*, 1264–65. For other formulations see Rosemond Tuve, *Allegorical Imagery: Some Mediaeval Books and their Posterity* (Princeton: Princeton University Press, 1966), 56–143, 442–43.

[72] 747 **spiritual Joy** *esperitale leesce*: the usual contrary of sloth or acedia (see next note) is diligence.

[73] 746 **wicked Sadness** *la male tristesce*: commonly referred to as sloth or acedia, it may be "sadness in the face of spiritual good": see E. M. Willingham, "Seven Deadly Sins," *ODMA* 4:1524–25.

The fountain of grace that surrounds the whole castle springs forth there. God gave his grace and distributed it with moderation, but he loved the Virgin so much that he gave her perfect grace,[74] whose abundance gives help to everyone. For this reason she is rightly called blessed, above all others.[75] And what, then, are the moats but voluntary poverty,[76] over which no siege-engine can hurl anything that could harm the castle. The devil is thus vanquished and has completely lost his power—whereas before, he had such great power that no man living could stand against him who was not cast into hell. This is the noble lady, of whom God said to the serpent that a woman would come who would crush its head.[77] (vv. 747–70)

Blessed be the blessed one, honored above all others, who is so fair and good that God made a throne of her soul for his use and lodging. He took flesh of her to save his people from prison. She is our defense. This lady is very beautiful because she has so much goodness, more than any other creature, but when the sun[78] rightfully impregnated her holy body, it made her a thousand times more beautiful. It entered through the closed door[79] and on leaving left it closed. No quarrel or complaint ensued, because whatever God wishes, is done. (vv. 771–88)

Noble Virgin, Queen, strong fortress of refuge, to you my soul has come which calls and shouts at your door, shouts and calls and shouts and cries out: "Sweet Lady, help, help! Lady Queen, open, open![80] Let me draw a little of this grace that heals the poor in spirit. I am beset outside your castle by three of my

---

[74] 752 **perfect grace** *pleine grace*: cf. Luke 1:28.

[75] 756 **blessed above all others** *Sur toutes autres beneuree*: cf. Luke 1:48.

[76] 758 **voluntary poverty** *voluntrive povertez*: A. Vermeersch, "Poverty," *The Catholic Encyclopedia* (New York: Robert Appleton Company, 1911), retrieved 1 June 2012: http://www.newadvent.org/cathen/12324a.htm

[77] 769–70 **a woman ... crush its head** *une femme ... sun chief enquassereit*: cf. Gen. 3:15.

[78] 782 **sun ... impregnated her holy body** *li soleil ... son seint cors enumbrat*: Wace, *La Conception nostre Dame*, ed. William R. Ashford (Menasha, WI: George Banta Publishing, 1933), vv. 1036–41 uses the image of the sun passing through glass as an image for the preservation of Mary's virginity both at conception and during childbirth; cf. Gérard Gros, "La *Semblance* de la *verrine*: Description et interprétation d'une image mariale," *Le Moyen Âge* 97 (1991): 217–57.

[79] 785 **the closed door** *la porte close*: the phrase comes from Ezechiel's (Ezech. 44:1–4) vision of the door of the sanctuary, closed because only God might enter it; it is a common metaphor for Mary's virginity, which Grosseteste has conflated with the image of the sun passing through glass (see previous note).

[80] 789–95 **Noble Virgin ... open!** *Franche Pucele ... ovrez*: on this passage see Whitehead, *Castles of the Mind*, 98–100.

enemies.[81] These are the devil, the world, and my flesh, which incites me continually to everything wicked. They do harm to my soul. They have held great assembly against me: first came the devil, who rose against me with three armies, that is, pride, anger, and sloth. The world has besieged me with two armies, that is, envy and covetousness; and the flesh, which inclines so readily to foolish pleasure and gluttony. They brought me harm: I am a vanquished champion. If your grace does not help me, I have lost control of everything. You, who raise up the weak, let me draw [water] from the moat, there where the castle is steadfast, and charity is constable." (vv. 789–820)

I have said a little about the castle and I would be delighted to say more, because all the good in the world comes from this castle. Indeed, I tell you, this is the ladder[82] by which God came down from heaven. From it he took the human nature with which he covered his divinity. Aaron's rod bore the flower[83] and the Virgin bore her Creator, and thus was the Child born, and this Son was given to us. The Child who was born for us is marvelous. But there is nothing so marvelous, it seems to me, as joining two natures together, so that each one clearly has everything that pertains to it, and nothing is diminished, but each may have its rightful nature.[84] It is sweet blessed Jesus who came down from heaven to reconcile his sisters[85] and to set his prisoner free. In sum, he has two natures—true God and true man. (vv. 821–46)

Blessed be the Virgin through whom we have the news of Jesus Christ, the fruit of life; now Mercy is heard. In heaven the angels sing praise and glory to the Almighty, and peace is proclaimed on earth to people of good will.[86] Then there was such peace on earth when our Lord was born; there was no war in all the world, nor any quarrel or discord; all were of one accord and governed by one prince. The man whose rule extended everywhere was named Caesar Augustus. Peace surely had to be maintained in anticipation of such a lofty coming that

---

[81] 800 **three of my enemies** *treis de mes enemis*: the soul's three enemies are a commonplace of medieval pious literature; cf. Paul Meyer, "*Le Roman des trois ennemis de l'homme* par Simon," *Romania* 16 (1887): 1–72, and Siegfried Wenzel, "The Three Enemies of Man," *Mediaeval Studies* 29 (1967): 47–66.

[82] 825 **ladder** *l'eschiele*: Mary occurs as the ladder of Heaven and the throne of God in Anselm of Canterbury's *Orationes* (no. 55, *PL* 158. 962B).

[83] 829 **Aaron's rod ... flower** *La verge Aaron porta la flur*: the allusion is to Num. 17:8, by which the tribe of Levi was chosen for the priesthood, seen as a type of the Incarnation; cf. Gertrud Schiller, *Iconography of Christian Art*, trans. Janet Seligman (London: Lund Humphries, 1971), 54.

[84] 836–40 **two natures ... rightful nature** *dous natures ... son dreit*: on Christ's two natures, see above notes to vv. 541–43 and to vv. 551–52.

[85] 843 **sisters** *sorors*: variant form of *soere*.

[86] 841–54 **In heaven ... good will** *En ciel ... bone volunté*: Luke 1:13–14.

sustains and establishes peace. Nature is greatly embellished[87] when the Creator[88] is joined[89] to nature; for then is nature[90] purified, a hundred times more than it was before Adam sinned. He is of great power and of free birth.[91] He can indeed plead for us and defend our rights. Now you have heard everything about how marvelous this child is. (vv. 846–78)

Now, in the name of God the Father, hear how he is a good Counselor. Imagine that you saw here a man who had been emperor of Rome but was now expelled from his country and remained this side of the mountains—mountains so high that the man could not pass them, either by cunning or by assault, nor could he go any other way: someone who saw him in distress might say to him by way of counsel: "Why are you so beggarly? Return to your own country. Go seek your friends everywhere, and recover your land."[92] That would be good advice, if he could follow it, but it is not true counsel, because there is no merit or help in it.[93] But the sweet blessed Jesus is a true counselor. (vv. 879–900)

You have heard how it happened, how he found man lost, thrown out of paradise; never could he return by himself or through his own power, had he not been raised up by God who wished to send his son into the world to save his people. He came to counsel us all, and to show us the way to heaven. But God is filled with truth, and wishes nothing but justice, and will save and heal only those who are willing to serve him. (vv. 901–914)

---

[87] 866–72 **Nature . . . sinned** *Mult est nature enbelie . . . Adam forfet aveit*: Murray, *Château*, 175 n. 866–72 explains that the passage seems to mean: Nature is embellished when God, without taking account of the ordinary course of nature, descends into the world, for the world then becomes a hundred times better than before the fall of Adam. On this passage, see Southern, *Robert Grosseteste*, 228.

[88] 867 **Creator** *nature naturante*: technical philosophical term translating the Latin *natura naturans* indicating Nature as the First Cause of the universe, i.e., God the Creator. Cf. Deferrari and Barry, *A Lexicon of Aquinas*, 723: "the nature that serves as the cause of everything that happens according to nature, by which is meant God."

[89] 868 **joined** *ignorante*: Mackie, "Robert Grosseteste's *Chasteau*," v. 872 (139) rejects this reading, substituting *ioygnante* from the Lambeth MS, f. 25ʳ.

[90] 869 **nature** *nature naturee*: this is a technical philosophical term (*natura naturata*), indicating nature as the created universe; cf. Southern, *Robert Grosseteste*, 227–28.

[91] 874 **free birth** *franche neissance*: because he is born free from the service to the devil, the Son has the status necessary to defend humanity. Cf. note to v. 186.

[92] 881–94 **Now imagine a man . . . your land** *Ki ke veïst ici un home . . . vostre terre*: this sounds like an exemplum, but a search of Frederic C. Tubach, *Index Exemplorum: A Handbook of Medieval Religious Tales* (Helsinki: Suomalainen Tiedeakatemia, 1969) turned up no parallels.

[93] 898 **no merit or help in it** *il ni a ne preu ne aïe*: the advice is not helpful because the sufferer has no one to aid him.

Gaze upon his power, man, and his eternal grandeur, which is without limit;[94] and see how he humbles himself, for he deigned to be born of a woman and to become a true man for us. And then, consider his counsel, how he leads us to safety in such a mild manner and says to us:[95]

"Dear sweet brother, I see you here, lost and exiled from your country, and you see clearly that in yourself you haven't the means to be restored. Do not despair and do not doubt, for if you believe in me, you will receive your inheritance; only hear me and follow my command. My yoke is easy to bear, my burden light to carry.[96] Pity for you has moved me, I have come here for you. I counsel you to follow me, and I will take up the battle for you. First, I will plead for you and lay claim to fight for your rights, for I am of your lineage and so I can claim your inheritance; and I am free born[97] and my speech will be heard. For you, I will undertake the battle and you will succeed, for I will be victorious in the end, and I will reclaim what rightfully belongs to you; you need think of nothing except loving God and your neighbor." (vv. 915–52)

God! What sweetness! And what generosity, since the one who rules everything shows us such friendship[98] and exemplifies humility. But this example is hardly followed and too rarely seen in the world, because the world always loves what is worldly, while the spirit of charity always loves humility. When the worldly man gives himself to the world and his wealth abounds, he thinks of nothing except what he has, and of acquiring more. When wealth has dominion, it binds him so firmly in its snares that he becomes harsh and proud, and arrogant to his neighbors. He desires generosity not at all, but only power and high estate. Because of his pride he completely forgets the example of humility. (vv. 953–74)

These men do not follow Jesus. Their behavior hinders them, for they do not want to believe his counsel. And how, or in what way, can they ask to have any of God's inheritance when they do whatever he forbids? They do nothing that he teaches, but always seek power and want nothing of humility. For this reason, Lucifer fell from heaven into hell. For this reason, I fear that they will also fall, all those who do such works. I do not say, however, that one cannot have possessions or great lordship and very high estate, castles and extensive woodlands.

---

[94] 917 **limit** *circumscription*: Murray, *Château*, 176–77 explains that God is without limitation or form, an idea similar to that of Eriugena, *De Divisione naturae*, Bk. 5 (*PL* 122. 896–902; ed. E. Jeauneau, CCCM 165 [Turnhout: Brepols, 2003], 52–61).

[95] 924 **us** *nus*: the reading in Murray's edition is found in seven other manuscripts; v. 928 of Mackie, "Robert Grosseteste's *Chasteau*" (142) reads "vus" from Lambeth 522, f. 26ᵛ.

[96] 935–36 **My yoke . . . carry** *Mon joc . . . sustenir*: Matt. 11:30.

[97] 945 **free born** *de franche nation*: i.e., born free of the servitude by which humankind is bound because of Adam's sin.

[98] 955 **friendship** *amisté*: on the friendship of Christ for mankind (cf. John 15:14–15), see McEvoy, *Robert Grosseteste*, 130–31.

One can still serve God very well, and do his will by living in humility, justice, and charity, because the Lord God holds nothing so dear as true and sincere love.[99] (vv. 975–98)

Now someone may ask how he intended to plead for us, and how he undertook the battle and how he won our rights. Now kindly listen and I will tell you how. When Jesus was born into the world, he was so hidden from the devil that the devil knew nothing of his coming. The devil thought to rule everything as he had done before, but his power was taken from him. He saw Jesus as an earthly man, but he did not know why the man had come to be born on earth, yet remained forever without sin. (vv. 999–1014)

Marveling, the devil said: "Who are you? Are you the son of God, then? I will give you all this world if you will agree to adore me."

And Jesus said: "Go, Satan; you shall not tempt your Lord God."[100]

And then the devil said:[101] "What do you intend to do? I am prince of this earth.[102] For a long time I have had the possession[103] of it, by charter[104] from the king most high. Unless I see your plan or know your secret, you will have much to do if you wish to win anything back from me. And even if I do not have power over you,[105] do you think you can take away my prey? No! the contract cannot be changed for it is written in multiple copies[106] in the court of God, saying that if Adam transgressed God's command, he would remain with me for all time and would finally die, and God, not wanting to commit an injustice, will honor the contract that was made earlier in his court." (vv. 1015–40)

Then sweet Jesus replied to him:

---

[99] 998 **true love** *fin amur*: as used in lyric poetry of the twelfth and thirteenth centuries, this usually refers to love between a lady and a knight. It is often translated in English as "courtly love" (see H. A. Kelly, "Courtly Love," *ODMA* 2:458–59). It is also used in religious context to indicate "true" or "perfect" love of God, e.g., the Nun of Barking's *La vie d'Edouard le confesseur* (ed. Östen Södergård, *La vie d'Edouard le Confesseur; poème Anglo-Normand du XIIe siècle* [Uppsala: Almquist and Wiksells, 1948]), v. 1360.

[100] 1015–20 **Marveling . . . tempt your Lord God** *En merveillant . . . Tun Seignur Deu ne tempteras*: cf. Matt. 4:1–4; Mark 1:11–14; Luke 4:1–3.

[101] 1021–110 **And then the devil . . . caught by the iron** *E cil dist donc . . . par le fer est atachié*: on the debate between Jesus and the devil, see Marx, *The Devil's Rights*, 69–71.

[102] 1022 **prince . . . earth** *Prince . . . terre*: cf. John 12:31.

[103] 1023 **possession** *seisine*: see above note to v. 131.

[104] 1024 **charter** *grant*: "grant, gift; grant of land, grant of a privilege or a right; grant, charter, legal document"; cf. Pollock and Maitland, *Law*, 2:93.

[105] 1024 **if I do not have power over you** *E se de tei puissance n'eie*: Mackie, "Robert Grosseteste's A-N Treatise," 171 translates this "And if I have none of your power."

[106] 1032 **multiple copies** *cirographer*: duplicate or triplicate copies are made on a single sheet; between the copies the scribe writes something—a word, motto, prayer, or alphabet—which is cut through when the copies are cut apart; see Olivier Guyotjeannin et al., *Diplomatie médiévale* (Turnhout: Brepols, 1993), 191, document 18.

"The contract was indeed enforced, but you violated it first, when you said to him treacherously, 'You will not die on that account, rather you will be as wise as God.'[107] You caused what happened. Now, listen to reason. Do you expect to gain from the contract when you do not maintain it?"

"Oh!" said the devil, "I am betrayed, when I am defeated while pleading my suit."

He continued:

"Where do you get such power, such virtue and knowledge, that you dare to dispute me, and reason with me? I have lost everything in arguing, but it won't stay like that![108] Man has transgressed so that he is in my prison and there will be no redemption for him. I will not be wrongly dispossessed."

Then said Jesus, the true king: "I will make payment for him."

And the devil said: "For what reason will you ransom this prisoner?[109] If you wish to buy him, it will cost you very dear."

"And how dear?"

"As much as he is worth, before he may go from my prison." (vv. 1041–68)

Then said sweet blessed Jesus:

"This is indeed justice and righteousness. I will take nothing from you by force, in breach of law. Therefore yield him to me willingly. What is it then that you ask?"

"I will tell you without fail. Give me what is worth as much as is the world now, and whatever may come after."

"Willingly will I do all this, for my little finger is worth more than are a hundred thousand such worlds with all the people in them."

The devil said angrily:

"Indeed I see that this is true, for I can govern all the world but I cannot come close to you in anything. And are you then willing to give your finger to buy such vile merchandise?"

"No," he said, "but my whole body." (vv. 1069–89)

"Before you have freed the prisoner, you will have to do much more, to suffer a great deal of pain and hurt. If you wish to make amends for his wrong, you must suffer death with as much suffering and as much pain as he would suffer for ever if he remained with me dwelling in hell." (vv. 1090–98)

Then sweet Jesus answered:

---

[107] 1043–44 **you will not die ... wise as God** *Tu ne murras pas ... cum Deu sachant*: cf. Gen. 3:4–5.

[108] 1055–56 **I have lost ... like that** *Tut ai perdu ... ne demora mie atant*: even if he has violated the contract, the devil does not admit defeat but turns to another line of argument, i.e., that he holds the prisoner.

[109] 1063–64 **And the devil said ... prisoner** *E dist li diables ... prison*: these lines occur only in Paris, BnF, fr. 902 and London, BL, Egerton 846B; Mackie, "Robert Grosseteste's *Chasteau*," retains them in her edition.

"Whatever you have said will all be carried out, for Truth determined it and Justice pronounced judgment. I will do more than you have said, and so the serf will be set free."

Then the Enemy thought that he would gain everything by Jesus's death. But the evil-doer was caught, like the fish on the hook when it swallows the worm and is caught on the piece of iron.[110] (vv. 1099–1110)

Now think about the kindness of the Savior's help, which is so easy to bear,[111] and from which healing may come. He takes all our misdeeds upon himself; on our account he is treated shamefully, the One who never sinned, nor was any wickedness found in him. In all the human limbs by which Adam first sinned, he wanted to punish his own members so as to pay our debts for our sins. For our iniquity he was crowned with thorns; and for our foolish glances he was blindfolded; they spat in his face and struck him with the palms of their hands; and for our foolish talk he was cursed and insulted; for our overeating he drank vinegar and bitter gall; for our wicked outward[112] deeds he was pierced in feet and hands; and for our bad thoughts he was pierced through to the heart. What more could he do for us? Tongue cannot recount, or the heart of man imagine[113] how he made himself suffer for us. Who is the man who would not be moved to pity for such great love? Such are the blows of battle he suffered for us without failing. (vv. 1111–45)

But when he delivered himself to death, he redeemed death by his own death, for he suffered a hundred times more pains and afflictions in dying than the power of the devils to burden human nature. For the soul so loves the body[114] that, regardless of any pain, it will never leave it before the body loses the power of all five senses, even if one wished to cut it to pieces. That is, it would lose all hearing and sight, speech, and its senses of smell and taste before it left the body, for Nature cannot allow the soul to leave the body before that. But the All-powerful multiplied his own suffering a hundred times, for when he hung on the cross he gave up his soul with a loud cry. It was then he showed he was God and

---

[110] As Mackie, "Robert Grosseteste's *Chasteau*," notes (vv. 1111–1114n.), Job 40:20 and the *Glossa ordinaria*'s influential commentary on it supported an iconographic tradition in which Christ uses a long-footed cross like a hook in the mouth of a Leviathan-like beast in order to release the inhabitants of Hell.

[111] 1112 **which is so easy to bear** *Ke tant est leger a suffrir*: cf. Matt. 11:30, alluded to in vv. 935–36; see note to vv. 935–36.

[112] 1133 **outward** *foreinz*: wicked physical (external) actions are distinguished from bad throughts in v. 1135.

[113] 1138–39 **Tongue ... imagine** *Langue ... penser*: an inexpressibility formula based on 1 Cor. 2:9.

[114] 1151 **For the soul so loves the body** *Kar tant eime l'alme le cors*: the relationship between body and soul is more often portrayed as an opposition; cf. Michel-André Bossy, "Medieval Debates of Body and Soul," *Comparative Literature* 28 (1976): 144–63.

accomplished our redemption. It was when he was incarnate[115] that he accomplished this, and thus he won the battle. The devil cannot require so much nor can Nature endure so much.[116] (vv. 1145–72)

Ah! most glorious Queen, Mary, Mother and Virgin, pity keeps me from naming your sorrows, or recalling them! But now the prophecy of Simeon[117] has been completely fulfilled, for your soul was more wounded by a sword than your body. But Jesus multiplied your joy a hundred times when he rose from the dead. The passion would have been worth nothing were it not for the resurrection.[118] You saw clearly the completion of his battle in which the devil was vanquished and the world helped, and our belief and our faith therefore remained in you. Everyone doubted, but you remained fast in your belief without doubting. Nothing could have changed your faith, Mary, Mother of pity, maiden full of goodness. Our belief was in you, therefore, as is now our hope that you will pray for us to him, our redeemer. (vv. 1173–1200)

You have heard about sweet Jesus, how by his great virtue he counseled us in goodness, how well he pleaded for us, how he fought for us, and how he finished his battle. Is he not the good counselor who thus redeemed us so dearly and who made a path for us so that we could come to the joy that was for so long blocked and closed to us by Eve? (vv. 1201–12)

Now consider as well how he is almighty God. Here you will hear clearly that he cannot be otherwise. One God created everything; this God redeemed us. There is no other god except him. This is the God of whom I tell you: three persons are named in him, but he is one God in unity. One can know and see the power of God in his deeds, for all his deeds were mixed with humanity and divinity. Whoever pays attention to his deeds can see that clearly. If anyone has a sword of sharp steel and puts it in the fire until it is red-hot, as long as it is red-hot no one can separate the fire from the steel, nor sever the steel from the fire. And whoever might strike with the sword would find two natures: the steel

---

[115] 1169 **when he was incarnate** *Vivant le cors*: although Christ's body suffered death, both his soul and his divine nature (united with both soul and body) continued to live; cf. Eriugena, *Adhuc de Christi resurrectione*, vv. 9–10 (*PL* 122. 1230B).

[116] 1171–71 **The devil cannot require so much ... endure so much** *Tant ne puet le diable charger ... tant endurer*: Christ's sufferings surpassed what the devil was entitled to exact, and exceeded what a natural being could endure.

[117] 1178 **Simeon** *Simeon*: Luke 2:35; the prophecy is fulfilled at the Crucifixion, and Mary is sometimes represented with a sword piercing her heart as she looks on her crucified son, e.g., in a fourteenth-century A-N manuscript, Paris, BnF, fr. 400, f. 43r: http://gallica.bnf.fr/ark:/12148/btv1b9009651g.r=.langFR

[118] 1183–84 **The passion would have been worth nothing ... resurrection** *Riens n'eüst valu la passion ... resurrection*: these lines are omitted in eight manuscripts, but retained as vv. 1187–88 in Mackie, "Robert Grosseteste's *Chasteau*," 157; cf. 1 Cor. 15:13.

cuts by nature and the fire burns; it is right,[119] and it all comes from one sword. So it is with Jesus Christ. He has fully two natures, truly God and truly man. (vv. 1213–44)

At the wedding of one of his friends, in Cana in Galilee, Architriclin[120] gave a banquet, where Jesus changed the water into wine. Six water-jars were brought and he commanded that they be filled with water. When Architriclin tasted the water, he found it to be good wine. As a man he commanded them to be filled, as God he changed the water into wine, and all this was the work both of man and of very God. Thus, wherever he went, so many people followed him that he fed five thousand men with five loaves of bread and two fishes; and twelve baskets were filled with the leftover scraps.[121] As man he divided the bread and as God he fed them all. (vv. 1245–64)

And look at Lazarus, whom Jesus raised after he had been in the tomb for four days and was all stinking with death; with a loud voice Jesus cried out: "Lazarus, come out from there."[122] As a man he shouted to him, and as God he restored him to life. In all his deeds we can see without a doubt that he is God. This God, who lodged himself in the Virgin, created everything. In him is our belief, our faith, and our hope; three persons in trinity, and a single God in unity. (vv. 1265–80)

You have heard clearly how he is God almighty, but no one can tell of his power, nor heart imagine, nor tongue describe. For this exalted name of Jesus has so much power in it, that everything in the highest heaven and on earth and in the abyss bows to this holy name;[123] for this reason a man who would describe his great power and his strength can only scratch[124] the surface. I wish to touch

---

[119] 1227–40 **Whoever . . . it is right** *Ki . . . c'est dreiture*: this image of the steel and the fire is a commonplace in medieval theology; see Murray, *Château*, 178 n. 1229–32.

[120] 1247 **Architriclin** *Architriclin*: name, from *architriclinus* "one who oversees the preparation of a feast" (Du Cange, *Glossarium mediae et infimae latinitatis*, vol. 1 [Lyon, 1688; repr. Paris: Librairie des arts, 1937]), given to the groom at whose wedding water was changed to wine (John 2:1–11, at 9); cf. *Biblia Latina cum Glossa Ordinaria* (Turnhout: Brepols, 1992), vol. 4, f. 228^v, col. 2: "Vocatur sponsus architriclinus." "Archedeclinus" was identified as the Cana bridegroom in vernacular texts such as Herman de Valenciennes's *Le Roman de Dieu et de sa mere*; see further D. A. Trotter, "The Influence of Bible Commentaries on Old French Bible Translations," *Medium Aevum* 56 (1987): 257–75. The name also occurs in the *Childhood of Jesus*, v. 1820 below.

[121] 1259–62 **he fed five thousand . . . were filled** *cinq mil homes a peüs . . . sunt emplis*: Matt. 14:15–21.

[122] 1270 **Lazarus, come out from there** *Lazere kar ça hors venez*: John 11:39–44.

[123] 1285–89 **For this exalted name . . . holy name** *Kar icest haut non . . . seint non*: Phil. 2:8–10; see below, part III of the *Seven-Part Meditation on the Passion* (Dublin, Trin. Coll., MS 374) for a meditation on the name of Jesus.

[124] 1292 **scratch** *rimer*: the reading *rongant* "gnawing" (Oxford, Corpus Christi College, MS 232, f. 26^r and London, Lambeth Palace, MS. 522, f. 36^v) seems superior.

on it clearly, according to what I understand. When the world was created, and Adam had first sinned, the Wicked One had so much power that he did what he wanted there because he had drawn Adam, for whom the world was made, into his power. The devil had so much power that he was prince of the world; no one, not for holiness, penance, or goodness, could strive so much as to escape hell. But the strength of Jesus Christ defeated and vanquished the devil. He was clearly vanquished, for he thought he could make Jesus do his will and submit him to his power as he could with other people. (vv. 1281–1312)

When the devil saw him hanging on the cross, he thought to take his soul. But the traitor failed;[125] instead, he was cast down in turn, for the holy divinity threw him into hell and went there himself with his soul and his godhead, and broke the gates of hell. He took a great bite out of hell,[126] and led out all his own people, those who believed in his coming and had served him willingly. Never had such power been heard of, nor indeed, except for Jesus, will there ever be such power, because he crushed the greatest power in the world. (vv. 1313–30)

The Wicked One was strongly armed against him and guarded his door very well, but when the stronger one[127] arrived, he took the devil's spoils from him; the devil was thrown out of the kingdom, and cast down into hell. For this reason Isaiah[128] said in his holy prophecy that Jesus would be named Powerful. No one could conceive of his strength, nor could tongue tell it, nor heart imagine it, nor intelligence describe it.[129] His strength causes fear but the kindness of his heart inspires love. He is our refuge, our strength,[130] our salvation, our faith, and our love, our help and our glory, the one who humbled himself so much and gave himself to save us, and one God alone did all this, Father, Son, and Holy Spirit. (vv. 1331–52)

You have heard how strong he is, but now, for God's sake, listen further and hear the story Isaiah tells us, that he would be called Father by people to come in the world to come. For this reason he wished to come into the world, so that all the holy prophecies might be fulfilled in him. You will indeed hear how he was the Father and how he begot us. In Adam, all sinned and through him all ate the apple: all who were begotten from him shared the curse upon him, for they

---

[125] 1316 **the traitor failed** *ad menti le traïtur*: the verb *mentir* "to lie" has a second sense of "to fail" (*AND* s.v. *mentir*). One manuscript indeed reads *failly* here (Mackie, "Robert Grosseteste's *Chasteau*," v. 1319n.).

[126] 1323 **took a great bite out of hell** *A enfern fist un grant mors*: the "bite" is Christ's liberation of souls from hell; cf. Hosea 13:14, "O death, I will be thy death; O hell, I will be thy bite." The pun (*mors/mors*) works in both Latin and French.

[127] 1334 **the stronger one** *li plus fort*: i.e., Jesus Christ.

[128] 1337 **Isaiah** *Ysaïe*: Isa. 9:6; see note to vv. 509–16.

[129] 1340–42 **No one ... describe it** *Nul ... descrire*: see above note to vv. 1138–39.

[130] 1345–46 **He is ... strength** *Icesti est ... force*: cf. Ps. 45:1.

shared it naturally, nor could it be otherwise, because Adam was our father and engendered us carnally. (vv. 1353–72)

But this begetting would have caused great and harsh suffering for us were it not for the grace of Jesus Christ, who engendered us in the spirit. All were condemned by Adam but redeemed by Jesus. He is rightly our Father; he begot us by washing us with his blood and redeeming our liberty. Never did a father show so much true love[131] for any child: he went straight into hell when he redeemed us and delivered us by his death. He remained there for forty hours, as Saint Augustine tells us,[132] until the morning of the third day. He rose again on a Sunday when dawn was first breaking. He took with him all his people who had ever been there since the time Adam was created until Jesus had risen. (vv. 1373–96)

He revealed himself to his disciples, eating and drinking with them. He remained there forty days, and preached the kingdom of God to them until the Ascension when his disciples were assembled in his name. Then Jesus appeared to them in order to test their lack of faith, because they had seen him risen but they all doubted, and did not believe it. But you should know that their doubt strengthened our faith, for Thomas's disbelief was greatly to our advantage — he who would not believe in resurrection for anyone until he had placed his hand in the wounds from Longinus's lance and then said: "You are my God." (vv. 1397–1417)

"Truly, Thomas," so Jesus said, "You believe it for you have seen it; and may he who believes without having seen it have the blessing that I give you for your belief."[133]

On that day he clearly wished to strengthen the faith of all people.

He ate with his disciples as he did before, and he talked about their travels, and that they should go into the world preaching to every creature[134] — that is, only man, of course — to believe in the Son of God and be baptized in the name of the Father and the Son and the most Holy Spirit, because whoever is not baptized will never enter heaven, but the baptized believers will be saved. He showed us clearly that it is fitting for us to be reborn; and since we shall be reborn we shall undergo conception. Jesus Christ begets us by water and the spirit;[135] he is truly our Father, and therefore we are his sons. (vv. 1418–47)

---

[131] 1384 **true love** *fin amur*: see note to v. 998.

[132] 1389 **Augustine** *Augustin*: *De Trinitate*, Bk 4, chap. 6: "Ab hora ergo mortis usque ad diluculum resurrectionis horae sunt quadraginta, ut etiam ipsa hora nona connumeretur" (*PL* 42. 894–95: Therefore, from the hour of his death until the dawn of the resurrection, there are forty hours, so that the ninth hour itself is counted in the reckoning).

[133] 1418–22 **Truly . . . give you for your belief** *Veire . . . creance te don*: John 20:28–29.

[134] 1429 **every creature** *universe creature*: cf. Mark 16: 15.

[135] 1443 **by water and the spirit** *Ce est del ewe e del espirit*: cf. John 3:4–6.

Indeed! Whoever does not give himself to such a father behaves like a wretch. He did not eat of the apple; through him we can indeed claim justice in heaven, for he kept the law, never infringing a point of it, the law that was never before upheld until his holy coming. The first man came from earth and through him we had war. The other man, who gave us back peace, came from heaven.[136] The first man, who did so much harm to all the world, was earthly. He was expelled from paradise, both him and all his lineage; but Jesus Christ our Father, who came down from heaven, gave us back our inheritance; he raised us up from low to high. (vv. 1448–68)

Whoever came of earth, returned to earth. The man who came from heaven went up into heaven, at the Ascension, in the sight of the people round about. He made a path for his subjects through the clouds and went away. He is the life and the truth and the way:[137] he leads the fair prey with him.[138] He took with him all who belonged to him, whom he had carried out of hell. He brought them to the joy that will never fail and he remains where he was before, with the Father, one God, three persons in Trinity and a single God in unity. One God made all things, Father, Son, and Holy Spirit, and if there is a distinction among three persons by name, nonetheless there remains one single God, Creator of creatures, to whom belongs all honor and glory, without end and without beginning. (vv. 1469–92)

How he is Father you have heard, and if you will continue to listen, you will hear shortly how he is the Prince of Peace. I have already recounted to you how he ascended into heaven. When he wants to judge the world he will come in a different way, in his divinity, in soul and in body, to judge everyone, living and dead, as surely as he used to walk the world. He will show the wounds that he suffered for the world, and how he was scarred for us; his skin was torn by scourges and the blood from his body flowed through his skin; he was led along shamefully and crowned with thorns, and was placed on the cross, his feet and hands pierced through; he was pierced through the heart whence blood and water gushed forth. And then he will then say to everyone:

"For you have I suffered so much disgrace and exceedingly great pain."

What shall we say in response? It will be worthless to plead, or answer him or oppose him. (vv. 1493–1520)

Neither castle nor tower will be worth anything, nor a great and handsome palace, for all things will perish that are the work of human hands. Then sinners will tremble, grinding their teeth with indescribable fear. Each one will see his own trial and his judgment before him. All his deeds will be written openly

---

[136] 1459 **came from heaven** *del ciel est venuz*: cf. 1 Cor. 15:47.
[137] 1475 **the life ... the way** *Vie ... veie*: John 14:6.
[138] 1476 **prey** *preie*: cf. v. 1030, where the devil refers in this way to the souls he has seized.

across his forehead,[139] and all the world will see them. On that bitter and dangerous day they will say with hideous shouts:

"Mountains, fall on us! Ah! lands, cover us, so that no one may see the horror of the Creator's anger."[140]

Afterwards they will see such signs by which all people will die.[141] (vv. 1521–40)

Then a fire will come before Jesus which will burn the whole world; it will burn all the plains, and the cliffs and the mountains. Heaven and earth will catch fire; the elements will dissolve. By fire will the air be purified and the waters dispersed. He will purify all the world, and there will be no more water, nor will there be fire in the world when this fire is extinguished. Then the Lord God will make for himself a new heaven and a new earth,[142] not different from what he made before, but he will put them into a better state. (vv. 1541–56)

Then the angels from heaven will come and sound the trumpets. All who have died in Jesus Christ will rise in soul and body;[143] and all those who will be saved will rise first. To these our Lord will say with great joy and great kindness:

"I was hungry and you fed me; you gave me shelter. I was thirsty, you gave me to drink, I was naked and you clothed me; I was sick and you visited me, and[144] in prison you comforted me. Come, my blessed sons, receive the joys of heaven which have been prepared for your use since the beginning of the world."[145] (vv. 1557–74)

Then the good will be transported into the air[146] toward him. The wicked will remain on earth and will not see the glory of God, but at this drawing up they will rise up together, these woeful, unfortunate wretches who are burdened

---

[139] 1531 **his deeds ... forehead** *ses fez .. sun front*: in Apoc. 9:4 the sign of God is written on the foreheads of the saved; in Apoc. 14:1 what is written is the name of the Lamb and his Father; Apoc. 20:12 specifies that the dead will be judged according to their works, as recorded in a book.

[140] 1535–38 **Mountains ... Creator's anger** *Muntaines ... l'ire a le creatur*: Apoc. 6:16.

[141] 1539–40 **signs ... will die** *signes ... murrunt*: on the Last (General) Judgment, see John McHugh, "General Judgment," *The Catholic Encyclopedia*, vol. 8 (New York: Robert Appleton Company, 1910), 2 Jun. 2012 <http://www.newadvent.org/cathen/08552a.htm>. For A-N texts on the signs of Judgment Day, see Dean with Boulton, nos. 637–639.

[142] 1554 **a new heaven and a new earth** *noveu ciel e novele terre*: Apoc. 21:1.

[143] 1559 **soul and body** *en alme e cors*: cf. 1 Thess. 4:15.

[144] 1570 **and in prison** *En en prison*: a misreading (or a scribal error) for "E en prison."

[145] 1571–74 **Come ... world** *Venez ... mund*: Matt. 25:34–36.

[146] 1575–76 **Then the good ... air** *Adonc serrunt li bon ... en l'eir*: cf. 1 Thess. 4:16.

with sin. Downcast, they will remain on earth until they hear the voice of the Judge. They will hear their wrathful and terrifying judgment:

"You wicked ones, go with the devil into the everlasting fire,[147] for you have earned nothing else from all the works of mercy."

They will fall head over heels into hell and be forever with the devil, blacker than mulberry or coal, and thus their name will perish. (vv. 1575–94)

Truly, the good will be glorified in both body and soul and they will be as bright as the sun.[148] Never more will they have to work, but they will have unending joy. Many were born at a propitious moment, so that they will be able to come to the feast that God will give for his own. There will be so much joy then that it will last forever and without end, more than could enter any heart, or any eye see or ear hear the joy that God has prepared for those who have loved him sincerely,[149] and that will never fail; and thus is he Prince of Peace. (vv. 1595–1611)[150]

And those in hell will never leave there, but will be tormented in its deep stinking abyss. There is nothing in hell that does not wound. The first torment will be sadness, and each [sinner] will press upon the others, which will double their pain. Another torment will be darkness, and the third will be fear. The fourth will be inextinguishable fire, and then the horror of seeing the devil. They will always have before them the thing that they most hate in the world, and repulsive[151] maggots, and they will see nothing that pleases them, for they will weep every day without end, gnash their teeth, and snarl. One will then say to the other:

"Wretch, what are you doing there?[152] Alas, I curse the hour you were born since your sins stink on me. My own sin makes me suffer here, and you double

---

[147] 1587–88 **Go, wicked ones . . . everlasting** *Alez, maleürez . . . pardurable*: Matt. 25:41.

[148] 1595–97 **the good . . . the sun** *Li bon . . . solail*: cf. Matt. 13:43.

[149] 1605–6 **More than . . . hear** *Plus ke . . . entendre*: cf. 1 Cor. 2:9.

[150] 1595–1754 **so much joy . . . the beauty of God**: Grosseteste's contrasting accounts of heaven and hell bear some resemblance to the influential Ps.-Anselmian *De custodia interioris hominis* (ed. Schmitt and Southern, *Memorials of St. Anselm*, 354–60), though the passages here are not so close in all details as to suggest Grosseteste had the text before him. Whereas homilists emphasized and developed the accounts of hell in such texts, Grosseteste here gives more detail to the joys of heaven (vv. 1651–1754). Unsurprisingly for a major pastoral figure, Grosseteste is himself credited (in the fourteenth century) with one such treatise in French: see Dean with Boulton no. 645 and Introduction, n. 9 above.

[151] 1625 **repulsive** *de mau plait*: *AND* does not attest this phrase, but has *de bon plai* "pleasing"; the context supports the opposite meaning here.

[152] 1629 **doing** *feïs*: an editor's error for *feis* (i.e., *fais*, present indicative); cf. Mackie, "Robert Grosseteste's *Chasteau*," 182, v. 1632.

my pain. But you, unfortunate wretch, I curse the hour that you came alive. Your wicked stinking sins make me snarl."

Thus they will bewail their sorrows, which will double each day. Love does not exist there, nor do joy, solace, and kindness. They will be confined to this abyss and will never leave it. The devil, who will torment them without ceasing, will be their prince. (vv. 1612–46)

But Jesus is the Prince of Peace.[153] His peace will never fail; rather joy and solace and love will be renewed day by day. The first joy will be that the man who is holy will see his Lord face to face there,[154] his God and his Creator. He will be mirrored in God's beauty and will see everything in him. He will be restored to so much joy that he will have whatever pleases him. Whatever he desires, he will find in looking at him. He will see the generosity of heaven, its beauty and nobility. Then he will see the glorious Mother of God, the precious, the most sweet Virgin Mary, and all the fair company.

He will see the nine orders of angels,[155] and each angel will greet him joyfully; the apostles and the martyrs will display endless joy. Then he will see the confessors and the virgins in beautiful raiment. There he will recognize his friends, those whom he once saw in the world, displaying such great joy, more than heart can imagine. Each one will be so powerful that he will do whatever pleases him, and he will be so light that he will think of a place and be able to go there. All will be so ethereal that they will pass through wherever they wish. One will say to the other:[156] (vv. 1647–80)

"Blessed be the one who created you and may the hour when you were born be honored before God, for in you I see joy so fair that it renews my joy."

The other will answer: "Blessed be the Almighty who has given you this joy by which my joy is multiplied; in you I have such great joy that all my own is renewed, with the great joy and love of looking at my Creator who formed me after himself and then deigned to redeem me. My joy is multiplied a hundred times. I have everything that I have desired." (vv. 1681–1700)

Such joy will remain with them and they will always be joyful. The less beautiful will be as bright as the sun, which will be seven times brighter than it is now and will shine more. The sun will have no purpose since everything is so

---

[153] 1647 **Prince of Peace** *Prince de Pès*: Isa. 9:6.

[154] 1652–53 **see . . . fact to face** *verra . . . Face a face*: cf. 1 Cor. 13:12.

[155] 1667 **nine orders of angels** *neuf ordres d'angles*: see M. Boyd, "Angels," *ODMA* 1:58.

[156] 1677–80 **Each one . . . will say to the other** *Chescun . . . al autre donc dirra*: in his 1231 letter to Richard Marshal, earl of Pembroke, Grosseteste described "bodies in heaven" as having "a lightness that cannot be weighed, a mobility that knows no hindering. . . a splendor like that of the sun. . . a state of blessedness untainted by envy. . .": Letter 6, in *The Letters of Robert Grosseteste, Bishop of Lincoln*, trans. F. A. C. Mantello and Joseph Goering (Toronto and Buffalo: University of Toronto Press, 2010), 71–72.

bright,[157] and whoever has most deserved it will be much more beautiful. He will see so many mansions[158] and legions of angels having varied kinds of joy. He will have even more joy at the sight. (vv. 1701–14)

And then he will see the most beautiful Queen and Virgin, the brightest and the purest of all creatures, the holy Virgin Mary. Her beauty is multiplied so much more than all other beauties because she has the greatest dignity. She has so much dignity because the Lord God is her child, and just as great as her beauty are her nobility and goodness. She denies her love, solace, or help to no one. For this reason, all in heaven welcome her. No earthly mind can describe her goodness or her nobility, her generosity or her simplicity, or her beauty. Nor could it be otherwise, since he, who foreordained everyone's beauty and illuminates all beauty, deigned to be born of her. (vv. 1715–38)

But anyone who meditates on her will be in joy and peace for ever; but the joy and the sweetness of gazing upon her Creator surpasses every other joy; there is no sum of joys to compare with that.[159] And if all the wisdom of all the men in the world were put into a single man, and he could live forever, as long as the world lasts,[160] still that man could not imagine so much or describe clearly and entirely one joy that the Lord God has prescribed for his chosen ones. How then can he imagine or describe the beauty of God? (vv. 1739–54)

But when we are glorified,[161] then we will see clearly how he is three in Trinity and one single God in unity, of whom, by whom, and in whom are all the joys in heaven. This Prince will guide his own in peace, and joy and peace will be forever; and may God in his mercy grant that we lead our lives accordingly and keep his commands so as to come into his peace. Amen. (vv. 1755–68)

---

[157] 1707–8 **sun ... bright** *Solail ... cler*: cf. Apoc. 21:23.

[158] 1711 **many mansions** *tant de mansions*: dwelling places prepared for the just; cf. John 14:1–3.

[159] 1741–44 **but the joy ... no sum ... with that** *mes la joie ... Envers cele ... nul acunte*: the joy of meditating on the Virgin is surpassed only by the beatific vision of God himself; cf. J. C. Hendrickson, "Beatific Vision," *ODMA* 1:239.

[160] 1749 **as long ... last** *Tant cum le mond poet durer*: omitted from Murray's edition, supplied by Mackie, "Scribal Intervention," 73 n. 19.

[161] 1757 **glorified** *glorifié*: the celestial bodies of the just are "glorified"; cf. 1 Cor. 15:40–43. See further Caroline Walker Bynum, *The Resurrection of the Body in Western Christianity, 200–1336* (New York: Columbia University Press, 1995).

2. "Jesus" from Grosseteste's Translation of 'Suidas'

Verse Prologue

In the name of the holy Trinity, I wish to translate the truth of the holy Nativity, and of the virginity of the virgin Saint Mary, so that she may give me strength and help to bring this to a successful end and finish this story well. I want to stop rhyming because I could exceed or distort the matter too much or alter the truth. But I should like to apply myself to translating the story in the written text into French from Latin, so no one can dispute anything. (610: 1–8)[1]

Text

This is the account of the book that is called *Suidas* in Hebrew, which[2] these wise men—Hendenus rector, Heradius, Eugenius, Eregius, Zonomanus, Tullius the sophist, Pamfilius, Julius, Zapathon and Pallion[3]—drew up in the time of Theodosius the Jew. In the time of Justinian the emperor,[4] a prince of the Jews named Theodosius was known to, and was the friend of several men known to, the said emperor. And in that time there was a Christian named Philip, a silversmith, who was the close friend of the Jew Theodosius and greatly admonished him that he should be a Christian. (610: 9–15)

One day it happened that the said Philip made the following speech to Theodosius:

"Why don't you want to believe in Jesus Christ and be a Christian, seeing that you are a wise man and know the religion and the prophets? Don't be guided

---

[1] The lines are numbered from the beginning of the A-N text on page 610, and start anew on each page.

[2] 610:9 **which** *de quel*: the Latin text in London, BL, MS Royal 8 B IV (f. 73ʳ "quem composuerunt") supports treating the relative pronoun as a direct object. *Suidas* was composed in Greek.

[3] 610:10–11 **wise men . . . Pallion** *sages homes . . . Pallion*: the list does not appear in the Greek text, and was probably added by Grosseteste; it is included in some Latin manuscripts, e.g., London, BL, Royal 8 B.IV.

[4] 610:12 **Justinian the emperor** *iustinien emperour*: the Eastern Roman emperor, who reigned 527–565.

by ignorance, for you know well what the prophets said by the inspiration of the Holy Spirit and about the coming of Jesus Christ. Now hasten to save your soul and be Christian and believe in Jesus Christ our Savior so that you may not be damned at the Last Judgment." (611: 1–6)

When the Jew heard the Christian's speech, he was grateful, thanked him, and answered:

"I accept what you said to me for the salvation of my soul, and I believe in Jesus Christ, who knows all the secrets of the heart of the Lord,[5] and I am certain that he came as the prophets told it, and I find it valid and recognize it, and I reproach myself. Now, I am a prince of the Jews, and I have great prosperity and an abundance of goods and of the things that are necessary in this life; and if I agreed to convert, I know well that your people would make me a patriarch or would give me a great office. And if I despise eternal life for the pleasure of earthly things, I act wrongly. And because I see and know that you are my friend, I will tell you a secret that is hidden among us Jews, by which we know that Jesus Christ, who is adored by you Christians,[6] was prophesied by the Law and the Prophets; and this secret is falsely hidden among us Jews. (611: 7–19)

"In ancient times, when the temple was built in Jerusalem, there was a certain custom among the Jews: in accordance with the number of twenty-two letters of the alphabet[7] there were twenty-two books[8] inspired by the grace of God and twenty-two priests were ordained who served in the temple. And this book, in which were written the names of the twenty-two priests and of their fathers and their mothers, was kept with great reverence. And when one priest died, the others convened in the temple and, by agreement, chose another in place of the one who had died. And then they wrote in the book that on such and such a day such and such a priest died, of such and such a father and mother, and in his place another one was appointed. (611: 20–26)

"This custom lasted among the Jews until Jesus lived in Judea, before he made himself known or called his disciples. One of the priests died and the others convened in the temple to choose another, as was customary. Each one pronounced his judgment, for they wished to have a type of man who was wise, led a righteous life, and was of the lineage of Levi. (611: 27–31)

---

[5] 611:9 **Lord** *domine*: the translator has retained the Latin word.

[6] 611:16–17 **who is hidden . . . by you Christians** *ki est rebot entre nous iuis, par quoi nus sauom ke jesu crist ki est aorez de vus cristiens*: the scribe repeated the entire sentence at the top of the page, perhaps confused by turning over his leaf.

[7] 611:21 **letters of the alphabet** *lectres*: there are twenty-two letters in the Hebrew alphabet.

[8] 611:21 **twenty-two books** *xxij livers*: perhaps the Pentateuch plus the seventeen books of Prophets; cf. Suda-on-line: www.stoa.org/sol-bin/search.pl?searchstr=iota,229&field=adlerhw_gr

"One priest rose and said to his companions: 'I have heard several men reproached as unworthy to serve in the temple. Now listen to me, if you please, for indeed I think that you will be well rewarded by what I say, for I advise and counsel you that you appoint Jesus who was the son of Joseph and Mary, in place of the one who has died; although he is young, Jesus is wise and leads a good life, and I do not think that there is his equal in Jerusalem in wisdom or effectiveness.' (611: 32–37)

"When the others heard this speech they were well satisfied and confirmed the decree. They agreed that the mother of Jesus should be led to the council and that they should know from her whether she was his mother, and the name of the man who was his father. When she was present they said to her: 'Since this priest has died, the son of such and such a father and mother, we wish to make your son Jesus a priest; now, tell us if Jesus is your son and if you bore him.'

"When Mary heard this speech she answered that he was her son, that she had borne him, that she had a good witness, and that he had no earthly father: 'For when I was in Galilee the angel of God entered the house where I was keeping vigil, not sleeping, and greeted me on behalf of God and announced to me that I would conceive and bear the son of God, by the Holy Spirit, my virginity unharmed—and I am still a virgin—and said that he would be named Jesus.' (611: 38–612: 4)

"When the priests heard this speech, they were amazed and sent for matrons and wet-nurses to examine Mary and determine whether she was a virgin. They were persuaded of her virginity and were most amazed; they asked Mary to tell them in confidence who was Jesus's father, so that they could write the truth in a book. (612: 5–8)

"Mary answered them that she had borne Jesus, that he had no father, that she had heard the angel call him the son of God, and that she was a virgin and not corrupted. (612: 9–10)

"When the priests heard this, they brought their book and wrote: on such and such a day such and such a priest died, son of such and such a father and mother, and by agreement and election, Jesus, the son of the living God and the virgin Mary, is made priest. And this book is kept in the temple with great reverence and the secret is not known to all. But it has been revealed to me because I am the master and the prince of our people. And we do not guarantee by the Law alone that Jesus Christ, who is adored by you Christians, is the son of God who came down to earth for the salvation of the world, but also by the inscription in the book, which is safe-guarded. (612: 11–17)

"But after the Passion, when our ancestors saw that they had condemned and crucified the son of God, they disloyally stole the book and deposited it in Tiberias."[9] (612: 18–19)

---

[9] 612:19, 21 **Tiberias** *tiberiade, tyberyaden*: a city in Roman Palestine on the Sea of Galilee.

When the Christian heard these words from the Jew, he was very happy and thanked our Lord; and he wished to go at once to tell these words to the emperor so that he would send him to Tiberias to recover the book to reproach the infidelity of the Jews. (612: 20–22)

The Jew answered the Christian:

"Why do you want, on the condemnation of your soul, to reveal this speech to the emperor and lose what you desire? For if he knew, there would be battle and bloodshed, and homicide, and the Jews would burn the place where the book is kept, and we would have wasted our pains. And I have revealed this secret to you because of the great love that I have for you, and so that you might know that I do not refuse to be Christian from ignorance but from vainglory." (612: 23–28)

When the Christian heard his speech, he did not reveal it to the emperor because he knew well that the emperor, who had great love for and great devotion to God, would bring about great bloodshed; but he revealed this speech to his close friends. And we find written that Josephus wrote about the capture of Jerusalem[10] and that Eusebius Pamphilus[11] revealed the capture in the *Ecclesiastical History* and recounted how Jesus ministered and kept holy in the temple with the priests. And we found the writings of Josephus,[12] a man of antiquity, and afterwards we sought the deeds of the apostles[13] and we found these words confirmed in the Scriptures inspired by God. And we find in the gospel of Saint Luke that God entered the synagogue of the Jews and was given a book in which he sought the prophecy of Isaiah, who said: (612: 29–38) "The spirit of our Lord is on me, and anoints me and sends me to preach the gospel to the poor."[14] And we have thought that if Jesus had no ministerial rank in the synagogue, no book would have been delivered to him to read in the presence of all the people. Even now among us Christians no man should read the books inspired by God if he is not ordained according to the statutes of holy Church. And from what we have learned from the gospel of Saint Luke, we ought to believe what Theodosius the

---

[10] 612:32 **Josephus ... Jerusalem** *josephus ... ierusalem*: Flavius Josephus, author of *De bello Judaico*, fought against the Romans in the campaign that led to the destruction of Jerusalem in 70 CE; cf. Josephus, *The Jewish War*, ed. and trans. H. St. J. Thackeray (Cambridge, MA: Harvard University Press, 1997); S. Bowman, "Josephus Flavius," in *ODB* 2:1075.

[11] 612:32–33 **Eusebius Pamphilus** *eusebius panfile*: Eusebius (c. 260–340), bishop of Caesarea, who wrote the *Ecclesiastica historia*, considered himself the spiritual son of Pamphilus; cf. Eusebius, *The Ecclesiastical History*, 2 vols., ed. H. J. Lawlor, trans. Kirsopp Lake and J. E. L. Oulton (London: Heinemann: New York: Harvard University Press, 1973–75); A. Kazhdan, "Eusebios of Caesarea," in *ODB* 2:751–52.

[12] 612:35 **Josephus** *joseph*: see above, note 10 to 612:32.

[13] 612:35 **deeds of the apostles** *fait des apostles*: perhaps a reference to the New Testament *Acts*.

[14] 612:39–40 **The spirit ... poor** *Lespirit ... poveres*: Luke 4:17–18, citing Isa. 61:1.

Jew revealed to his friend Philip, for he did not say it from any deceit, but revealed in good conscience the secret hidden by the Jews. (612: 39–613: 3)

The narrating of the book called *Suidas* in Greek is finished; the wise men mentioned above wrote it. (613: 4–5)

3. The Childhood of Jesus Christ
(*Les Enfaunces de Jesu Crist*)

Prologue

I wish to relate something that should be pleasing to you; henceforth I shall ask you to listen to this account. If you agree to listen, you will hear about the childhood[1] of Jesus Christ the blessed, who must be honored. It does one good to listen to this; do not be half-hearted, for everyone, great and small, can find pleasure and profit in it. You have heard many romances by very diverse people that were to your liking. Now listen well, for you shall hear much that is pleasurable and profitable. Indeed, this text will show that everything comes from Jesus Christ.

Now commit this text to memory[2] without hesitation. This story of youthful deeds will undoubtedly please you, for I will not say or show anything except what can be verified, as shown in Latin and found entirely in books. I will not recount the gloss, but only the completely truthful text,[3] as I have found it in books; thus I will describe[4] everything to you in detail. (vv. 1–32)

When Jesus Christ the blessed was born of his mother, as the angel had announced it, Mary had joy in abundance. Soon afterwards he was put straight into

---

[1] 6 **childhood** *enfaunces*: a standard term for a work dealing with the childhood and education of a hero, especially in the epic tradition.

[2] 22–22 **commit . . . memory** *metez . . . remembrance*: *AND* glosses the phrase "mettre en remembrance" as "record," but the context here does not support this meaning; it seems to be used more literally as "remember."

[3] 30 **truthful text** *tiste*: *tiste*, "text," can often refer to the gospels: the author declares that he will refrain from adding interpretative glosses.

[4] 32 **describe . . . in detail** *destincterai*: *AND* glosses *destincter* as "distinguish, specify, describe in detail;" in *Lumere as Lais*, ed. G. Hesketh, III, ANTS 58 (London: ANTS, 2000), 185 it is glossed as "to treat under separate heads"; it is related to *distinction*, which can mean a subdivision of a book. In the scholastic compilations known as *Distinctiones*, words found in the Bible are arranged along a more or less alphabetic principle with their various definitions; see Beryl Smalley, *The Study of the Bible in the Middle Ages* (Oxford: Blackwell, 1952), and R. L. H. Lops, *La Bible de Macé de la Charité*, 7: *Apocalypse* (Leiden: Presse Universitaire de Leyde, 1982), xxvii–xxxi.

a manger where an ox and an ass were eating: both knew that it was God who was placed there,[5] and that he was sent to earth to save all his friends. Here he was circumcised and then presented in the temple, and he was greatly desired by Simeon the blessed[6] who had spoken so much of him. (vv. 33–48)

Then, because of this event, three kings[7] from a foreign land went with their gifts to seek that child, so that they might inquire about everything and whether it was God who was born, for a star of great brightness, which had revealed the birth, had guided them from their land: by dint of the star[8] that they saw they knew the truth. They all agreed that they would then go to the child. They immediately made their way toward Bethlehem, but they went too far into the land of that tyrant Herod, who was king and lord and governor of the whole kingdom. (vv. 49–66)

With very great anger toward the kings he at once said:

"Who are you and where do you come from? And who brought you here? You have a crazed look about you."

"Sire, we are crowned kings; we are from a foreign land and we are searching and seeking if we can, by any means, to see the God who was born on earth."

"What now, sir king, is there another god besides me? I see clearly that you are wronging me." (vv. 67–79)

"Mercy, sire, listen to me: we know plainly that God almighty was born, and he will save all the people, know that for the truth. Thanks to a star of great brightness we know unambiguously that he was born; he has led us here from our lands with our complete agreement. We have truly lost the bright star and its light ever since we entered this kingdom; for that reason, sire, we ask your permission to leave here." (vv. 80–94)

"There is nothing further to say, for I wish to send for my scholars and learn the whole truth."

Herod then sent for all his scholars and explained to them what he wanted to know about the child. Each then took up his book; they found in their law that a king had been born who would attract everyone to himself.

"And will he be greater than I am?"

Each of the doctors answered:

"Yes, sire, and rightly so, for no one anywhere could be greater than he is." (vv. 95–108)

---

[5] 40–41 **both ... placed there** *E l'un e l'autre ... la fu mis*: traditional exegesis of Isa. 1:3.

[6] 47 **Simeon the blessed** *Siméon li bonuré*: Luke 2:25.

[7] 49 **three kings** *treis reis*: the account, vv. 49–152, is very similar to that in Matt. 2:1–12, but is enlivened with dialogue.

[8] 57 **by dint of the star** *l'esteile*: usually *a l'esteile*.

"Oh! By Mohammed's head,[9] shall I then be under his jurisdiction? He will indeed be of great renown if he is such a powerful man."

Then wicked Herod, with cruel intention, spoke to the three kings: "Go, lords, with my leave, to the child who has now been born and when you have given presents to him, return at once directly to me and to my people, for we will make him a very handsome gift."

Without further delay, the three kings, greatly alarmed, immediately saw the star; it was not a jest. (vv. 109–23)

What shall I tell you beyond that? When they had all gone forth from the land of the wicked man, they looked at that star that gave such great light. They came to Bethlehem and made offerings to sweet Jesus since they had indeed recognized him as God: gold, incense of great strength, and, indeed, myrrh as well, for they knew most certainly that he had so much power in him that he would vanquish his enemy. (vv. 124–36)

When they had presented their gifts,[10] they all wished to sleep straightaway, and so indeed they did. While they were sleeping, an angel announced to them that they should not go on toward Herod the tyrant. They turned back from there and continued on their way; they journeyed home to their country and praised God the blessed: had they returned through the land of the wicked man Herod, all three would surely have been killed by him. (vv. 137–52)

Herod was harsh and extremely angry when he could not find them, whatever he did, for he desired to kill them. He then had all the children below the age of two and a half brought before him, as I tell you; I can assure you that he had them killed. The wicked man mistakenly thought he had killed the child Jesus when he killed the recently born, as I have recounted to you.[11] (vv. 153–64)

Mary was very sorrowful; she begged her husband Joseph to listen attentively to the voice of the angel without argument. Indeed, that angel told them everything that Mary was to do. She was, he said, to carry her son into Egypt and remain there.[12] I will now leave that matter and speak of the many deeds that he did during his childhood on earth. (vv. 165–76)

Mary went with her son and Joseph, who loved her very much. They met many dragons, but each one bowed before Jesus.[13] Then Mary took her child and held him in her lap. She was very afraid of the beasts, because she saw so many of

---

[9] Herod's anachronistic oath places him indiscriminately in the category "pagan," which included Muslims, or "Saracens."

[10] 138 **their gifts** *lur present*: the French form is singular, but the context confirms that each king made a separate gift.

[11] 153–64 **Herod was harsh ... recounted to you** *Mut crüel Herode esteit ... vus ai counté*: Matt. 2:16–18.

[12] 169–76 **that angel ... remain there** *Icel angle ... demor[er]ad*: Matt. 2:13–14.

[13] 179–80 **many dragons ... bowed before Jesus** *Muz de dragons ... l'enclina*: see Ps.-Matt. chaps. 18–19 for a much fuller account.

them coming. Many lions came, and other four-footed animals; sheep and wolves roamed there and did no harm to each other. Afterwards, everyone understood that everything that Isaiah told us when he revealed his prophecy was indeed true; he had explained by his words that when Mary had a son, the wolf would eat with the sheep without harm or strife.[14] (vv. 177–96)

The third day after they had gone forth from the land of the wicked, fearsome Herod was very hot, for the sun was blazing. And Mary immediately called Joseph and said to him:

"Lord Joseph, know truly that this heat bothers me a great deal. For that reason, lord, set me down beneath that tree that you see."[15]

"With pleasure," he said to her. Joseph brought Mary straight to the tree and lifted her down from the mule on which she was seated. Then Mary indeed rested beneath that tree and gazed upon it; she took great delight in it because of the fruit that it bore so plentifully. She showed clearly by what she was thinking that the fruit pleased her greatly and she said to Joseph, laughing:

"Now would I have my fill of it!" (vv. 197–220)

Then Jesus, who knew everything, spoke to the tree (his mother was then holding him for she loved him most tenderly):

"Tree, bend down at once and bow to my mother; hand over to her in great abundance the fruit you bear!"

At his voice, the tree that bore the fruit then bent over and Mary ate of it, as did Joseph, who loved her greatly. When they were sated and had had enough of the fruit, they rejoiced and thanked Jesus very much. Jesus loved his mother greatly and she him, very appropriately so, for he carried out her request just as she asked. Blessed Jesus, who did so many good deeds, said:

"Tree, now be raised and stand up straight!" Without waiting, the tree stood up and was as straight as it had been before; so much was the tree ready to humble itself. (vv. 221–48)

Then as Mary held her child in her lap, she took very great joy in him and in the many deeds that he performed.

"Mary, my dear love,[16] I am overcome by thirst[17] and our water is already gone; I must tell you that." Mary answered him:

"And I am also very thirsty, as is the mule we have with us."

---

[14] 191–96 **everything Isaiah . . . strife** *Ço ke Ysaÿe . . . estriz*: Isa. 11:6.

[15] 197–220 **On the third day . . . my fill of it** *Le terz jur . . . ma saülee*: Ps.-Matt. chaps. 20–21.

[16] 253 **Mary, my dear love** *Marie ma bele amie*: the speaker is Joseph: the *Enfaunces* omits the lines introducing his speech; they appear in the Continental *Évangile de l'Enfance*, vv. 371–73.

[17] 254 **overcome** *prent pur la mestrie*: *pur la maistrie* may be a variant of the more common *par maistrie*, but may also have been influenced by ME *for the maistrye*, "extremely" (*OED*, VI, 218c).

Jesus heard this. Listen! listen to how he spoke to the tree that had righted itself! As you will hear, he commanded and required the following of it:

"For the love of my good mother, whom I love and hold most dear, give her some clear water and answer her prayer. And I wish, and so command, that in return you shall be equal in paradise henceforth, by my authority forever; and from your roots may there be many clear springs and pure water abundantly given!" (vv. 249–76)

When Jesus, full of goodness, had thus commanded, they found abundant beautiful springs that came from the roots. Mary drank her fill of this water which satisfied her, as did Joseph, who loved her; her thoughts were happy and Joseph was delighted for her and for his animal; this deed pleased her more than any meat, salted or fresh.[18] Mary held her son and she thanked him for all that he did and she loved her son always. Once more, Jesus the blessed said of this tree:

"May your branches be planted in paradise!" Straightaway, an angel came and took branches from the tree and planted them in paradise, as Jesus commanded. (vv. 277–300)

But when the angel was seen and observed by the people, everyone was terrified and moved to fear. Indeed, there was such intense brightness, since the tree shone all around and in front, that all were transfixed. Those who saw this miracle fell down flat as though dead, they had never seen such brightness; they gave thanks to Jesus Christ for it. Then Jesus Christ said to everyone:

"Why were you so fearful? You may know for a fact that my command will be obeyed."

Then Joseph said to Jesus, who was full of goodness and virtue:

"We have suffered great heat, for it burns us just like fire, and if you agree, let's go by the road along the sea which is refreshing to us, and in that way we would make good headway."

Blessed Jesus answered:

"Now, Joseph, do not fear; your road has been made shorter by thirty days straight." (vv. 301–28)

When Jesus had spoken thus, Joseph quickly looked toward the mountains of Egypt, but he was much amazed. And he saw wicked people in this country, as it seemed, for I tell you that the land of Sotinen[19] was placed under the devil.[20] And in this country there were fully three hundred idols before whom all the wicked people came to adore the devil who had enchanted them to such an

---

[18] 288 **any meat salted or fresh** *Ke nule char, salé u reste*: *reste* means "rancid" but *fresche* is usually found in such expressions: see the examples in *AND* at "salé."

[19] 336 **Sotinen** *Sotinen*: the city in Egypt to which the Holy Family fled; *Ps.-Matt.* chap. 22.

[20] 335 **under the devil** *al deble*: explained in the next sentence, i.e., they are all idolators.

extent, and Frondise,[21] their protector, acknowledged as lord by all. And then Jesus, the son of Mary, cast down all that deceitful idolatry[22] without violence. For Jesus Christ entered [i.e., the pagan temple] and looked around and saw that everyone honored the demons that were there. But once Jesus Christ had entered, there was great sorrow: all the idols fell down like dew. The people made a great outcry, for all the gods they adored tumbled down on all sides and their idols, so honored by the people, were dashed to pieces. (vv. 329–60)

Frondise was grief-stricken for his gods and for his people, but nevertheless he knew well that Jesus did it deliberately and that he was God, with complete power to destroy his enemies, about which the prophets of old spoke truthfully in their writings: Pharaoh, who was a king and a powerful man, came to a bad end; he had Egypt under his jurisdiction and all the surrounding lands. Not for anything would he believe that God might have been born on earth, nor indeed, on any account would he ask for mercy. Rather he behaved pridefully in everything, so that in the end he drowned in the sea;[23] he will always be in hell, he will have much suffering and punishment. Frondise, greatly afraid at that, came at once to Jesus Christ, the sweet child, crying for mercy for his sins. Jesus Christ took great pity on him and from that time pardoned his wicked deeds. And in truth, Jesus Christ is so merciful to his people, so loving and so very sweet, that he abandons his anger toward all sinners. It is very good to serve him and to do his pleasure, for he is ready to reveal his joy to those who wish to come to him. (vv. 361–96)

The fifth year after God was born,[24] he accompanied the children of the city; it was, in fact, a Saturday.[25] While they walked together, they enjoyed themselves and exchanged talk so that they finished by playing together. Then they went to the river where there was a little clear water; but Jesus Christ, as he was wont,

---

[21] 343 **Frondise** *Frondise*: the governor of Sotinen; *Ps.-Matt.* chap. 22.

[22] 346 **idolatry** *mahomerie*: the illustration that accompanies this miracle in the manuscript (f. 8ʳ) shows demons flying out of a temple. However, in the text, as in its source (*Ps.-Matt.* chaps. 23–24), and in many other illustrations of this miracle, idols fall from their pedestals as Jesus enters the building.

[23] 369–78 **Pharaoh . . . came to a bad end . . . drowned in the sea** *Il mesavint a Pharaon . . . en mer nea*: cf. Exod. 14:9–28.

[24] 397 **The fifth . . . born** *Le quint . . . né*: from this point on, the miracles are derived from a Latin version of the *Infancy Gospel of Thomas*, published by Tischendorf as "pars altera" of the *Pseudo-Matthew*.

[25] 401 **Saturday** *samadi*: *Ps.-Matt.* chap. 26–27: insistence that the miracle was performed on the Sabbath is found in the Latin. The point is to show Jesus breaking with Jewish law.

drew the water back. Jesus constructed[26] seven pools and put water in them. But one Jew hindered him and ruined all his pools. Jesus snapped at him:

"Oh, you vicious son of Satan! Why have you done that to my pools? Indeed, you will die right now!"

When Jesus Christ had said this, the Jew died without a moment's delay. The other children were not pleased at this; they all, big and little, left him. They all went at once to their parents and gave them to understand that Jesus had killed their[27] child. The parents came to Joseph to complain and make a great argument about what Jesus had done; everyone said that he was guilty. (vv. 397–428)

Joseph was very sad, for they each threatened him. Joseph told everything to Mary, for he didn't dare to criticize Jesus. Mary knew about the whole affair and went immediately to ask Jesus, her noble son, if he might be willing to undo what he had done. Jesus said:

"My dear mother, I love you and hold you dear. In the way that I do, I was drawing back a bit of water, when a wicked Jew came and put his stick in it, and with his little stick he completely disrupted everything I did. Lady, I tell you all this so that you may know that he did wrong, and that's why the evildoer is dead. But he will have a reprieve, Mother, because of your love. He'll get his life back, that traitor. I do not want you to be dishonored hereabouts or anywhere."

Jesus touched the dead boy with his foot, that is all, and at once he came back to life, but he did not beg for mercy. (vv. 429–56)

Then blessed Jesus returned to his pools straightaway, and with the mud that he found, he made twelve sparrows—this on a Saturday. Some Jews came with him; one of them was astonished when he realized what Jesus was doing. At once the Jew became angry, and made great complaint to Joseph. He reproached Joseph because his child did such a thing. He reproached him repeatedly, and harshly, and most grievously about this:

"For our law," he said, "forbids anyone to work on the Sabbath." (vv. 457–72)

Joseph asked Jesus why he did it on the Sabbath. He clapped his hands and laughed:

"Fly, sparrows!" he said to them.

Then, in his sight and everyone else's, they flew. Some there praised God willingly. But immediately afterwards, others appeared before the princes in their palace; they said to those vile people that Jesus scorned their law. Jesus was

---

[26] 409 **constructed** *compassoit*: the Selden manuscript (f. 9ʳ) has an illustration showing Jesus drawing seven circles with a compass, a detail apparently drawn from the French verb; the Latin text at this point reads simply *fecit*.

[27] 424 **their child** *lur enfant*: the possessive stresses that the child was one of the community.

in the middle of the courtyard, as was Annas,[28] the priest. His son came up at very great speed and struck Jesus. Jesus was angry, but he spoke not a word; yet he was truly avenged, because the boy died forthwith, sprawling in front of his father.[29] Joseph was very fearful at this, for everyone threatened Jesus. For fear of the people, Joseph took sweet Jesus away from there, for they all hated both of them bitterly. (vv. 473–500)

Another Jew[30] then ran up and came close to Jesus; he bounded onto sweet Jesus's shoulder and hit him. At once Jesus called him the devil's son:

"You must not leave here undamaged, for it is fitting that you be brought low."

Indeed, after this incident, all the Jews and the priests caused great disquiet in the land. They could not refrain from speaking ill. Small and great, they all complained to Mary and admonished her to punish her child. She and Joseph begged Jesus and requested repeatedly that they go before the princes, and they exhorted him with fine words. (vv. 501–20)

Then all the masters said:

"Joseph, what are you doing? Give us your son and he will leave behind what he receives from you.[31] We will teach him to read, his master will be Zachary; he has understood all our law."

Joseph then begged Jesus to go and learn from them, and that he speak no evil, and that for love of him, he agree to cease harming them.

"Joseph, know for a fact that your son is excessive. Truly, he has done us more harm than anyone else ever has; he has killed a little Jewish boy who was once greatly valued. You must make amends to his friends, or go forth from the country, for otherwise they seek to do you great harm in this land. And if he were willing to back away, it would be good to ask him."

At that, Joseph asked Mary to speak to Jesus Christ about this. And she did so at once, very gently; and he then took that little Jewish boy, who was certainly dead, by the ear.

"Get up, scoundrelly fellow!"

So said Jesus, who worked a miracle. The dead child then rose up and got away quickly. Everyone who saw this marveled greatly. Joseph was very happy when the boy had been raised from the dead, because he had indeed been much

---

[28] 486 **Annas** *Anne*: the priest's name anticipates the high priest named at the beginning of Jesus's ministry in Luke 3:2 and identified as the father-in-law of the high priest in the Passion account of John 18:13.

[29] 488–94 **struck Jesus . . . sprawling in front of his father** *feri Jesum . . . sun pere en trebuchant*: Ps.-Matt., "pars altera," chap. 28.

[30] 501 ff. **Another Jew** *Un autre Giu*: Ps.-Matt., "pars altera," chap. 29.

[31] 524 **what he receives from you** *Si lerra ço k'il a en vus*: the Old French *Évangile de l'Enfance* (v. 706) has "Si lessera tous ses forfais" (he will eschew all his transgressions).

threatened by all the people of the city, and Mary likewise. And yet, Jesus Christ remained unrecognized by the people; they were very often blind. (vv. 521–64)

Zachary,[32] a great master who was most learned, was quite envious of Joseph and spoke to him very foolishly:

"You do not see to your son's learning to read and write. Really you should be taken to be burned or hanged."

"Fair and gentle master, take him and keep him with you; you were wrong to have misspoken to me, master, and you shall indeed be made aware of this."

Jesus hardly delayed at all before challenging that master: very soon indeed he asked him what he was studying:

"Master, I see you look in your law books very often, and yet you are not able to tell me what I am thinking or indeed what its subject is; and yet you are truly more learned than anyone in this country; you are renowned in the law;[33] your friends consider you as a god.[34] Can you say when you were born? No indeed, you do not know. Why indeed have you reproached Joseph, who brought me here? Now come a bit this way. Do you know what is written there? 'A God will be born on earth who will rule everything.' Now he has been born on earth, and you have seen him very often. How then does it happen that you do not recognize him?" (vv. 565–600)

When Zachary listened to him and had heard his speech, he considered himself beaten and completely humiliated, as did all the others with him.

"How is it," they said, "that this child could ever have been born? He knows more than our master, and now he is beginning to grow."

Then Jesus said:

"Now listen! Among you, you are very well aware that Abraham was appointed to you, and you consider him a father; and your ancestors did so, and they praised him in his time, for they all loved him sincerely and honored him more than any god. This Abraham, of whom I speak: I have seen him plainly and have often spoken with him, know this for certain." (vv. 601–20)

To this, Levi the great responded:

"Indeed, you are nothing but a child; you will lie like a thief[35] when you are fully grown. You have already begun to lie, for we can all hear it well. Tell more lies at your leisure and you will do our sweet pleasure!"

---

[32] 565 ff. **Zachary** *Zackarie*: Ps.-Matt. "pars altera," chap. 30.

[33] 587 **law** *lei*: i.e., Jewish religious law; cf. the expression "the law and the Prophets," Matt. 22:40 and Luke 16:16.

[34] 588 **as a god** *Cum deus*: this statement of esteem that Zachary enjoys seems exaggerated, but is confirmed by the *Old French Évangile de l'Enfance*, v. 794: "Pour Dieu vous tiennent vos amis."

[35] 622 **like a thief** *cum truant*: Hindley et al., *Old French-English Dictionary*, 595; *AND* gives "good-for-nothing."

"And you, white-haired master Levi, you have failed to recognize me. Before Abraham, I was.[36] And you have lied to me. You are all blind, seeing that I have been among you so often and explained your law and set [it] out right."

Levi then felt confounded and all the masters likewise; no one wished to stay any longer because each one considered himself defeated. (vv. 621–40)

Jesus scarcely waited[37] after that before going away to play with the Jews whom he found on the hills where he passed. They were all pretending to jump; but Jesus jumped from one steep and high hill to another, and after that each child did the same. But none of them was able to jump without breaking his neck or shattering his arm or having some other misfortune befall him, so that in the end, all died. In an evil hour had the little Jewish boys who came there learned to jump. One child did not want to jump on any account, because he could not. He loved Jesus very much and followed him everywhere. Jesus noticed him, and at that, he spoke to him. He said this to him: (vv. 641–62)

"Stay there! You have no business over here."

The others had all died immediately, except that one child. It was much talked about; the people threatened Jesus. Indeed, Joseph was not there, nor Jesus's mother, holy Mary, and nevertheless everyone denounced them loudly, solely out of envy. All the Jews who were the leaders of the land fiercely threatened harm. For that reason, Mary went to ask Jesus, her blessed son, if he would take pity on all those who lay dead and wounded, and bring them back to life:

"This I beg you of my own free will."

Jesus loved his mother very much and for that reason, at her entreaty, he went back to that hill and worked a miracle. He called all the dead Jews by name, and said to them:

"Now, come here! Tell me now what happened to you."

Each said what he wished. And then he brought them straight to where his mother was standing. Mary had great joy at that. (vv. 663–92)

Jesus came carrying a water pot leading many other children to a very pure spring where there was a river nearby and good grass, fine and lush and, it is said, of many kinds. Before them all, he made a show of wanting to fill his pot first. The others refused to permit it, but competed with him; they said, indeed, that they would break his pot, and afterwards they did so. Then, Jesus became very angry that his pot was smashed and for that reason he threatened all the children gathered there. Jesus remained calm, for he did not want to sow disorder, but he gathered the pieces, and said to them all:

---

[36] 631 **I was** *jo fu*: cf. John 8:58, which uses "I am." This allusion is not found in *Ps.-Matt.*

[37] 641 ff. **Jesus scarcely waited** *Guers apres ne demora*: the source of this episode is unknown.

"Now listen to me! You see here the pot that, in truth, you smashed; let no one be ill-disposed and all resentment pardoned."[38] (vv. 693–716)

From that time, the children I have told you about became good friends. Then each one took his pot, so that none was left behind. Each one filled his pot to the brim from the spring I've told you about. Jesus let them do all this, but also filled his own pot. (vv. 717–724)

The sun was very warm and it was very hot that day; Jesus looked at the sun and hung his water pot on a sunbeam.[39] Everyone who came to get water wanted to do likewise, for they thought they could hang their pots in this way without harm. They did it in vain, for when they took their hands away, not a single one of the pots filled with water[40] remained undamaged. Jesus's pot remained whole, just as it had been when he placed it the way he wished; he did it intentionally so that one of them came and told the people of the city what Jesus had done, and how they left all their pots beneath the beam completely smashed. Many people ran there and looked at Jesus's water-pot, and saw it clearly, still hanging there. Everyone marveled when he saw that pot, then recounted the wonder to each person that he met. (vv. 725–52)

Afterwards the children joined together and begged Jesus to make whole the pots they carried; this they asked. Then he raised his hand and blessed the pots that were there, so that he made them all whole. Everyone found his pot undamaged and completely sound and full of water; and each one who had before hung it in vain put his hand on it. Afterwards they went away carrying their pots full of water as before, and recounted to their parents what Jesus had done before their eyes. (vv. 753–68)

Now I will tell you about a child who plainly seemed to love Jesus, and often went to play with him. The child's father hated his son very much because the child would go to [Jesus] and keep him company. He intended to lock up his son so that Jesus could not find him. Therefore he threatened his son and said that he would lock him up because he was with Jesus so often and loved him so intensely. The Jew, the father of the child, made so many threats against his son that the boy wept all day and was downcast. The father immediately took a big broom into his hand; the detestable man took his child and beat him three times. When he had beaten and struck him hard, he said that because of the boy's love of Jesus,

---

[38] 712–16 **Now listen . . . pardoned** *Ore oëz . . . pardoné*: this speech is meant to show Jesus's patience in the face of gratuitous violence.

[39] 728 **sunbeam** *rai*: the miniature in the Selden manuscript (f. 15ʳ) shows a wooden beam with one pot and three handles suspended from it and broken pots below. See Maureen Boulton, "The *Évangile de l'Enfance*: Text and Illustration in Oxford, Bodleian Library MS. Selden Supra 38," *Scriptorium* 37 (1983): 54–65, plate 8c and the cover of this volume for a reproduction of the miniature.

[40] 735 **filled with water** *d'ewe porta plein*: this detail is added for the rhyme, but becomes significant below when the broken pots are repaired and their water restored.

he would be locked up forever. Then, for no other reason, this traitor took his son by the chin and put him in his prison, which was in a very strong tower with but a single door. The boy remained there like a dead thing: there was no one who treated him well. The father had sworn repeatedly that the boy would be locked up forever and that he would never in his life be released or moved. He went away and the boy remained, looking very wretched. His father took the key away with him and immediately put it in a safe place. (vv. 769–808)

Because Jesus was aware of the whole situation, he did not wait but went at once to the child without being summoned, for he wanted to make him happy. Jesus went to him quickly and said:

"Friend, I have come to free you from the torment that you have borne for my sake. Give me your finger through this opening and be troubled no more."

"I do not think I can," he replied to Jesus. "The opening is too small, I will never get through, I think."

Jesus answered:

"What have you said? You shall get through instantly!"

Then the boy put his finger through and Jesus drew him to himself.

"I see that you are very weak; nevertheless, follow me now!"

When Jesus Christ brought the boy outside, just as he had hoped to do, the child loved him even more, indeed, than ever before. Once the child had been freed by Jesus and gone away,[41] the father returned, thoroughly angry, thinking he would find his child. He unlocked the door and called his son repeatedly; when he did not hear him speak, he looked inside the prison. When he had looked everywhere and could not find him, he was most woeful and enraged; he would almost have put out his own eyes. In his torment, he wanted to kill himself, so full of anger was he. That wicked man[42] was brought to great sorrow and suffering, for he understood correctly that Jesus had surely freed the boy, and secretly, by some true enchantment. (vv. 809–52)

In their envy, the great masters of the clergy[43] came to Joseph and said to Mary that Jesus was doing too much mischief, and they ordered them to bring Jesus to school and to entrust him to wise Master Levi. So Jesus, who had so much power, came to school. Jesus greeted the masters and Levi took charge of him and questioned him; Jesus listened readily, but in truth, he had no desire to answer. Instantly, therefore, Master Levi became very angry with Jesus, who, by refusing to engage in disputation, was not taking him seriously. The master considered him clever, and for that reason wanted to hear from him what he desired:

---

[41] 833–34 **freed ... gone away** *esteit alez ... deliverez*: I have reversed the order of the verbs to improve the sense.

[42] 848 **man** *sire*: the French word suits the rhyme of the quatrain, but seems incongruous here.

[43] 853 ff. **In envy ... the great masters** *Les grant mestres ... par envie*: *Ps.-Matt.* "pars altera," chap. 31.

what he did not know himself. The master had heard enough: he was filled with knowledge.[44] Without a warning sound, he struck Jesus cruelly. At that, Jesus became angry and said to old Levi: (vv. 853–82)

"And why have you struck me? You have failed to recognize me. Know now for a fact that the one whom you have struck knows a thousand times more than you, or indeed, than any of the masters. All your knowledge is worthless and sounds like brass or shrill cymbals.[45] Answer at once now: you strike me because of your authority, and only in spite. But do not commit an act of folly: answer rather with learning. You cannot answer me, because you do not understand the force of your law, as you will find out. Why was Aleph named first of all the letters, and Bet the second, and Gimel the third and Dalet thus the fourth?"

The master sat and stared. He turned his face toward Jesus and kept changing what he thought. Finally, in utter anger, he spoke:

"And who has taught you so much book learning? You are still only a child!"

Thereupon Jesus answered:

"The one who taught me is all-powerful and he and I are one in outward manifestation, without separation, and indeed we have one power and will have it forever, without end.[46] If you want to know more, I can show you; and I can offer so many questions that we'll never finish. Earlier, you were questioned about Aleph, Bet, Gimel and Dalet; now tell me, if you know, about He, Vav, Zayin, Chet, and what each letter means, since you are so learned!"[47] They then heard each letter; there was not a single one that he did not name and describe in detail,[48] and whose meaning he did not reveal. Everyone listened carefully as Jesus defeated him completely. Then Jesus said to these heretics:

"O you wicked hypocrites, haven't you written laws, which I have explained to you? But you don't know how to answer the questions I raised! You are indeed completely blind, since you do not understand your own law!" (vv. 883–940)

Then one of them shouted out loudly so that everyone heard:

"Be advised that this one cannot live among us thus, for he'd be put on a cross at once, given that he casts down all our laws!"

---

[44] 877–78 **The master ... knowledge** *Le mester ... repleni*: the idea here, which is expressed more clearly in the *Old French Évangile de l'Enfance* (vv. 1153–58), is that the teacher, who has already heard and learned quite a lot before Jesus's arrival, would like Jesus to teach him something new; Jesus refuses to share this with the teacher.

[45] **All your knowledge ... shrill cymbals** *Tut vostre sen ... cymbales cri fesant*: an echo of 1 Cor. 13:1.

[46] 913–16 **He and I are one ... without end** *E il e mei ... sumes un ... sanz terminance*: Jesus declares here his essential unity with the Father, in terms that echo John 10:29–30.

[47] 921–24 **Aleph ... Hez** *Aleph ... Hez*: the Hebrew alphabet begins with the letters "aleph, bet, gimel, dalet, he, vav, zayin, chet"; *Ps.-Matt.* "pars altera," 101.

[48] 929 **describe in detail** *destincta*: see note 4 to v. 32.

He said in a loud voice:

"I do not know which devil engendered him, who it was who bore him or the mother who nursed him. Truly I think he twisted[49] everything."

Jesus bore this most patiently and said no more to those people; he had no desire to, and he did it deliberately. (vv. 941–56)

That day there were many sick people in great need of help, so that Jesus in his kindness healed them, to great renown: he made the lame walk and the mute speak. He greatly frightened the masters by the signs of his healing. To the blind he gave sight, so that everyone understood that he could certainly do his will, as I have told you. Jesus was feared the more as he performed so many miracles; and he is and was worthy, and is well known for that. (vv. 957–72)

Then Jesus Christ went to the city of Nazareth.[50] He found relatives there, given that Joseph brought him: Joseph was very well received because he was known by everyone. Mary took her son Jesus, and they were very welcome. Jesus went to play with many children of the city, and they all entered an upper room by a flight of steps. There the children quarreled:[51] some threatened others, and they fought so much that they struck each other. Jesus always held his peace and, whatever they did, he looked on. Then one Jew came to another and threatened him violently, and as they quarreled,[52] one took hold of the other cruelly. With anger and ill will he pushed him forcefully down the steps so that he fell down and broke his neck. Jesus spoke not a word but kept his distance and just looked on.

It was in fact a Saturday when the boy was killed in this way. A great cry went up about that, as the relatives and friends of that child arrived. When they saw him lying dead, everyone indeed, both small and great, immediately said that Jesus Christ killed him and pushed him like that. Everyone in the city threatened Joseph a great deal. Joseph then said to Mary: (vv. 973–1013)

"What shall we do, my dear? Everyone is shouting against us now, and I think they're acting foolishly toward us."

Thereupon, Jesus spoke:

"Now, Joseph, do not be afraid, because the child that you see here was not touched by me. Be advised that in truth these people reproach you wrongly, and it will certainly be clearly proven to them now."

He brought the dead boy back to life, and then asked:

---

[49] 952 **twisted** *besturna*: according to *AND*, *besturner* means "to turn upside down or back to front." Figuratively, it can mean "transform," but usually with negative connotations.

[50] 973–74 ff. **Then Jesus Christ went ... Nazareth** *Jesu Crist est puis alez ... Nazarez*: Ps.-Matt. "pars altera," chap. 32.

[51] 985 **There the children quarreled** *Les enfans si estriverent*: the edition should read "s'i."

[52] 993 **quarreled** *tencerent*: I have omitted the translation of *nekident* after this word.

"Now, Zeb, tell the truth! Were you pushed by me?"
Then Zeb, who had been dead, said:
"No, indeed, in no way, but Solomon[53] threatened me and he himself pushed me. No one else did it, be aware of this, sweet Jesus Christ, and the one who accused you—God knows—was mistaken. You have such great power that you can bring the dead back to life, and then fulfill each man's wish. You return to me the life that Solomon took from me; you have given me a great gift, for my life is sustained by you."

This child's relatives rejoiced and were happy; they thanked Jesus for honoring them so much. (vv. 1014–48)

Then Jesus went to Jericho with Joseph, who guided him. They found many people there who became their close friends. Jesus was six years old when he went there, and he performed many miracles, which made Mary joyful. Mary called to Jesus:[54]

"Dear sweet son, now come here! I'll need to drink from that spring there. Take this jar and go quickly; bring me water from the spring. Make haste, dear sweet son, and come back very soon!"

Jesus ran to the spring carrying his jar in his hand; he filled it at once and started back. As he returned, Jesus met a wicked little Jewish boy, who threatened him and smashed his jar. When his jar had been broken and the Jewish boy had run away, Jesus abandoned all the pieces; he gathered all the water to himself by his power, and took it and put it into his tunic. He did it to such effect[55] that nothing remained on the ground. Then he ran to the house carrying all the water like that. He came to his mother immediately, showing her all the water. He recounted this incident to his mother and how it came about, and she marveled greatly and had great joy in her heart. (1049–88)

One day after that, Jesus found a bit of barley while he was walking along, and as he handled it he threw it into a field. At that very moment the field bloomed: very good barley was growing there. Jesus did not take notice of it. Afterwards the people marveled that they found such good barley there; then they cut it down and carried it into their houses.[56] (vv. 1089–1100)

Jesus, filled with goodness, went from Jericho quite alone, in truth. He asked the Jews where the children of the country had been put, the ones he used to play with. They said to him:

---

[53] 1031 **Solomon** *Slomo*.

[54] 1057 ff. **Mary called to Jesus** *Marie Jesum apela*: *Ps.-Matt.* "pars altera," chap. 33.

[55] 1079 **to such effect** *a cel' hure*: *AND* provides *a tel hure*, "to such effect"; given the great similarity between *c* and *t* in many manuscripts, it is possible that the edition should read *a tel hure* rather than *a cel' hure*.

[56] 1089–1100 **After that, one day . . . carried it into their houses** *Un jur aprés . . . lur osteus le carïerent*: *Ps.-Matt.* "pars altera," chap. 34.

"Dear friend, we do not know where they are, nor indeed, where they may be found."

But know that they made a mistake and would pay dearly for it. All the Jews, small and great, had put their children in a closed oven,[57] so that they would not go around with Jesus, as was their custom, because the Jews feared his ways and spoke ill of him whenever they could. Jesus knew of their wickedness and how the children had been locked up; in a friendly way he asked the Jews to be shown the children. He said that he wished to play quietly with them. The Jews swore that no one had seen them since the day before. (vv. 1101–28)

Then Jesus went to the oven with deliberation, and he asked the Jews: "And who is locked in there?"

The Jews swore that, truly, there were pigs inside. Then Jesus said to them: "And pigs they shall certainly be."

As soon as he said that, each one became a pig; and they ate like pigs and grunted continually. When Jesus had gone away, the ovens were[58] unbarred: those who had been pushed inside had indeed all turned into pigs. When they all came out and the Jews saw pigs, they considered the children to be dead, for they were ashamed of their pigs' bodies. Forever after that, the Jews considered every pig as a brother in its way, and so this was a powerful miracle. From that hour no Jew ever ate or roasted a pig, nor indeed will they ever, for the religion has forbidden it.[59] (vv. 1129–56)

On another occasion, Jesus went from Jericho without permission. He met other children. Jesus gazed at these children because there were so many; and indeed, when he left, they all followed him. Jesus Christ, who knew everything, went to a sunbeam[60] and took off his coat; each child did likewise. When blessed Jesus Christ had taken off his coat, he left it on the sunbeam; everyone stared at it. After that, Jesus sat down, and they saw him and thought they would do the same. For that reason, each one tried, all except one; all but one wanted to sit near Jesus. But they were too eager, and they all fell down at once. One and another jumped up quickly onto the sunbeam, but it turned out badly for them, since each

---

[57] 1115 oven *furneis*: in an Arabic version, the children are changed into kids but restored to human form at the end of the episode; for English translations, see Roberts and Donaldson, "The Arabic Infancy of the Savior," chap. 40 in *The Ante-Nicene Fathers*, 405–15, at 413, and Elliott, *New Testament Apocrypha*, 100–7.

[58] 1142 were *sun*: the edition should read "sun[t]."

[59] 1153–56 **Forever after that ... forbidden it** *Pus cel' hure ... defendu l'a*: this fanciful explanation of the Jewish prohibition of pork does not occur in the Arabic Infancy story. See further Claudine Fabre-Vassas, *The Singular Beast: Jews, Christians and the Pig* (New York: Columbia University Press, 1997).

[60] 1165 ff. **sunbeam** *rai de solail*: cf. *Armenian Infancy*, chap. 15; trans. Abraham Terian, *The Armenian Gospel of the Infancy with Three Early Versions of the Protevangelium of James* (Oxford: Oxford University Press, 2008), 67–76, at 68.

one broke his neck, except one who escaped and recounted the incident to people as he went; a great outcry arose everywhere because of it. All the masters of the city quickly asked for Joseph and told him what Jesus had done. At that, Joseph was very sad, and replied to those people that Jesus's behavior certainly grieved him deeply; but he could not discipline him; then he swore that Jesus was indeed too wild.

"I could not punish him, and indeed, lords, he is very wise: he has known everything even though he's a child. If I were so angry that I said something embarrassing to him, he would soon pay me back for it, and rightly so. I do not know so learned a person as would dare to say wicked things about him." (vv. 1157–1208)

"And so how will this turn out? Does he then wish to make war against us in this land?"

"Certainly not, but I will ask him gently, without rudeness, to stop his violence, and Mary, his mother and his friend, will do likewise."

"Now Joseph, be aware that if you do not take him away soon you will be chased from here, because you may no longer remain here."

"I don't care where I go! I have had too much trouble on his account, and you can be sure that it grieves me, for his mother suffers because of it."

Jesus climbed down from the sunbeam and looked at the people. He kept his counsel, not yet revealing his intention; he brought the dead boys back to life, and then departed. Everyone thanked him for what he did and then went away. (vv. 1209–32)

Jesus was seven years old when he revived the dead children. He returned home afterwards and Joseph said to him:

"I can't excuse you any more, nor can I keep you any longer; be aware that I do not dare, nor, for my pleasure, do I even wish to, for all the masters of any renown, and everyone in this country, and all my friends as well, have required and charged me to evict you, so that you not be seen here for any reason. Otherwise, I will be driven out of the land. You are fully seven years old[61] and nimble-minded enough; you were never wild or slanderous of anyone."

"I am what I am. Don't worry about me, for I will soon find shelter in some place." (vv. 1233–56)

Jesus was quite lighthearted and did not wait any longer. He came to a cloth dyer,[62] and said that he knew the man's trade. Immediately, the dyer laughed at the child because of his speech and his manner, and he said to him:

---

[61] 1249 **fully seven years old** *set ans pleners*: in the Middle Ages, the age of seven marked the end of infancy and the beginning of childhood. The duties of parents lessened at this point, and a child could enter minor orders (e.g., as a chorister) or be engaged to marry (though not actually marry). At seven, boys typically were active outside the house, although most apprenticeships started later.

[62] 1259 ff. **dyer** *teinturer*: cf. Roberts and Donaldson, "Arabic Infancy of the Savior," 412, chap. 37; and Terian, *The Armenian Gospel of the Infancy*, chap. 21, 99–107, at 100–4.

"Now, come here and tell me, if you please, do you wish to serve me willingly?"

"Yes, sir, that's the truth."

"I see that you are very young; if I give my cloths to you, how will you proceed? Tell me."

"I will do well, if I have the means."

"If you do well, you will be rewarded; we shall see what you can do. You will take these three pieces of cloth and put them in three cauldrons, for I have decided that one cloth will be blue [and] the other green. Have you understood?"

"Yes, very well," said Jesus.

"I will see the third [piece] scarlet,[63] for I have paid dearly for it. Now do well, for I shall leave and I shall return, and I forbid you, upon your life, to let any of the cloths you have in your possession touch one another, because you would be doing a stupid thing; they would be completely ruined. But each one must be put separately into a cauldron by itself; take good care of this, young man." (vv. 1257–92)

Jesus answered:

"Do not fear; go off confidently, for I will do well, and you will know that when you return."

When the owner had gone away, Jesus quickly took the three cloths and put them straightaway into a single cauldron. Jesus was very sure of his trade as a dyer, and he wanted to work as he pleased. As I told you, he put the three cloths into one cauldron and boiled them together—anyone else would have ruined them! When he had done so, Jesus Christ went away. The master who had given him the cloths soon returned. When that lord came and failed to find Jesus, he realized then that Jesus would not come back. Instantly he went looking everywhere for his three cloths. He became thoroughly sad and downcast, and he shouted and wailed repeatedly: (vv. 1293–1319)

"Alas! Oh God," he said, "I am ruined by this little rascal, for he has completely betrayed me; I will always be in a sorry plight. I am too foolish, and showed it when I hired him to do anything at all, for he is scarcely seven years old and yet he is very surly, treacherous and thieving, this little Jesus! And that's why I can promise you, he has stolen all my pieces of cloth; but I do not know where he has gone nor indeed where he took them, for I have looked everywhere. I will search the cauldrons again right now. I have looked carefully in two of them, but I didn't find a single cloth. Now, I will search the third in case I find something. For if I could find anything, it would be of great value to me." (vv. 1320–44)

In that cauldron, he saw a good cloth that seemed blue; when he noticed that, he was not wholly dejected. Now his sorrow was diminished, because he

---

[63] 1281 **piece of scarlet** *e[s]carleite*: the French word indicates cloth of fine quality, often dyed scarlet.

then saw another color: a very good, well-finished green, as he had planned. "It's important to put my hand into the last cauldron."

He found a cloth of scarlet, rich and good and clean. And when he found these three to be just as he had planned, he praised God frequently for having restored the cloths that he had given to Jesus and which he thought he had lost when he returned to his house; but now he was not disappointed. (vv. 1345–64)

Jesus came back to his mother, who greeted him gladly, and Joseph, whom he considered to be his father, received him with undivided joy. They looked very happy now because they had found their child. They led him away and remained no longer. Jesus was seven years old[64] when he exercised such power.

Then they saw lion cubs, which Joseph feared greatly. They followed in his path, each one as vicious as a mastiff; in short, they very often harmed pilgrims.[65] Joseph was very afraid and showed it clearly. Jesus hastened to say:

"Joseph, don't be afraid!"

All alone, Jesus went toward them; each one honored him with its tail,[66] and each one came up to him. They showed great joy; like the beasts that they were, they played before him continually. They knew well that he was God. And Jesus remained among them for a long time, as long as he liked. Joseph was indeed deeply troubled then, because Jesus stayed so long. It grieved Joseph very much, partly because he feared greatly for the child, whom he loved very much. (vv. 1365–1400)

Many people of the city watched Jesus and told Joseph that Jesus would be devoured by lions where he was, for each of them was big.[67] And for that reason Joseph feared that one of them would seize Jesus by the throat. Jesus was well aware of Joseph's thought, but the power came to Joseph to explain clearly everything that Jesus wished to reveal.[68] Many people had gone to Joseph earlier and told him that blessed Jesus had been devoured, and that they indeed had seen the

---

[64] 1373 **seven years old** *De set ans*: see above, n. 61 to v. 1249.

[65] 1375–1380 **Then they saw lion cubs . . . in short . . . pilgrims** *Liunceus si unt dunc veü . . . pelerin . . . ço est la fin*: cf. *Ps.-Matt.* "pars altera," chaps. 35–36. The syntax of this passage is unclear; *liunceus* is obl. plural, but *il suit* is singular, while *damagerent* is plural; *checun* also implies more than one. The inconsistency may arise from the compression of a longer passage (vv. 1763–88) in the Continental *Évangile de l'Enfance*, which describes Jesus among a group of wild animals before relating his encounter with a single lion.

[66] 1387 **honored him with its tail** *de sa coue l'onura*: this is explained in the Continental *Évangile de l'Enfance* which reads "Entre ses piéz sa queue tint" ("Held his tail between his legs," ed. Boulton, v. 1772).

[67] 1401–6 **Many people . . . were big** *Mut de gent. . .grant estoit*: in the *Évangile de l'Enfance* this group of Jews loves Jesus and therefore warns Joseph as an act of kindness (ed. Boulton, vv. 1809–14).

[68] 1409–12 **Jesus . . . reveal** *Jesu . . . mostrer*: text is unclear. In the Continental *Évangile de l'Enfance* vv. 1819–20 Joseph reacts with anger when the Jews, having urged Joseph to send Jesus away, report that Jesus has been killed.

lions seize him violently by the throat. And they said publicly that it was because of his sin that Jesus had been killed and that by rights Joseph should indeed be drawn as a criminal.[69] When they, great and small, had spoken thus in spite to Joseph, he was not pleased but sad, for he feared their ways; they did not love Jesus or his mother, nor would they in the future. As the people remained quarrelling with Joseph and also threatening him, some of them saw Jesus coming. Then they were afraid, because many a lion, standing on its hind legs,[70] treated Jesus courteously.[71] When people saw Jesus coming, they all wanted to leave because they had no desire to carry out their threats. So Jesus made them wait; no one dared to leave. He assembled all the lions before them without causing harm. (vv. 1401–48)

"O! you most treacherous people, so full of deceit, you know treason only too well! Look at these lions, who are wiser, by their own law, than you, for each of them sees his Lord and recognizes him, and greets him as he knows how."

Before them all, he said to the lions:

"Return, all of you, I command you! Do no harm whatsoever to anyone until you have returned to the place whence you came."

With that, the lions went away in great joy. (vv. 1449–64)

Joseph was capable of good work.[72] For his trade, he needed what was required for a plow, [for] a young man had come to him and described a job to be done and had spoken to him about it. When he had made the agreement, Joseph called his apprentice and said:

"Listen here! This young man described to me something that you shall make with this piece of wood before you. He stipulated that this beam should be cut and the two pieces measured against one another, so as to be sure that they have been done correctly." (vv. 1465–80)

Joseph said to him that the two pieces should be equal, and that he should make them so, lest he ruin them. His apprentice promised him that he would do it as he instructed. And when Joseph had departed, his assistant took an axe used in his trade, and began to work. He thought he was working very well, for he was

---

[69] 1412–24 **Many people ... indeed** *Mut de gent ... pur verité*: this group of people acts malevolently, unlike the one above. Cf. *Évangile de l'Enfance*, vv. 1825–30.

[70] 1439 **hind legs** *rampant*: the lion rampant, a heraldic figure, is a symbol of lordly authority.

[71] 1438–40 **They were afraid ... courteously** *Idunc estoient mut dotant ... bel semblant*: lions are noted for their ferocity, hence the reaction of the villagers. But the lion is also a symbol of Christ and was also thought to possess virtues such as compassion and moderation; see T. H. White, trans., *The Book of Beasts, being a Translation from a Latin Bestiary of the Twelfth Century* (New York: Putnam's Sons, 1954), 7–11; R. S. Sturges, "Bestiary," *ODMA* 1:253–54. For the facsimile of a Latin manuscript see Christopher de Hamel, *Book of Beasts: A Facsimile of MS. Bodley 764* (Oxford: Bodleian Library, 2008).

[72] 1465 ff. **Joseph ... work** *Joseph ... overer*: Ps.-Matt. "pars altera," chap. 31.

quite nimble; but in truth, he failed, for he cut one piece of wood at least a whole foot less than had been stipulated. When Joseph realized that, becoming aware of the situation, he grew nastily angry because he could not fix it. Joseph was cruelly angry for sure, and reproached him horribly. Then Jesus said courteously:

"Joseph, do not be upset any longer, because this will easily be set right. By the faith that you owe me, hold your peace now!" (vv. 1481–1508)

Joseph did not speak; for the moment, he did not dare to reproach his apprentice for fear of doing wrong; he did not want to anger Jesus. And Jesus loved Joseph greatly, and Joseph feared him greatly. Jesus said to him:

"Now, come here, for I want to be over there; you hold on to this end and don't move anywhere; I'll be over there so that you can see me easily. Hold firmly to what I have given you; pull when I pull, and do it when I do."

Now, all at once and without waiting, both pulled so much that the pieces indeed became equal, and they were worked as stipulated. Joseph was very joyful that he had made them equal. The young man came by afterwards; he wished to see the work. When he had inspected it carefully, Joseph was paid well for it; he rewarded Joseph most willingly. (vv. 1509–36)

The masters of the region asked Jesus once more to learn the Scriptures,[73] of his own accord and ungrudgingly, so he agreed and entered the school. As he looked at a book, a master asked Jesus, what he could say about Aleph,[74] and if he could describe the range of its power and nature; but Jesus remained silent. He looked at the teacher and then said, feigning:

"If you explain what Bet is, I will tell you all about the true nature of Aleph."

The master grew angry, threatened Jesus, and questioned him once more, as follows: "Now, say, if you know, why Aleph was so named in Hebrew and explain in detail[75] why it comes first in the alphabet." (vv. 1537–60)

"Again, I respond as before, master. I will explain even more than you are asking. As you wish, I will explain Aleph. But first of all, I would know from you, if I may, what Bet is and what it says, and what is its use in writing."

The teacher answered immediately:

"You wicked little rascal, where do you get the nerve to pose such a question?"

Then, without waiting, the teacher struck Jesus viciously. When the teacher struck him, Jesus became very angry indeed and said to him:

"You grey-beard, that will avail you little! I will pay you for it, for I shall be avenged very soon; I will leave here immediately, asking you no further questions."

Then the teacher fell down dead before everyone, just as I tell you. A great outcry went up after Jesus had left. (vv. 1537–88)

---

[73] 1537–38 **The masters . . . Jesus . . . Scriptures** *Jesu . . . des mestres . . . escris*: Ps.-Matt. "pars altera," chap. 38.

[74] **Aleph** *Aleth*: *sic* in the manuscript, here and in the rest of the passage.

[75] 1566 **explain in detail** *destincterai*: see above, n. 4 to v. 32.

The news came to Joseph, and it did not seem at all good to him. He called Mary and they had a long conversation about it. After that, Jesus went back[76] to the school, and was seen and recognized by all the teachers: for he was certainly noticed.

Jesus held a book in his hand. He looked it over well, but did not say a word about the knowledge that he found in his book; there was much learning in it, but he spoke about something else, preaching about the Holy Spirit.[77] When one of the teachers heard him, he fell at Jesus's feet and cried out:

"Have mercy on me, O God!"

When that teacher prostrated himself sincerely before Jesus, all the others asked Jesus's mercy of their own accord, for they had all reached understanding and showed it clearly: they knew they had heard the truth, that he was the powerful God, by the veritable signs he had given in his childhood in both word and deed. From that time onward, everyone, small or great, considered him to be God almighty, and some were fearful. (vv. 1589–1624)

One of the teachers then went to Joseph and told him that Jesus had revealed to the teachers so much of what he had learned through scholarship that he showed great authority. And then indeed, without further discussion, each one begged his mercy.

"His mind is such that no one can keep him from anything that he wishes to do, because there is no one in any land who might ever, by any power, say what Jesus has just said: what he revealed through his power converted everyone to salvation.[78] He is God, I promise you, because what David once said in the psalm *Flumen Dei*,[79] where he told everything about Jesus, is now fully evident

---

[76] 1593 ff. **After that, Jesus went back** *Uncore aprés entra Jesu*: this incident and the preceding one present very different views of Jesus's career at school. In the second one, Jesus does not wait to be questioned, but expounds on his own authority and impresses the teachers. Both episodes are found in the *Ps.-Matt.* "pars altera," chap. 38–39.

[77] 1604 **Holy Spirit** *Seint Espirit*: this pointedly anticipates the later, distinctively Christian doctrine of the Trinity and the existence of the Holy Spirit. The incident is perhaps based on Jesus in the temple at the age of twelve, Luke 2:46–47.

[78] 1633–41 **His mind . . . He is God** *Sun sen . . . Il est Deu*: the punctuation of the edition is wrong; there should be an open quotation mark at the beginning of v. 1633; these lines should be read as part of the master's speech (vv. 1641–48 in the edition). The open quotation mark at the beginning of v. 1641 of the edition should be suppressed. The sense of vv. 1638–40 is clearer in the Continental *Évangile de l'Enfance* vv. 2021–22: "Car che qu'il dit est verités: Il nous a tous a lui tornés."

[79] 1643 **Flumen Dei** *Flumen Dei*: the allusion is to Ps 64:10 (Douay). The psalm is a hymn of praise to God, who gives all good things to his people. This is an example of Christian reading of the Hebrew Bible as prefiguring, as often as possible, the coming of Christ: in this case the banquet prefiguring the Eucharist: e.g., Cassiodorus *In Pss.*, PL 70.448.

and completely realized in him. Joseph, I tell you this now, in truth, without any deception."

Joseph rejoiced greatly when he had heard that. The teacher left immediately, and so did Joseph. (vv. 1625–52)

After this incident,[80] Jesus, Mary, and Joseph went to another land, to Capharnaum, as I have heard, where people were seeking the great physicians of the country, because a man had fallen ill who was very well-bred, and was greatly esteemed. He was named Joseph and there was much goodness in him, and he had been beloved by everyone; but, to tell the truth, he had died. When that Joseph had died, everyone who knew him grieved greatly for him, and for the kindness that was in him. Jesus then called the other Joseph [his father], whom he loved, and commanded him to go at once to the dead man, since he had explained sufficiently to him that the man had borne his name, so that Joseph would go and comfort the dead man. Then Joseph said quickly: (vv. 1653–77)

"Now, how shall I help him or restore his health, since I do not know how to do that?"

"Joseph, now listen to this! The cloth that you are wearing—put it on the dead man and afterwards say: 'I have come to you, Joseph, on behalf of the child Jesus, and through him you will have health, because he is filled with power.'"

Joseph got there immediately and found the man lying dead. Men, women, and children were grieving mightily for him, because the dead man was loved by all the people of the city; he was rich and much feared because of his family connections. When Joseph arrived there, he greeted the man: he had come on behalf of Jesus, of limitless power. He touched the dead man with the cloth, and he came back to life. He thanked Joseph profusely and asked him at once who was the Jesus whom he mentioned:

"Because by him I have been restored to life, as it is proven; now tell me the truth."

Joseph answered instantly:

"Jesus is the one true God."

"Indeed, that is true, and I know it, and for this reason I will believe in him."

The man named Joseph and his relations were very joyful. Thereafter Jesus was much beloved and honored everywhere. (vv. 1678–1716)

After that, Mary, Joseph, and Jesus came to Bethlehem.[81] There they saw their relatives, who received them very well. The son of the family was named Joseph, and he was ordered to fetch plenty of cabbages. This Joseph was related to Jesus and went quickly to gather cabbages. In the vegetable garden into which he went, a poisonous snake bit Joseph's hand, and he cried out and returned to the

---

[80] 1653 ff. **After this incident** *Aprés tut icest afere*: *Ps.-Matt.* "pars altera," chap. 40.

[81] 1717 **After that . . . came to Bethlehem** *A Bethlehem . . . puis venu*: *Ps.-Matt.* "pars altera," chap. 40.

house. Jesus met him and asked him why he had cried out so much. And Joseph told him that his hand was badly injured by a snake. Jesus swiftly said to him: (vv. 1717–39)

"Let's return to the snake! You will be avenged at once, so that you have no harm from it."

He said to the snake:

"Come here! Burst in two right here!"

The snake burst in two pieces immediately, right where he was. Joseph was overjoyed and went at once to Jesus, who called him and rubbed his hand. Jesus blew on it a little; then nothing hurt Joseph. Joseph took the cabbages, and Jesus did too. When he had what he had come for, Joseph returned to the house and told how he had been injured and how Jesus had healed him. Everyone was very happy about it and thanked Jesus. (1740–60)

They then went to a feast; they found some of their relatives there and many others who greeted them warmly. Seated around a table in the house were James and Sir Simeon, Joseph and also Jude, and two Marys of the region; one was called "of Cleophas," and the other was called by kinship "mother of Joseph."[82] They all received sweet Jesus, their kinsman, courteously. They had heard of his power and knew about his deeds. Each one there loved Jesus very much, and honored him greatly. He gave his blessing at the table, and then ate. While he was seated at the table, the house was filled with light, I tell you this, and so say the Scriptures. (vv. 1761–84)

Joseph and Mary went to the city of Jerusalem. They later returned, but [for now] left Jesus behind.[83] Jesus entered the Jews' school and examined their books, debating every day with the Jews, defeating all their objections. Jesus was twelve years old when he debated thus with the Jews. [Then] Mary sought her son for three days and was very sorrowful about him; on the fourth she found him arguing with the Jews. Then she called to him at once and he came away looking happy.

"Be aware that Joseph and I and all our friends have looked for you and we have been distressed on your account."

Jesus answered with kind words:

---

[82] 1766–72 in the house were James . . . by kinship "mother of Joseph" *en la maison Jacob . . . Mere Joseph de parenté*: this episode is omitted from the Continental *Évangile de l'Enfance*, but is close to *Ps.-Matt.* "pars altera," chap. 42. These lines refer to the Holy Kinship resulting from the three marriages of Mary's mother Anne; cf. V. F. Koenig, "'La Généalogie Nostre Dame' and the Legend of the Three Marys," *Romance Philology* 14 (1960–61): 207–15. Mary Cleophas, the mother of James the Less, Joseph, Simon, and Jude, is also mentioned in John 19:25. The author seems to have confused the second Mary (mother of James and John, the sons of Zebedee), described here as the "mother of Joseph."

[83] 1785–88 Joseph . . . left Jesus behind *Joseph . . . Jesum derere i unt lessé*: Luke 2:42–50.

"Dear mother, I was concerned here with my father's affairs and I took care of them because he ordained all that, and commanded that they be done."

At that time, Mary did not understand the meaning of Jesus's words, but she paid careful attention to them because she understood that he was powerful. (vv. 1785–1812)

In the region of Nazareth many people of the city were assembled who had been summoned there; a woman was being married to a worthy man of the region. At the wedding,[84] talk of the renown of Architeclin[85] and his household was great. Indeed, Jesus was there with his disciples.[86] Mary was received joyfully by those people; all their closest friends were seated at the tables. Everyone from the area was happy and laughing. They were quite joyful, and the people had drunk freely, but the wine ran out at the wedding. The cupbearers came to take counsel with Mary.

Mary immediately told everything to her dear son: that the wine had run out and there was no more. Jesus told her that he would do everything he ought:

"The onus, I tell you, is not on me, but on others, but I will act like a friend when an opportunity arises, this I promise you."

She called the cupbearers and ordered: (vv. 1813–46)

"You, cupbearers, do everything according to the will of my son."

At that, Jesus stepped forward and called a servant:

"Go now," he said, "and bring me the vessels great and small, and fill all six of them with water. When they are filled with water, take a goblet straight to Architeclin."

At that time Architeclin was a good judge of wine. The end of this was that he drank it and it seemed to him the best wine that he had ever drunk or tasted. He therefore asked for the man who had kindly organized the wedding and spoke to him:

"I don't know how you have done it, since you refused to give the best wine that you had; it has been saved until now. You ought, indeed, to have given the best at the beginning; you would have acted honorably. I say this to you out of love." (vv. 1847–72)

"I beg your indulgence, dear sweet lord, for I cannot really give an account; and I shall try to explain the truth of the matter to you, how the wine came to us, for it had been drunk up before, and we all saw that. But then I saw that Jesus had the jars filled with water and spoke to the servants that my wife hired, and one of them then took the goblet and brought it to you. I have told you what happened. Dear sir, it will be clear that it is going to make me very happy! I have

---

[84] 1819 ff. **wedding** *noces*: this incident is essentially the miracle at Cana (John 2:1–11), transferred from the public life of Jesus to his childhood.

[85] 1820 **Architeclin** *Archeteclin*: see above, n. to v. 1247 of *The Castle of Love*.

[86] 1822 **disciples** *disciples*: Jesus's disciples, not mentioned earlier in the *Enfaunces*, nonetheless figure in this gospel episode.

already drunk so much that I am quite tipsy. You will see the others in the same state before you leave!"

Everyone from those parts had a good time; the people drank well, and were indeed tipsy when the feast was over. Each rejoiced in it, and marveled at the miracle that Jesus performed. They then left there, all very happy. But some fled because of the bright light that they saw wherever Jesus went; it made them very fearful because they could not look at his brightness or his power. (vv. 1873–1908)

Both Mary and Joseph were often sad on account of Jesus. They were hated by the people and frequently threatened but were saved. In truth, it was thus because they accepted their troubles willingly. Blessed be sweet Jesus, who acted with such power! By his deeds, he is well known, and he was and always will be. Indeed, when his mother requested anything of her son, sweet Jesus Christ, he did it immediately, as soon as she asked it. Jesus loved his mother very much and honored her everywhere. And blessed be the one who loves her sincerely and serves her and both of them openly from now on, with a noble heart. And blessed be those, small and great, who honored him in his lifetime! (vv. 1909–32)

[Epilogue 1]

Now, with your consent, I take my leave of you, for there is truly nothing more to tell, you may be sure. But you have heard about the childhood deeds of Jesus; you have received great comfort from what he did by his power. Now we must pray sincerely and gently to Jesus that he may give us the strength and power to serve him and to love him well, and his mother holy Mary. May each one of us now pray that she grant us her love and friendship in this life! And let us pray sincerely to the angels and all the apostles to give us protection; let us pray to the holy virgins, and ask all the saints with profound devotion, that we may readily have pardon for our sins and offences committed knowingly against God and his chosen ones: we will be in a sorry plight if God, who made and formed us, does not take pity on us, because we have indeed sinned against his will too much and too often. But sweet Jesus, you hear each person readily, whoever is sad and weary, if he is truly prepared to make amends for his misdeeds. And may God give us contrition and love for all people and pardon our sins freely and completely. Amen. (vv. 1933–72)

[Epilogue 2]

The story that you have heard is about Jesus, the son of Mary, about the childhood deeds that he performed during his lifetime, which was filled with joy. And with it you have seen illustrations that greatly adorn the text. The mixture of text and illustration is very fine; there is much profit in it, great joy, and a moral lesson. Hearing it and believing it willingly is a great delight. (vv. 1973–84)

I wish to tell you,[87] and will take pains in the telling, about some wicked people—may God give them sore affliction all their days without end: about the Jews who were most envious of Jesus, the son of Mary. I cry my prayer to Jesus, that he may confound and curse them if they do not repent of their misdeeds, begging mercy of Jesus Christ who is all-powerful, to whom they did such great harm. Now I will leave the treacherous Jews, and tell you about something else. I shall soon end, leaving you with a brief word about the man who wrote the story and did the pictures. Out of charity, pray to Jesus Christ with an undivided heart that he may give him his blessing and true forgiveness for his sins, so that he may have his portion of joy God's realm, and may he protect him from the prison of the devil, full of great treason! For whom do you pray? His name is John; God keep him from shame! And here below you can truly see Jesus Christ raise his right hand to give his blessing to him, who holds the scroll in his hand—it is shorter than a hand's breadth.[88] He prays to Jesus for a balm, that he may receive his soul. (vv. 1985–2020)

---

[87] 1985–86 **I wish to tell you** *vus voil conter*: there is an error in punctuation in the edition: the dash should come at the end of line 1986, not 1985.

[88] In spite of this clear description, the miniature below the text on f. 36ᵛ shows only a kneeling man holding a (blank) scroll; the right-hand side of the picture is empty.

4. The Vengeance of Our Lord
(*La Vengeance de Nostre Seigneur*)

When Tiberius was emperor of Rome, Jesus was betrayed by the Jews, but Tiberius did not know of it. At that time Titus, who was king of Aquitaine in the city of Bordeaux and the vassal of Tiberius,[1] had a cancer in his right nostril that had eaten away his face up to his eye. (ll. 1–4)

It happened that Nathan, the son of Nahum,[2] went out of Judea to bring tribute up to Rome to the emperor Tiberius, who was raging and covered with sores, but a wind brought him and his ship to the city of Libourne.[3] When Titus saw him approaching, he knew that he was from Judea and he wondered at that, as did all his knights. Then he commanded Nathan to come before him and asked him who he was. Nathan answered:

"I am Nathan, the son of Nahum, of the lineage of the Greeks; and I am subject to Pilate in Judea, who sent me to Rome to bring tribute to the emperor. But the wind brought me here and I do not know where I am."

Then Titus said:

"If you heal me of this wound that I have on my face, with herbs or by some other means, I will lead you safely to Tiberius."

Nathan replied: (ll. 5–14)

"I know nothing about that. Had you been in Judea, however, you would have found a wonderful prophet named Jesus Christ. He saved his people from their sins by his word alone: he cleansed lepers, gave sight to the blind, raised the dead, and did many other things in the sight of his disciples. He raised Lazarus, who had lain in the tomb for four days, and a maiden in the house of her father; he gave a young man back to his mother, and spared a woman taken in adultery whom the Jews wished to stone. And he cured another woman who had suffered hemorrhages for twelve years when she simply touched the hem of his garment.

---

[1] 2–3 **Titus ... vassal of Tiberius** *Tytus ... huem Tyberii*: the historical Titus was born two years after Tiberius's death in 37 CE.

[2] 5 **Nathan ... Nahum** *Nathan ... Naüm*: Nathan's name recalls any of several biblical personages, while his father's name echoes the name of the prophet Nahum, whose prophecy deals with the fall of Nineveh.

[3] 7 **Libourne** *Lure*: the exact location of this city is uncertain, but Libourne, near Bordeaux, was an important port of medieval Aquitaine.

And he fed five thousand men with five loaves and two fishes.[4] All this and many other things he did before his Passion. After his resurrection we saw him in the flesh as he had been before."

Then Titus asked:

"How did he rise if he had not died?"

Nathan answered:

"I swear to you that it was a public execution, and that he was hung on a cross and put into a tomb where he lay for three days, and then he rose. And he freed the prophets of human lineage from the devil in hell and raised them.[5] Then, forty days later, we saw him ascend to heaven, and he sent the Holy Spirit from heaven to his disciples and gave them knowledge of seventy-two languages.[6] You may be certain that everything I have told you is true." (ll. 14–31)

When Titus heard this, he and all his household believed, and he said to Nathan:

"Oh, Tiberius, how unfortunate you were when you sent your kings into the land where my Lord God was born, whom they took and killed and did not let come to us, for he would have cured you of your leprosy and me of my wound."

When he said this, the wound vanished from his face and his flesh, which until then had been ugly, was healed. Then he cried out in a loud voice:

"Oh, you my Lord and my God, I have never seen you and you have made me whole. Command that I may go across the sea where you were born, and I will make your enemies see that I can destroy them."

When he had said this, he commanded that they baptize him. And he called Nathan, to whom he said:

"How do you baptize those who believe in God? Come and baptize me in the name of the Father and the Son and the Holy Spirit, for I believe with all my heart in Jesus Christ, who has healed me even though I have never seen him." (ll. 31–42)

Then he commanded his brother Vespasian to come to him and to bring with him all those able to bear arms, and Vespasian came with seven thousand men. When he arrived at Libourne, he asked his brother why he had sent for him. Titus answered:

---

[4] 17–23 **He saved ... two fishes** *Icist fist salf ... dous peissons*: for accounts of these miracles, see John 9:32–44, Mark 5:22–24 and 35–43, Matt. 9:18–26, Luke 8:41–56, 17:11–16, John 8:2–11, Mark 5:25–34, Luke 8:43–48, Matt. 9:20–22, 14:15–21, Mark 6:35–44, Luke 9:12–17.

[5] 27–28 **And he ... hell ... human lineage ... raised them** *Et li ad ... emfern e suscitat ... humeine lignee*: a reference to the *Gospel of Nicodemus* and the Old Testament prophets (as opposed to Sibyls and other kinds of classical prophets and oracles).

[6] **Then forty days ... ascend into heaven ... languages** *puis muntat el ciel ... aprés quarante jurz ... setante dous langages*: for the Ascension and Pentecost, see Acts 1:9 and 2:1–5.

"Dear brother, Christ came into this world in the land of Judea; he was born in Bethlehem and betrayed by the envy of the Jews, and crucified. They saw him then in his own flesh on Golgotha where he rose on the third day, for his disciples saw him then in his own flesh as he had been before. And in the flesh in Galilee, he performed the first of his signs so that his disciples might believe in him. And we wish to be his disciples. Let us go to Judea to destroy his enemies and to make them understand that there is no God but him." (ll. 43–52)

When they had taken counsel, they went forth from the city and entered their ships and sailed until they came to the land of Jerusalem. And they surrounded the kingdom and destroyed those whom they could capture. When the kings of the country heard that they were destroying their kingdom, they were greatly afraid. Archelaus said to Pilate, his son:[7]

"Son, I turn the kingdom over to you; take counsel with other kings of this land as to how you may escape from the hands of Titus and Vespasian, for I was the one who captured Jesus Christ, on account of whom they want to kill us."

When he had said this, he cut the staff of his lance and stuck it in the ground so that it leaned against his chest. Then he impaled himself on it and so died. Pilate, his son, took counsel with the other kings, and they shut themselves up in Jerusalem with their people and remained there for seven years. (ll. 53–63)

In the meantime the power and governance of Titus and Vespasian grew and they occupied the whole realm. At the end of seven years, there was such famine within it that the people ate dirt for lack of bread. Then all the knights of the four besieged kingdoms took counsel and said:

"We will all die and we know well that God does this to us. What are our lives worth if the Romans destroy us and our people? It is better that we kill ourselves than to have people say of us 'The Romans killed and vanquished us.'"

When they had said this, they killed some eleven thousand of their own. Then there was such great fear among them, because they could not bury the dead or throw them outside, that they could stand it no more. Instead they said:

"What shall we do? We delivered Christ to his death and now we are to be handed over. Let us surrender to the Romans, for we are dying."

And when they had said this, they climbed up onto the walls of the city and said:

---

[7] 57 **Archelaus ... his son** *Archelaüs ... sun filz*: the historical Archelaus was not the father of Pilate, but a son of Herod the Great, and ruled Judea from 4 BCE to 6 CE; he was exiled by Augustus to Vienne, south of Lyons in France; see Ford, *Vengeance* (1993), 199 nn. 57–61.

"Titus! Vespasian! We yield the keys of the city of Jerusalem to you, for God wishes it. Now we know that our kingdom will last no longer but is given to us by the Messiah who is called Christ."[8]

Thus they surrendered themselves and their kingdom to Titus and Vespasian and said to them:

"Judge how we must die, because we killed Christ." (ll. 64–80)

When they had said this, they were taken and bound. A large group were stoned, and another group hanged or pierced with lances; still another group was sold, and another was let go. Thus they were divided in four parts as they had divided the clothing of Jesus.[9] Then Titus and Vespasian sold thirty Jews for one piece of silver.[10] After that they took all the land and searched for the portrait of Our Lord until they found a woman, Veronica by name, who had it.[11] Then they took Pilate and put him in an iron chest and sent him to prison in Damascus and had him guarded by his men. Then they sent messengers to Tiberius in Rome and asked him to send to them his provost, Velosian, through whom they would report what the Jews had done to Jesus. (ll. 81–91)

When Tiberius saw the messengers, he summoned Velosian and had him come to him and told him:

"Take whatever you need for a sea voyage and go to the land of Jerusalem. Seek one of the disciples of Jesus and say to him that he should come to me, in the name of his God, to heal my wounds, and so he may condemn my kings to death as they condemned Christ. And if you bring me a man who can cure me, I will believe in Christ, the son of God, and I will be baptized."

Then Velosian said:

"Lord, if I find such a man, what shall I promise him as a reward?"

Tiberius answered:

"I will put all my kingdom into his hands."

Then Velosian departed and set sail. (ll. 92–100)

After a year and seven days, Velosian came to Jerusalem and summoned before him all those who had known Jesus, and he asked them what had been done

---

[8] 75–79 **Titus ... the Messiah who is called Christ** *Tyte ... Messiam qui est dit Crist*: the Jews are portrayed here acknowledging that Jesus was the Messiah, which they had denied during his lifetime.

[9] 83–84 **Thus they were divided ... Jesus** *E firent de els ... Jhesu*: cf. Matt. 27:35, Mark 15:24, Luke 23:34.

[10] 84–85 **thirty Jews ... one piece of silver** *trente judeus ... un denier*: the punishment meted out to the Jews is an inverted form of Judas's betrayal; cf. David Hook, *The Destruction of Jerusalem: Catalan and Castilian Texts* (London: King's College London Centre of Late Antique and Medieval Studies, 2000), 132–33.

[11] 85–87 **After that ... who had it** *Emprés iceo ... ki aveit le vult*: this is the first mention of Veronica and the portrait.

The Vengeance of Our Lord

with Jesus. Then Joseph of Arimathea came and Nicodemus[12] with him, and Velosian ordered them to say what they knew of Jesus. Nicodemus said:
"I saw him and I know that he is the savior of the world."
And Joseph said:
"I saw him before his Passion; he was truly the son of God. I took him down from the cross and put him in the tomb that I had carved in stone and guarded him until the third day. Then I put my head inside to see him, and I saw nothing. But I saw two angels in white tunics, one at the head, the other at the foot, and they asked me: 'Joseph, whom do you seek?' And I said that I was looking for Jesus who had been crucified. And they said to me: 'Go into Galilee; you will see him there.'[13] Then I saw him in the same flesh as before, and his disciples believed in him. I saw him and I believe that my God lives and that I will rise on the last day and I will see God my Savior in his true flesh."[14]

Afterwards there came old man Simeon who said:
"I knew him as an infant and received him in the temple. I worshipped him on the cross and I know that he rose again. Then I saw him ascend into heaven. And I know well that he was the son of God."[15] (ll. 101–16)

Then came a woman, Veronica, who said:
"For twelve years I suffered from hemorrhages and when I touched the hem of his garment, I was cured.[16] I believe that my God lived and will live again."

Then Velosian said to Pilate:
"Why did you kill the son of God?"
Pilate answered:
"His people delivered him to me."
Velosian said:
"You will die shamefully."
Then he had him put in an iron chest.

Then he requested that Veronica give him the portrait of Our Lord. She answered that she did not have it. He tortured her until she was willing to give it up to him. When she had suffered enough, she said:
"I enclosed it in a coffer and I worship it each day."
Velosian said:

---

[12] 103 **Joseph of Arimathea and Nicodemus** *Joseph de Arimathie e Nicodemus*: John 19:38–42 mentions both disciples; the other gospels name only Joseph.

[13] 108–11 **But I saw . . . there** *Mes jo vi . . . iluec*: cf. Luke 24:4–6.

[14] 112–13 **I saw him . . . God my Savior in his true flesh** *Jol vi . . . en sa charn verrai Deu mun sauveur*: Job 19:25–26.

[15] 113–116 **Afterwards . . . Simeon . . . God** *Emprés . . . Symeon . . . Deu*: cf. Luke 2:22–38.

[16] 116–117 **Then came Veronica . . . I was cured** *Dunc vint Veronices . . . si guarai*: cf. Matt. 9:20–22. On the legend of Veronica, see Ford, *Vengeance* (1984), 3–18; S. Riches, "Veronica, St.," *ODMA* 4:1693.

"Give it to me and I will adore it."

And so, of necessity, Veronica turned over the portrait. When Velosian saw it, he knelt and worshipped it sincerely; then he got up with great reverence and took it and wrapped it in a fine cloth embroidered with gold. Then he enclosed it in a golden container and sealed it with his ring and swore that he would not look at it again until he saw Tiberius his lord. When he had said this, he told those in his confidence who were with him:

"You shall not see it again until you have brought it to where you will see it with me, for I will not leave you until we are before my lord Tiberius. And you will tell him everything that you have said about Christ."

Then he said to them: (ll. 116–32)

"Surely you have heard what God said: 'Blessed are the peaceful for they will be called sons of God.'"[17]

Then he commanded Pilate and all the others to go with him and he took the portrait and entered his ship with his disciples that same day. But Veronica abandoned all she had for the love of God and entered the ship in order to follow the portrait. Then Velosian said:

"Woman, whom do you seek?"

She answered:

"I seek my Lord, whom God gave me, not because of my merit but through his great compassion, and whom you have taken from me against the law. If the Jews killed Christ, what guilt do I have for it? Give me back my Lord! And if you do not give him back to me, I will follow him as long as I must, wherever you put him. And I will adore him and serve him as long as I shall live. I believe that my redeemer lives and I will see my Savior in the same flesh that I have now."[18]

Then Veronica's husband and her sons and daughters and her neighbors wept greatly when they saw her go away. Then Velosian said:

"Oh you daughters of Jerusalem, do not weep for us but for yourselves.[19] Surely you have heard God say: 'Whoever leaves everything behind for the love of God will receive a hundredfold in eternal life?'"[20] (ll. 132–46)

Then Velosian departed, leaving Titus and Vespasian in the land of Jerusalem, and sailed until he came to Rome, within a year. Then he left his ship in the Tiber and came to the city and notified the king by messenger that he had come. The emperor summoned him and asked:

"Velosian, what have you found out in the land of Jerusalem about Jesus Christ and about his disciples? If you have found someone, let him come to me and heal my wounds. I will put my kingdom in His hand." (ll. 147–53)

---

[17] 133 **Blessed . . . sons of God** *Beneurés . . . Fiz Deu*: Matt. 5:9.
[18] 141–42 **I believe . . . I have now** *Jo crei . . . ore ai*: cf. Job 19:25–26.
[19] 144–45 **O you daughters . . . yourselves** *O vus filles . . . vus*: Luke 23:28.
[20] 145–46 **Whoever leaves . . . eternal life** *Ki lairat . . . vie pardurable*: Luke 18:28–29.

Velosian answered:

"Everything that I have heard and learned I will tell you, for I found Titus and Vespasian, your faithful subjects who fear God and are cleansed of all their infirmities. And I found three kings hanged, Caiphas stoned, Archelaus dead by a lance, Pilate bound in an iron chest and imprisoned in Damascus. And I heard such words about Jesus Christ as I shall tell you now: how the Jews came to him by night with lances and clubs and lanterns, and took and bound him, and killed our light who was meant to enlighten us, and did not let him come to us, but put him on the cross. Then the faithful followers of God, Joseph of Arimathea and Nicodemus with him, took down Jesus's body from the cross and anointed it with a hundred pounds of myrrh of aloe and put it in a tomb. But Jesus, as true God, rose on the third day and appeared to his disciples in the very flesh that he had had before. Then his disciples saw him ascend to Heaven. And again, know that he performed many signs before his Passion that I do not know about and many that I shall tell you: he cleansed lepers and gave sight to the blind; cured the paralytic, cast out demons, made the deaf hear and the mute speak. And he raised Lazarus, who had lain in the tomb for four days, and a girl in the house of her father, and he gave a young man back to his mother; and a woman, Veronica by name, who had hemorrhages for twelve years, was cured merely by touching the hem of his garment. These miracles, and many others about which we are not informed, Jesus performed in the sight of his disciples. (ll. 153–73)

"Then it happened that God was angry on account of his son, whom they killed on earth. So he sent his angel to Titus and to Vespasian and not to us, for we were unworthy sinners, and he inspired them to go into the land of Jerusalem. When they came they took three kings and judged how they were to die. And I heard a report of how they acted. When they had taken them, Vespasian said:

'What shall we do with them?'

Titus answered:

'They took our Lord and bound him. We will take them and bind them.'

And they did so. Vespasian said:

'What else shall we do?'

Titus answered:

'They scourged our Lord and insulted him. And we shall scourge them and insult them.'

And they did so. Vespasian said:

'What else shall we do?'

Titus answered:

'They hung our Lord on green wood and pierced him with a lance. We will hang them on dry wood and pierce them with lances.'

And they did so. Vespasian said:

'What shall we do with those who remain?'

Titus answered:

'They took the clothing of our Lord and divided it into four lots. We will divide them in the same way into four groups and I will have one and you another; and my men the third, and yours the fourth.'

And they were so divided. Vespasian said:

'What then shall we do with them?'

Titus answered:

'They sold our Lord for thirty pieces of silver. And we will sell them and will give thirty for one piece of silver.'

And so it was done. Then they looked for the portrait of our Lord and they found it with a woman, Veronica by name, who had it. And they put Pilate in an iron cask and delivered him to me. I have him here as well as the portrait and the woman." (ll. 173–93)

Then Tiberius said:

"Uncover the portrait and I will look at it and worship it, for many blind men and lepers, and lame and mute and deaf people, have great confidence in it."

Then Velosian unwrapped it. When Tiberius looked at it, he worshipped it. When he had seen and adored it, the leprosy fell from him, and his flesh was whole and clean like the flesh of a small child. And all the other sick people who were there were cured along with him. Then Tiberius bowed his head and bent his knees and remembered these words:

"Oh, you, Christ, blessed is the womb that bore you and blessed the breasts that nursed you, and blessed are those who hear your word and keep it."[21]

Then he raised his eyes toward heaven and wept with his heart and his eyes and said to our Lord in a low voice:

"God, Lord of heaven and of the earth, do not let me die but comfort me, for I have great faith in your name."

When he said this, he remembered the words of the prophet David and said:

"Lord God, deliver me from wicked men and from evildoers,[22] and deliver me from this kingdom as you delivered Daniel from the lion's den and Jonah the prophet from the belly of the whale.[23] And so deliver me from the hands of my enemies."

When he had said this, he called Velosian and said to him:

"Velosian, are you not one of those who saw Christ and who can tell me how he performed a baptism? Come to me and show me."

Then Velosian said:

---

[21] 200–3 **blessed is the womb ... keep it** *beneïz est li ventres ... la gardent*: cf. Luke 11:27–28.

[22] 205–6 **Lord God ... evildoers** *Sire Deus ... feluns*: cf. Ps. 58:3, 70:4, 139:2.

[23] 207–8 **Daniel ... whale** *Daniel ... baleine*: cf. Daniel 6 and Jonah 1:15–2:11.

"Here is someone who was a disciple of Jesus and his name is Sylvester.[24] Call him, for he will baptize you willingly."

Tiberius said:

"Oh you, blessed Sylvester, I commend my spirit into your hands."[25]

And Sylvester baptized him in the name of the Father and the Son and the Holy Spirit. Afterwards he confirmed him. (ll. 194–214)

Then Tiberius stood up on his platform and blessed the Lord God as follows:

"Blessed be you, God, who were and are Lord of our fathers, and praised be you and glorified by all worlds.[26] Blessed be the name of your kingdom, for your holy kingdom has power of damnation. And I am cleansed of my sores and of my sins, for all my life I had sinned before you. For that reason I was not worthy to see your face, but nonetheless you visited me, not because of my merit but because of your great mercy. The wicked men who killed you, and because of whom I could not see you, are destroyed. And may they be before me on the last day so that I may see them. Lord God, deliver me from this mortal kingdom so that I may bless you and your kingdom eternally."

Then he commanded Velosian to come to him and said to him:

"Bring me Pilate, the wicked man who prevented me from seeing my Lord, who made me whole and whom I never saw; and have him put in the city of Vienne, where the condemned remain. Let him be enclosed there under the seal of your ring so that he may never appear on earth." (ll. 215–28)

This vengeance was taken for the death of Our Lord. Blessed be all those who avenge the death and the shame of the one who lives and reigns for all ages. Amen. (ll. 229–31)

---

[24] 211 **Sylvester** *Silvestre*: no first-century disciple by this name is known, but there were two popes by that name: the first (314–35) is associated, especially in apocryphal sources, with Constantine's establishment of Christianity as the official religion of the Roman Empire; the second (999–1003) was the first French pope. Cf. Ford, *Vengeance* (1993), 204, n. 211.

[25] 213 **I commend my spirit into your hands** *li men espirit comant jo en tes mains*: cf. Luke 23:46.

[26] 216–17 **Blessed be you . . . worlds** *Beneït seies tu . . . siecles*: Daniel 3:26.

5. Little St. Hugh of Lincoln
(*Hugues de Lincoln*)

Now hear a fine song about the Jews of Lincoln, who treacherously committed the cruel murder of a child named Hugh. The child was in the Dernstall[1] quarter of the rich city of Lincoln. On the evening of the first of August, he was kidnapped by Peitevin[2] the Jew. No sooner had he been taken than his mother noticed that the child was lost; she went searching for him in many places. All evening until the ringing of curfew she cried out:

"I have lost my dear child whom I have always loved so much." (1–16)

That night the mother slept very little. She scarcely lay in her bed; she prayed fervently to God that he might help her by his mercy, if it pleased him. When she had finished her prayer, she quickly suspected that the theft of her son had been done treacherously by the Jews. At daybreak, the woman went weeping throughout the Jewish quarter, asking at the doors of the Jews:

"Where is my child?"

I do not doubt that the gate through which the child had entered was tightly locked, so that no Christian born could know about the Jews' private affairs. (17–32)

The report soon spread throughout the whole city that the child had been stolen; but no one knew the truth except Jesus Christ and the excommunicated Jews.[3] Because of her suspicion of Lincoln's Jews, she scarcely ceased all night until she came to the royal court, as it pleased God. (33–40)

When the woman had left the city of Lincoln, those who had kidnapped the child were very happy. They thought that she had fled from Lincoln for fear of her life, since she made such a great noise. Never fear, you shall hear something

---

[1] 6 **Dernstall** *Dernestal*: an area south of the castle, around St. Martin's church, adjacent to the junction of the Strait and High Street; see J. W. F. Hill, *Medieval Lincoln* (Cambridge: Cambridge University Press, 1948), 233; the name may derive from OE *dierne* "hidden," and *steall* "a place" (Hill, *Lincoln*, 34). Its identification as the Jewish quarter (Jacobs, "Little St. Hugh," 59) relies on popular belief (Hill, *Lincoln*, 233). Michel (*Hugues*, 60–61) derived the name from *Dernetal*, a place name found in Normandy (Seine-Inférieure) and in the Pays d'Auge.

[2] 7 **Peitevin**: possibly Peitevin ben Beneit, who was the Jewish creditor of the abbey of Bardeney (Jacobs, "Little St. Hugh," 62).

[3] 36 **excommunicated** *escomengé*: ecclesiastical judgments do not apply to those outside the Church (Michel, *Hugues*, 61 n.7); an example of a Christian-centric attitude.

else. When she came before King Henry (may God guard and keep his life), she fell at his feet at once and piteously begged his mercy:

"Lord, please listen: my son was kidnapped by the Jews of Lincoln one evening; pay heed to it, if you please, for charity."

He swore a truthful oath:

"By the pity of God, if it is as you have now recounted here, the Jews will die without mercy; and if you have lied about the Jews, for such a crime, by St. Edward, never doubt that you shall receive the same judgment."

The woman replied very gently:

"May Jesus Christ almighty fulfill it for you on the day of Judgment, should you find the truth to be otherwise." (41–67)

Soon after the child had been kidnapped the Lincoln Jews assembled the richest Jews born in England,[4] as had been agreed before. Jopin[5] the Jew brought the child before them, bound with a cord. They stripped the child naked, as the Jews had once done to Jesus. All the Jews there rejoiced to see the child naked; very little pity did they have for him. Then said Jopin the Jew, who thought he spoke worthily:

"It is fitting that the child be sold like Jesus for thirty coins."

Chaim[6] the Jew then replied like this:

"Give me this child for thirty correctly-weighed coins—here they are; but I want him to be condemned to death and delivered to me, so that I may do my will, since I have bought him." (68–91)

The answer of the Jews, quickly giving their support, was very harsh:

"Let Chaim have him. There's no wrong in it, but let the child be put to death quickly."

And then the wicked Jews of Lincoln said a harsher word. They all shouted with one voice:

"Let the child be put on the cross."

The Jews of Lincoln immediately fetched a cross. The child trembled greatly that day, but said nothing at all. The child was unbound and soon was hung vilely on the cross, as Jesus was, who died for our benefit. Now hear great profit or

---

[4] 72 **the richest Jews born in England** *Des Jus plus riches d'Engleterre né*: according to the annals of the abbey of Burton-on-Trent, a large number of Jews had come to Lincoln for a wedding (*Annales Monastici*, ed. Henry Richard Luard, Rolls Series, Rerum Britannicarum Medii Aevi Scriptores 36 [London: Longman, Green, 1864], 1:340–48); cf. Jacobs, "Little St. Hugh," 55–56 and Hill, *Lincoln*, 226.

[5] 73 **Jopin**: Matthew Paris, *Historia major*, gives the name as *Copinus*; cf. Michel, *Hugues*, 29.

[6] 84 **Chaim** *Agon*: the usual form in the manuscript is *Agim*: cf. lines 94, 121, 324; Jacobs, "Little St. Hugh," 61 states that Agim is an English form of Chayim or Chaim.

sorrow[7] (may God have mercy!). Hear how the young child was afraid at the hour when he was placed on the cross. His arms were stretched out on the cross, as he was bound, and his feet and hands were pierced by many of the Jews with sharp nails. Thus the hands and feet of the child were attached to the cross, as you hear, and he was crucified alive on the cross. (92–119)

Now hear the great sorrow[8] of the child when Chaim the Jew came forth, because he said:

"The child shall die at once."

Chaim the Jew took up his knife and pierced the side of the innocent child and cut his heart in two; then the wicked people sprang up.[9]

When his soul went forth from his body, the child shouted out, called his mother and said:

"Pray to Jesus Christ for me."

Immediately angels of heaven, all singing, carried the good soul of this child into the presence of God Almighty. (120–35)

When this child had died on the cross, the wicked Jews of Lincoln said:

"Let the body be carried outside the gates. May he be buried deep[10] within the earth, so that no Christian born of woman may know where he is buried; then it will be our secret."

When the body was buried, a Jew said mockingly:

"Now may his mother rejoice in him today!" (136–47)

The next morning, when the Jews passed by where he was buried and found him above the earth, they were greatly astonished at that. When the Jews of Lincoln heard about the great marvel that the others had seen,[11] they assembled that very day, and decided upon a plan: that the body of the child should be thrown into a stinking privy. They were very foolish and unbelieving. (148–59)

Indeed the next day the treacherous Jews found the body on the seat of the privy; whatever they did was in vain. The Jews of Lincoln were[12] full of sorrow and fear when they could not ever hide the body, night or day. A Jew came and said:

"Let the body of the child be carried out of Lincoln at once, for it is already stinking. Indeed, a woman who is a close friend, who nursed me, has agreed, for

---

[7] 108 **profit or sorrow** *pru u dolur*: this contradictory statement refers to the account of the martyrdom that follows: the "profit" is the creation of a saint; the "sorrow" is the suffering undergone by the child.

[8] 120 **sorrow** *dodel*: = *duel, doel*; the form is not attested in *AND*, but it may be a scribal error.

[9] 127 **sprang up** *gurristrent*: misreading for *surristrent* < *sordre*. The scribe's compact form of round 's' occurs again at v. 365.

[10] 140 **Deep** *par fond*: MS *parfond*.

[11] 153 **had seen** *vi*: MS. *virent*; edition is incorrect.

[12] 164 **were**: MS *firent;* see Michel, *Hugues*, 62 n. 16.

a bribe, to carry the body away in secret. But before it is carried out of Lincoln, let all the wounds be filled with well-boiled yellow wax." (160–79)

The stinking body was carried by a wretched nurse and thrown into a well behind the castle of the city. The woman was considered a Christian; for that reason she feared nothing. She thought to escape, but was adjudged baser than a dog. (180–87)

The next day another woman came to draw water from the well and found the body, but she scarcely dared to touch it with her hand, so soiled was the body with the filth of the privy. The woman was astonished that such a body was found there. She thought at once of the woman whose child had been stolen; she went into Lincoln, to Dernstall, where the child was born. When she came to the house of the child Hugh's stepfather, she said quickly to the man:

"Listen to me: this morning I found the body of a child outside the city of Lincoln beyond a well; I think that you should examine it." (188–207)

Immediately the man agreed because of his great suspicion that the kidnapping had been done treacherously by the Jews. The woman went through the city saying:

"I have found a child lying naked in a well behind the castle; let it be inspected[13] at once."

Those who heard the woman's cry all went to the well; there they found the body of the child, and they all prayed for his soul. No sooner were the coroners summoned than they came willingly to inspect[14] it honestly, according to the law. When the body had been viewed, it was recognized by all the people, and everyone said:

"Let the body be carried today to the place where it was born."

The body was soon brought to Dernstall,[15] where it had been born; because it was so filthy it could not be examined by the priest. (208–31)

At that moment a woman, who many days before had happened to lose the sight of one eye, came along, as God our Lord wished it. The woman said at once:

"Alas! Hugh, young child who was once so fair, why are you lying here?"

She touched the body with her hands and afterwards touched the eye that she had lost; God showed her his grace and gave her the sight of her eye. When the woman became aware of the grace and the wonder that had been shown her, she said:

"By God's mercy, I can see!"

All the people who were there saw the miracle; they all gave thanks to God; they did whatever they heard. (232–51)

---

[13] 215 **inspected** *l'aü seit fet*: MS. *aü* is unattested in *AND*; in the context it seems to be a scribal error for *la vu[e]*; cf. the phrase in v. 223.

[14] 223 **inspect** *fere la we*: *we = vue*.

[15] 229 **Dernstall** *Desternal* is a variant of *Dernestal*.

At that moment a convert came forth and said:

"Do you want to know right now how this child died? Let his filthy body be washed with hot water; how the child was tortured will be revealed, I think."

No sooner was the body washed than the convert saw he was right: he showed them[16] how the treachery done by Jewish scheming was visible. The same wounds by which God was tortured were found on the child. Throughout the city of Lincoln the report spread quickly. (252–67)

Those of the mother-church heard of God's miracle, seen by the others; everyone went to the holy body and carried it away with great ceremony into the mother-church of Lincoln, where, with great joy, they put it in a tomb[17] which once held holy bodies: they did well, it seems to me. In the entire city there was not a canon who failed to process toward the body of little Hugh. It was put into the tomb with great devotion. Soon afterwards his mother came from the courtyard with a sorrowful face because she could not see the body of her dear son, whom she had cherished. (268–83)

The widespread report of the slaying of this child caused much to be said about the Jews, who were seized immediately. After the Jews of Lincoln had been arrested, they were put in a secure prison; then they thought, "We have been betrayed by treachery."[18]

Every one[19] of the Jews of the city of Lincoln remained in prison, except for women and children, who were released by grace and pity, until the next day, when King Henry (may God guard him and protect his life) came to Lincoln with his knights, as God wished by His mercy. The Jews were summoned in shackles before the king so that the truth might be sought about whether the child had been crucified.

A wise man who was present there now spoke before the king:

"The Jew who reveals the truth to the king will have his life."[20] (284–307)

At once Jopin the Jew arose, who first undertook all the treachery:

"Today you will know in whose house everything was done. The boy was kidnapped by Peitevin[21] the Jew on the evening of the first of August; when the child came through my door he was tightly bound. He was imprisoned within my house until all the English-born Jews knew the secret, and everyone said that he should be crucified. In all England there was nary a Jew or his advisor

---

[16] 262 **showed them** *mustra a us*: editor's error for *vu* written *w* by the scribe; cf. v. 223 where the same form occurs.

[17] 274 **tomb** *tumbe*: Hugh was buried in a stone coffin inside the cathedral; cf. Jacobs, "Little St. Hugh," 57–58, with an illustration of the coffin and remains.

[18] 291 **treachery** *Falsim*: the word should not be capitalized in the edition; it is a form of *fausine*.

[19] 292 **Every one** *chescon peé*: = *chescon pé*.

[20] 307 **will . . . life** *vi avera*: the edition omits *vi*.

[21] 312 **Peitevin** *Partenin*: a scribal variant for *Peitevin*; cf. v. 7.

who was not there. By common consent he was hung on the cross, as Jesus was. Chaim, the Jew to whom the child was sold for thirty coins as Jesus was, came along afterwards, and I received the coins in my hands. With his knife he killed the child as he hung there on the cross; the child called out loudly in pain when his soul left his body. The child could not be buried within the house or in secret, which amazed and eventually frightened us. A Jew's nurse carried the child by night[22] — she was considered a Christian — to a well, I know where, behind the castle, to the west; I know that it is deep, and there he was plunged in headfirst. Now judge as you will." (308–43)

When Jopin the Jew had spoken, what he said was written down in the presence of the king. King Henry said straightaway:

"By the pity of Jesus Christ! He did great wrong who killed him."[23]

The Jews went immediately to their council and tried Jopin the Jew, whom they sentenced to death; they readily turned him over to the bailiffs.

"Let the body of Jopin be dragged through the city of Lincoln by strong, well-shod horses until the life has gone out of him. Then let him be hanged cruelly and swiftly as a traitor and a thief so that all people may see why he is hanged, and what the meaning of it is."

As justice ordained, the body of Jopin the Jew was dragged by strong horses and then hanged outside Lincoln, I know where: on the Canwick[24] side, on a high hill where people who commit theft and treason are hanged. The Jews had much to be ashamed of. (344–68)

---

[22] 336 **by night** *nutanté*: editorial error for *nutante*; cf. *AND nuitantre*.

[23] 344–48: stanza has five lines.

[24] 365 **Canwick** *Canevic*: situated on a hill about a mile south of Lincoln, still a suburb of the city; cf. Michel, *Hugues*, 63, n. 27.

6a. *Seven-Part Meditation on the Passion*, in prose (Dublin, Trin. Coll., MS 374)

Prologue (London, BL, Arundel MS 288)[1]

[1]   The prayers and meditations that follow are taken in part from Saint Anselm, in part from other writings,[2] to enkindle the hearts and thoughts of those who read them with the love and fear of God, and to know themselves: and they are not to be read when you are upset, but in tranquillity; not while on the run or while moving about, but little by little, with great perseverance and with great understanding of heart. The one[3] who says these prayers should not apply herself or himself to read the whole of each one but as much as she or he[4] feels might be useful, with the help of God, to ignite in them intense desire to pray as much as they please. Whoever begins should not graze each time only at the beginning, but where it pleases them most. Indeed, for that reason each prayer is divided by illuminated letters,[5] so that one may begin or end where one would like and so that the prayer may not become boring from excessive length and by frequent re-reading, but so that the reader may read the prayers for their original

---

   [1]   ¶ 1 **Prologue:** a translation of the Prologue to Anselm's *Orationes sive meditationes; S. Anselmi Cantuariensis Archiepiscopi Opera omnia*, ed. F. S. Schmitt (Edinburgh: T. Nelson, 1946), 3:3.

   [2]   ¶ 1 **Saint Anselm . . . other writings** *Seynt Auselyn . . . des autres escritz*: *C* reads: in part from St. Augustine, in part from St. Anselm, in part from St. Bernard, and in part from the Holy Scriptures.

   [3]   ¶ 1 **The one** *cele*: the Arundel manuscript addresses the one prayer it includes to a female reader, but the Cotton manuscript uses a masculine pronoun, and the Dublin text is addressed to a male reader, perhaps a religious.

   [4]   ¶ 1 **she or he** *il*: from this point the Prologue in the Arundel manuscript uses only the singular masculine pronoun, translated here by the plural.

   [5]   ¶ 1 **illuminated letters** *lettres enluminees*: although not strictly illuminated (i.e., gold), the different sections of the text are marked with large initials, painted either blue or red, indicated in the edition (below, pp. 175–88) in boldface.

purpose: that is, to stimulate pity of heart and desire to love God, and to know oneself. *Jesus mild, Jesus virtuous, do not forsake me.*[6]

Dublin, Trinity College, MS 374

I. [2] Good Jesus, I see you with the eyes of true belief that you have opened for me. I see you where you go after the Last Supper with your disciples to the place of your Passion. There, willingly, you are betrayed by your own disciple, and all for me; taken by cruel hands, and captive and tied with bonds, beaten with scourges, and struck with slaps, and all for me. Your face is covered with filthy spittle, you are mockingly clad in purple and the royal scepter is put in your fist; nails driven in, pierced with the lance, hung between thieves, and all for me. Slaked with gall mixed with vinegar, you bent your head to the right and gave up your soul, and all for me. Good Jesus, all these humiliations and all these torments were done to you by my sins and my mortal wounds, which would be without hope of cure if the precious balm of your sweet blood had not been shed for me, and upon me. But now it is shed and poured over my wounds, and the cure of my soul is the result, thank you! Henceforth I am most wretched if, through my folly, I should lose that health that the son of God bought so dearly for me.[7]

[3] Lord God of heaven, look[8] at your sweet son, how he suffers a great thing for me! Remember, dear Father, for whom he suffers it—it is your own son, whom you delivered to death for us, to whom you cannot fail to answer any request. Who is it for whom he suffers? It is I, N_____,[9] full of sins and nevertheless trusting in your mercy. Truly he is the son of God who was here obedient to you unto death.[10] And truly he is a man, who suffers in human nature a horrible death like that on the cross. Lord Father, cast your eyes on your dear son and see how his body is stretched on the cross, and pardon me all my sins that I have committed with my whole body. Look at these innocent hands that never sinned, how they run with blood, and pardon me the great wrongs that my hands

---

[6] ¶ 1 Jesus . . . forsake me *Jhesu . . . me relinquere*: a variant of a line from the hymn "Juste Judex Christe."

[7] ¶ 2 *Arundel adds here*: "This prayer is to be said before the crucifix of the church or above a crucifix painted in a book."

[8] ¶ 3 **Lord God of heaven, look** *Sire Deu del ciel, esgardez*: from this point to the end of ¶ 6 the text is based on the *Meditatio* (chap. VI-VII) attributed to Augustine but actually written by John of Fécamp: *PL* 40. 901–42, at 905–7; CPPM 2:700–1 (no. 3072). Cf. A. Wilmart, "Les méditations réunies sous le nom de saint Anselme," in *Auteurs spirituels et textes dévots du Moyen Age latin* (Paris: Bloud et Gay, 1932; rev. ed. 1971), 898–942.

[9] ¶ 3 N *N*: from Latin *nomen*; the following blank space in the manuscript allows the reader mentally to insert their own name.

[10] ¶ 3 **obedient . . . death** *obedient . . . mort*: Phil. 2:8.

have brought about. Look at this innocent side, how it is pierced with the cruel point of the lance, and wash me with the holy stream that runs from it. Look at these innocent feet, that never took a false step, how cruelly they are pierced with nails; and pardon me the wicked steps that I have taken with my feet.

[4] Then, don't you see, dear Father, how your sweet son bends his head and gives up his soul? His naked chest[11] whitens with death, his side is all red with blood, his entrails all stretched out begin to dry up. The fair eyes begin to fade, his bright face begins to grow pale, his fully extended arms become completely stiff, his thighs and his legs, which were better colored than marble, begin to wither. His feet, pierced through by nails, are all soaked with the blessed blood. Look, glorious Father, at your sweet offspring, how all his limbs are torn, and lighten my misery, for whom he suffers all this.

[5] O sweet child, the sweetest that ever was born, what did you do wrong that you were so shamefully condemned? O sweet young man, the kindest that there ever was, what did you do wrong that you were tormented so harshly? What was your crime? What is your guilt? What is the reason for your death? I am, and my sins! I sinned with my sinful flesh: You therefore afflicted your flesh. I sinned through pride: You therefore humbled yourself unto death. I sinned through covetousness: You therefore suffered the cross. Now you can hear how wonderful is God's ordering: the son of God pays for the sins of man. The sinner does evil, and the just man suffers the punishment. The slave is guilty, and the lord is punished.[12] And for this reason, there is great need for us to keep within us the gift that God has given us, for the more he has suffered, the more harshly we will be condemned if we fall into the sins for which the son of God suffered bitter death.

[6] O you wretched, sorrowful madman N._____ , why is your heart so hard that you cannot understand how great were the sins for which the son of God himself must suffer such a cruel death? Now think about how dreadful were those wounds for which the son of God must suffer such painful wounds. If those wounds had not been mortal, and even now worthy of eternal death, the son of God would never have had to suffer that death to heal them. Thus, through the magnitude of my cure, may I understand the magnitude of my wounds. And nevertheless, from that very fact I may indeed have the beginning of good hope; on the one hand, just as I see that my illness is so great that it cannot be cured except by the death of the son of God, so I can see, on the other hand, that it is not so great that it cannot be healed with such potent medicine as it has made use of. For otherwise Jesus would not be a wise physician if he applied

---

[11] ¶ 4 **His naked chest** *Sun nu piz*: for this and the next sentences, see the *Meditatio* of Pseudo-Augustine (*PL* 40. 906) "Candet nudatum pectus," also found in the *Oratio ad deum patrem* attributed falsely to Anselm (*PL* 158. 861).

[12] ¶ 5 **The sinner ... punished** *Li peccheur ... penist*: cf. Ps. Augustine (i.e., John of Fécamp), *Meditatio*, *PL* 40. 906.

in vain such valuable drugs and such a precious medicine as his body and his blood, were he not certain that I could be cured. Henceforth these drugs are applied to me. Now I can be healed, if I wish. I am most wretched if I do not forget about the pleasures of my flesh and the delights of this world; and I must abandon the heaviness of my heart[13] in order to concern myself with this ransom.

II. [7] Lord Jesus Christ, now let me debate with you a little, and reveal to you what lies in my heart. Dear sweet Lord, the death that you suffered, you suffered it for me. You cannot deny this. You suffered it in order to save me, to deliver me from everlasting death—you cannot deny it—and to lead me to life everlasting. Therefore your death and your passion are given to me and ordained for my salvation.

[8] Jesus Christ can truly say:
"If you love him, follow his example and lead your life on his model."

Dear Lord, because of this very thing, I must have your help and your grace, for I am disturbed by the sins I have committed, and by other sins by which I am often tempted. Truly, your mercy and your grace draw me upwards, but my sins drag me down. Now it will become evident which will win—your mercy or my sins. For certainly, I do not believe that my sins have more power and strength to damn me than your mercy has to save me. Anyone who believes that should be ashamed! Rather, your mercy is much more exalted than all the sins of the world, and you can pardon more in a single day than I could sin in all my life. And you wish to pardon more than I wish to sin, for if I think rightly, in the hour and the place where I am ever more encouraged to sin, you would be even more ready to pardon me and to save me.

[9] Truly can Jesus Christ say:
"And I find in you three things that I require: the intention to leave off and to stop [sinning], the intention to confess completely, and the intention to make amends."

Dear Lord, I bear witness through you yourself who see in my heart all three of these things, both in will and in intention, that I do not renounce everything as firmly or as fully as I ought, and for this reason I must beg mercy and ask your grace. As regards stopping, you see well that I would prefer to die than ever do the evils that I have done; and if they were now to do, I would not do them for all the world, it seems to me, neither these nor others, according to the intention I have now. Regarding confession, I am ready. I have told my priest all the wickedness that I am able to recount or relate about myself, and if I could remember any more I would say it, in such intention as I now have, you see this well. Regarding making amends, I will fast when I want to eat and drink. I will keep vigil when I

---

[13] ¶ **the heaviness of my heart** *la grossure de mun quer*: as an organ of feeling and thought, the medieval heart could alter its physical condition in response to different affective states. Heaviness of heart here signifies a grudging and sullen disposition: see *AND grossur [de cuer]*.

want to sleep. I will be quiet when I want to speak. I will be at peace when I want to go from place to place. I will endure discipline,[14] hardship, and troubles; and above everything I will restrain my own will out of respect for you and for those who are in your place. If all these things are not sufficient for me to have pardon for my sins and be saved, I will take a greater share of your death, Jesus Christ, suffered because of me and on my behalf; and I will pay in full with your death what I cannot provide with my own.

[10] Then can Jesus Christ say:

"Now do not be too confident. You have not yet escaped from my judgment; you still do not know which way you will turn."

Dear Lord, I am truly afraid of your judgment, and less than I ought to be; this I know well. But the love and the confidence that I have in your Passion is greater than the fear of anything else. Indeed, I believe with certainty—whether I am happy or sorrowful, in peace or sadness, or tribulation, or when I am afflicted, in good health or bad, whatever accident may befall me—and if I remember and love perfectly your cross and your Passion, I cannot take any wrong path, whether in this life or in the next.

[11] Jesus Christ, it seems to me that there is still more reason why you ought to have mercy on me. For in that blessed hour, and at the very moment when you had to give up your soul on the cross, you prayed for those who crucified you. Doubtless you were heard in that prayer; it could not have been otherwise. And I recognize well that, at the hour when you endured such an extreme sacrifice for us as the soul and the body of the son of God, as great as their[15] sin was, your mercy was far greater; and as great as it was then, it is now. And your death is still as powerful as it was then, and my sin is not as great as was the sin of those you prayed for then. Why would a repentant sinner, safe and trusting in God's mercy, not be as good as those who crucified you, who did not believe in you as I do?

[12] Dear Lord Jesus Christ, sweet, gentle, meek, see me here before you, wretched with all my sins, who never crucified you with my own hand. Although I have angered you enough with wicked deeds, say for me and for my sins to your dear Father in heaven what you said for those who crucified you:

"*Father, they know not what they do.*[16] Dear Father, pardon them what they do, for they do not know what they are doing."

Indeed it is the truth that when I committed sins, I did not think that they were as great as I have since seen, any more than those who crucified you knew that they sinned as much as they did. By the power of the blood that you shed for me, and by the power of the death that you suffered for me, together with the

---

[14] ¶ 9 discipline *disciplin[e]s*: can mean the religious way of life or (in the plural) punishment as well as moral exercises.

[15] ¶ 11 their *lur*: i.e., of those who crucified Jesus.

[16] ¶ 12 Father...they do *Pater...faciunt*: a variant of Luke 23:34.

trust and the hope that I have in your mercy, each time I ask you to have mercy on me.

[13] Jesus Christ, I see you all covered in blood for me, for in the beginning when you were circumcised, that part of your body was doubtless bloody. Good Jesus, you were very young when you first suffered pain for me: you were not even eight days old. Afterward when you were beaten with the scourge, then your back was bloody. When you were crowned with thorns, your head was bloody. When you were attached to the cross with nails, your hands and feet were bloody. And after death when you were pierced with the lance, your side was bloody, for the cruel ones who tormented you did not spare you even after your death. The other parts of your body were bloody, with the bloody sweat that you produced when you prayed so intently before you were arrested. Dear Lord, I must give that blood back to you. If I cannot return it by shedding my blood for you, give me compassion so that I may return it by shedding my tears. Through compassion for your blood, draw out tears from my heart and from my eyes, so that I may lament and weep for my sins.

[14] Now let us speak a little more about the prayer that you prayed. The gospel tells me that when you were on the point of being arrested, you felt great sadness and trouble and fear of the Passion, so that the great anguish and sadness that you felt came forth from your body like drops of blood dripping to earth.[17] Then you prayed long and intently and said to your Father:

"Father, if it is possible, let this chalice pass from me; in truth, however, let your will, not mine be done.[18] That is to say, dear Father, if it can be, turn away from me the draught of this Passion that I am willing to drink. And nevertheless, if it is necessary that I drink it, may your will take precedence and not mine."

Dear sweet Lord Jesus Christ, what is it that you say? We read of Saint Andrew the apostle, that when he saw the cross prepared for him, he was so happy and joyful before it that he was almost beside himself with joy. And because of the great happiness he had, he shouted far and wide:

"O precious cross that I have desired so much and have always loved, and which I have now regained later than I would wish, receive me with great joy as I receive you, since through you I can come to him who has redeemed me."[19]

Merciful Jesus, holy and full of mercy, why didn't you ask yourself for the great strength and daring that you gave to Saint Andrew, for he had none except by your gift, you from whom come all good things? You were his Creator;

---

[17] ¶ 14 the great anguish ... earth *la grant anguisse ... tere*: cf. Luke 22:43–44.

[18] ¶ 14 Father ... your will, not mine, be done *Pater ... non mea voluntas fiat sed tua*: a variant of Matt. 26:39.

[19] ¶ 14 O precious cross ... redeemed me *O precius croiz ... me reinst*: the life of St. Andrew in the *Golden Legend* reports a similar speech; cf. Jacobus de Voragine, *The Golden Legend: Readings on the Saints*, trans. William Granger Ryan (Princeton: Princeton University Press, 1993), 1:17.

why weren't you as bold as your creature? You were his Lord; why weren't you as bold as your servant? You were his Master; why weren't you as steadfast as your disciple?

[15] I marvel still more that the gospel says that when you were in your greatest anguish, an angel, who comforted others, came there and comforted you;[20] that the messenger of God comforted the son of God; the creature comforted the Creator; the angel comforted the God of all angels. Dear lord Angel, why did you undertake to comfort him? Didn't you know well that he was the sovereign Comforter, without whom comfort can be worth nothing? Why didn't you know that it was he who had been born miraculously of the Virgin, who changed water into wine, who cured the lepers and the feeble, who walked on water, who raised the dead? It is he who made heaven and earth and created all things, who maintains and governs the whole world, without whom nothing can last—even, lord Angel, you yourself, who comforted him.

[16] But now it should be known why the son of God wished to become so fearful before his death that he needed the comfort of an angel, he who could have had more than twelve thousand angels to protect him, if he wished.[21] He did it to show us how he loved us and why he loved us, why he didn't want to suffer anguish of body alone, but also anguish of the soul, just as he said:

"Brother N._____, you ought to be mine, for I have ransomed you with myself. I have bought your whole body with my body and I have bought your soul with mine. I suffered death in order to make you live; I became weak in order to make you strong. I became fearful to make you bold; I became sad to make you happy. I suffered anguish and discomfort within myself in order to make you healthy and comforted."

[17] Dear Lord, I will not despair henceforth. I, wretched N._____, when I am assailed by temptation, when I am weak of heart or when I am moved by tribulation or illness, by harshness of the rule,[22] or by other conflict that is mine by fear or by fault, since you, who are our sovereign refuge, our chief comfort, said and prayed that you might be delivered from anguish. Dear sweet Lord, what you prayed, you prayed as if it were from my mouth and the mouths of others like me, for you who are our head[23] took into your person our weak members, as the hen opens up its high-pitched voice to attract and assemble its chicks.[24] And since it is here that I find my voice in my Savior, why should I despair of my salvation? No, dear Lord, since I say after you what you said:

---

[20] ¶ 15 **an angel . . . others, came there . . . comforted you** *la vint un angle . . . vus conforta . . . autres*: cf. Luke 22:43.

[21] ¶ 16 **he who could . . . if he wished** *ki poiet . . . si il volsist*: cf. Matt. 26:53.

[22] ¶ 17 **rule** *ordre*: i.e., religious or monastic rule.

[23] ¶ 17 **you are our head** *vus ke estes nostre chief*: cf. 1 Cor. 11:3.

[24] ¶ 17 **hen . . . chicks** *geline . . . poucins*: cf. Matt. 23:37.

"*Not my will but yours be done.*[25] Let not my will go forth but yours." That is to say, not man's will but God's will; not the will of the flesh but the will of the spirit.

III. [18] This name of Jesus means savior. Learn how this name was given to him: The gospel tells us that when Saint Joseph, the spouse of Our Lady, first noticed that she was pregnant, because he knew well that no one else had touched her, he thought indeed that the Lord God had begun to perform some great miracle in her. Therefore he did not consider himself worthy to see it or to know it, and for that reason he left her secretly without speaking and without having sexual intercourse with her.[26] While he was in this state of mind, an angel of the Lord God appeared to him and said:

"Joseph, son of David, do not fear to take Mary as your wife, for what is within her is from God and by the work of the holy Spirit. She will bear a son whom you will call Jesus, and for that reason he will be named Jesus, for he will save his people from all their sins."[27] Fortunate is he among his people who can be saved from his sins; and unfortunate is he among his people who does not have a mortal sin.[28] And we find this name of Jesus in the book of Solomon called the *Song of Songs*,[29] for the spouse of the Lord God says to her husband (that is, holy Church to Jesus Christ) and here is what she says:

"*Your name is oil poured out.*[30] Your name is like oil that is poured out." Hear why the comparison is made between the oil and our spouse. In the oil there are three kinds of goodness, for by burning brightly it is good for light; it is good for flavoring meat; it is good as ointment for soothing pain. All three of these things we find in the name of Jesus: By the light of this name is the whole world illuminated and taken out of shadows and misbelief; by the light of this name each man who turns to God is taken out of sin into the light of knowing and amending himself. By the power of this name we may be comforted and restored in spirit to the service and the love of God. There is nothing in the whole world that can nourish our spirit like this name, Jesus: When we think sincerely about

---

[25] ¶ 17 *Not my will . . . be done Non mea voluntas . . . fiat*: Luke 22:42.

[26] ¶ 18 **first noticed . . . in her** *aparceut primes . . . en ele*: cf. Matt. 1:19.

[27] ¶ 18 **Joseph . . . all their sins** *Joseph . . . tuz lur pechez*: Matt. 1:20–21.

[28] ¶ 18 **Fortunate . . . mortal sin** *Boneuré . . . mortel peché*: the idea is that he is fortunate to have a sin from which he can be saved by the sacrifice of Jesus Christ, and would be unfortunate to be unable to profit from it. Cf. *C*: Fortunate is the one of his people [who] can be washed of his sins; unfortunate is the one of his people who does not have such a sin. The idea is similar to that of the "felix culpa"; i.e., Adam's fall was happy in that it elicited the miracle of salvation.

[29] ¶ 18 **Song of Songs** *Cantica Canticorum*: the remainder of this paragraph is based on Bernard of Clairvaux's *Sermones in cantica Canticorum*, 14.8 and 15.4–7: *PL* 183. 843, 846.

[30] ¶ 18 **Your name is oil poured out** *Oleum effusum nomen tuum*: Cant. 1:2.

the sweetness of this name, good things delight us, and the evils that we suffer for God become pleasing to us. Just as the oil flavors all meat, so strife has no savor if I do not hear the name of Jesus. Jesus is honey in the mouth, melody in the ear, and happiness without measure in the heart.[31] That is to say, it is as sweet as honey if you speak of Jesus yourself; if you hear another speak of him it is very sweet. And if you think of him often, there is still in the name of Jesus most effective medicine. And hear what kind: whoever is sad or disconsolate, or whoever may have fallen into sin, or who begins to despair that his sin is so great that God could not or would not pardon it, whoever lets himself run from sin to sin because he thinks that God has no concern for him, or whoever finds himself in an unfortunate situation: let him remember the saving name of the merciful Jesus, and from his heart it will leap to his mouth so that he calls him devoutly. Behold, a brightness will dawn suddenly in his heart so that he will at once begin to breathe in life, when before he was entirely turned toward death.

[19] Any man in the world in whose soul had lodged hardheartedness, rancor of heart, languor of sadness—once he has called earnestly on the helpful name of Jesus, (had there been lack of tears so that he could not weep for his sins)—as soon as he calls upon the name of Jesus, tears will flow more sweetly and more copiously than they had ever done before. Or if he had wandered from something that he ought to do, as soon as he names the name of Jesus, he will be certain of what he had doubted before. Or if he is completely exhausted from adversity or ready to give up, strength and help and comfort would come to him as soon as he called upon the name of Jesus. All these things that I have set down are maladies of your souls, and Jesus is the true medicine and the one thing in the world that is most useful in checking pride, soothing envy, restraining lust, moderating avarice, and repelling all evil, malice, and wickedness, in the name of Jesus. And I will tell you why.

[20] When I put before me the name of Jesus, I see before me a meek and loving man, compassionate and full of mercy, and so full of every holiness and all honesty as ever a man could be. I think that this very one is all-powerful, that he could save me and comfort me with his help; all these things are shown to me when I hear him named. Therefore I will hold fast to the example of the man on the one hand, and to the help of God on the other—the one, as if it were the drugs with which one makes a medicine; the other, as if it were the goad by which I must be driven. From these two things I must make a medicine so precious and so effective that no physician in the world could make one more precious. This medicine, which is sufficient to cure all the wounds and all the illnesses of my soul, I have stored in the vessel of the name of Jesus. I must carry this medicine forever in my hand or in my bosom, according to the example of

---

[31] ¶ 18 **Jesus is honey . . . mesure in the heart** *Jesus est mel . . . al quer . . . mesure*: cf. the hymn "Jesu dulcis memoria" attributed to Bernard of Clairvaux.

my Savior. In this name my soul has what may make amends for sin, if it is in a state of sin.

[21]   One customarily puts into a writ of safe passage[32] carried by sailors and pilgrims a name that is called the highest name of the Lord God, that should not be named except in peril of death. One does this to help simple people understand, but you should know that it is against God and against holy belief, for no name in the world is as high as the name of Jesus. You can know this from the word of Saint Paul, who said:

"Christ became obedient for us unto death, even unto death on the cross; because of that God exalted him and gave him a name which is above all names, so that at the name of Jesus every knee should bend, in heaven and on earth and under the earth."[33] That is to say, Jesus Christ was obedient unto death on the cross, and for this reason God raised him up and gave him a name which is above all names. It is the name of Jesus which must be adored by whatever there is in heaven, and on earth and in hell. He did not say this about *Agla*[34] nor about *Eloy*[35] nor about *Adonay*,[36] nor about any other name except only the name of Jesus. One must call on this name when in danger of death, and not only then, but in every need.

IV. [22]   After the five *Our Fathers* that you say in honor of the five wounds that our Lord suffered, say this:

"Jesus Christ, who allowed yourself to be bound, to be scourged, to be crucified, to be nailed hand and foot to the cross, to be pierced in the side with a lance so that blood came forth, and in the end you bowed your head and gave up your soul, for the mercy and the pity that you were willing to suffer so much for me, and not unwillingly but willingly, so that your great charity brought you to death because of me, thank you! Do not permit me, sorrowful N_____, through my misdeed and my sin, to lose your grace and your kindness. Do not permit me, through my folly, to lose the profit of this Passion and the fruit of those wounds. I know and fully understand, and indeed, I am in no doubt that I am most worthy and have well deserved not only to lose the benefit of the death and Passion you suffered for me. May it not only not be turned to my profit, but let it be turned to my harm and torment and to increasing my damnation and perdition. All this have I deserved today, when you gave me these favors and I have scorned them and not paid them heed. But I beseech you for mercy, dear

---

[32] ¶ 21 **writ of safe passage** *bref*: cf. *AND* "document," "official letter"; a safe-conduct is usually expressed as "bref de passage" or "bref de passer". The context suggests that the word is used metaphorically.

[33] ¶ 21 **Christ ... under the earth** *Christus ... infernum*: Phil. 2:8–10.

[34] ¶ 21 **Agla** *Agla*: a kabbalistic acronym for *Atah Gibor Le-olam Adonai*, meaning "You, O Lord, are mighty forever."

[35] ¶ 21 **Eloy** *eloy*: an Aramaic interjection meaning "O God."

[36] ¶ 21 **Adonay** *Adonay*: Hebrew for "Master," a way of referring to God in Judaism.

Lord, who were holy then and are still holy now, who were merciful then and are still so now, who were concerned for me then and still are, by the power of these five wounds, restrain and govern and bind in love and fear of you the five senses of my body. That is to say, my eyes, my ears, my nostrils, my mouth, my hands and feet; do not allow them to serve anyone but you. And put the sign of the holy cross in my heart so that it may always be armor and defense for me against the devil and against his snares and assaults, so that he may have no power over me, and I may consent to him in nothing."

[23] Think, think, brother N_____, and think often and think again, how you might make return to Jesus Christ for the torments he has suffered for you, for if you do not take the trouble to make return, you are then guilty of two things, of the sins that you have committed that are not forgiven, and of the death of Jesus Christ, that you made him waste for you, since it does not profit you. Just as he had had in mind when he suffered, he did a great thing for you and gave something great for you, and you have prepared everything and have therefore begun well what he asks of you. For he asks nothing else of you in all the world except that you not take from him what is his rightful possession; and that you, his serf, not hand over what is his to another lord (your soul is his serf; your body is his rightful possession). It is your soul since he put up his soul for it; he made your body his serf when he gave his own body over to death for it.

Now pay close attention to what he asks of your spirit and what he asks of your body. Both, therefore, must rightfully be his serfs. Love him with your whole heart and you will have given what he asks of your spirit. Give all your limbs to serve him, and you will have given what he asks of your body. His blessed eyes darken in death because your eyes ought to have turned away from every empty trifle. His tender ears were opened to taunts and bitter words because your deaf ears ought to be closed to the idleness and vanity of this world. His sweet mouth drank bitter gall and vinegar because your lying mouth ought to practice speaking the truth. His clean hands were stretched out on the cross because your dirty hands ought to be opened to doing good works. His innocent feet were pierced with nails because your wicked feet ought to become accustomed to walking the straight path. And what more shall I say? His whole body suffered the anguish of death because our rotten bodies ought to become part of the body of Christ.

[24] These are the things that our Lord lamented in you, for which he redeemed you, and which he requires of you. He placed your body so that you can deserve from him what you wish, either torment or joy. If you are a wicked servant, you will experience the effect of his anger endlessly with the evil spirits. If he finds that you are a loyal servant, you will rejoice with his angels and with his

children in the joy that will never end.[37] *Which may he deign to grant us, who lives and reigns God forever and ever. Amen*[38]

V. [25] When you see the crucifix in front of you, either in church or painted in your prayer book, and you see Jesus in the middle between the figure of Mary on one side and that of John on the other, then you should reflect that God has provided for you, as if these were three authorities through whom you might ascend from good to better, and in your heart approach your Father in heaven. The first step is Saint John the apostle, through whom you must gaze at the Lady that he has in his care, as Christ's chamberlain and personal servant, and ask Saint John assiduously for the sweetness he had in the company of the Lady when each was commended to the other,[39] so that he might be more prompt to your needs.

[26] When you are reasonably reassured by the confidence that you have in Saint John's merits, then go to the Lady and fall at her feet sincerely and with good will. Ask the Lady for the sweetness she felt within herself when she had the son of God in her womb; for the pity that she had when she first saw him tormented and crucified; for the joy that she had when she saw him risen from the dead; for the joy that she had when she saw him ascend to heaven; and for the joy that she has now from him and with him in his kingdom without end, that she may assist you before her son, who can refuse no request from her, so that he hears your prayers through the merits of his mother, since they are not worthy to be heard through your own merits. Prove to the holy Lady that the great honor she has came to her for you and by reason of your sins. For in order to heal your sins and those of others, the son of God took flesh and blood from her, and for that reason particularly did he exalt her and make her lady of everything that there is in heaven and on earth and in hell, in order to be prepared to help us and all other sinners.

[27] When you have thus debated with the Lady and you have shown her so earnestly that in your heart you feel she could not fail you in any request, then go forth confidently to the hanging Jesus, and seize him by the foot, if you can reach it, given the weight of your sins, which, if they drag you down, accept them most carefully as true; and lick, if you can, that blessed blood. And beg him, for the love of his sweet mother, that he reconcile you to his dear Father in heaven, with whom you have been so fiercely in disagreement, that by yourself, without other help, you could never be reconciled. Thus you can have great assurance about yourself and about all other sinners, when Jesus sees that two such noble

---

[37] ¶ 24 **If you are ... never end** *Si vus estes ... ja ne faudera*: cf. Matt. 25:14–30.

[38] ¶ 24 **Which may he deign to grant ... Amen** *Quod ipse prestare dignetur ... Amen*: the first part of the phrase occurs frequently at the conclusion of episcopal blessings; see V. Leroquais, *Les Pontificaux manuscrits des bibliothèques publiques de France*, vol. 1 (Paris: Protat, 1937), lvii; cf. *The Golden Legend*, 2:395. C ends here.

[39] ¶ 25 **when each ... other** *quant l'une ... l'autre*: cf. John 19:26–27.

messengers intercede for him, and two such good advocates plead before him, as is the Son before the Father and the mother before the Son. The Son bares his side and shows his wounds to his Father as he says to him:

"Dear Father, see here the wounds that I suffered at your command. Have mercy on these wretches for whom you made me suffer them."

The mother bares her chest and shows her breast to her son as she says to him:

"Dear Son, see here the breasts that nursed you.[40] I beg you as lord, and command you as son, that you never cease to pray for these wretches who rely on me."

Here there can be no refusal, so that our need might not be met. If our unfortunate life does not interfere, these three images, to those who reflect well on them, signify all these things for us.

[28] This name John means the grace of God, or the one who has the grace of God. Hear what the Lord God did. The first grace was that he summoned him when he was prepared to take a wife, and so he kept his chastity. The second grace was that he made him his apostle, in common with a number of the other disciples; and not only apostle to preach the gospel but also evangelist to write the gospel. The third grace was that when he had the Last Supper with his other disciples, John put his head on Christ's chest and rested there[41] and learned doctrines that he later taught us. The fourth grace was that when Jesus Christ was on the cross at the time of his death, he put his dear mother into his care.[42] The fifth grace was that in that place where he was in exile God comforted him by the most heavenly vision that he showed him.[43] The sixth grace was that when he was thrown into a vat of boiling oil, he was delivered without harm or pain. The seventh grace was that when he was to leave this world, Jesus Christ himself came and gave him his death without pain,[44] and each year on his feast day there still comes forth from his tomb a food called manna.[45] And since he had

---

[40] ¶ 27 **see here ... nursed you** *veez ci ... vus aleistates*: a frequent image: see J. M. Davis and F. R. P. Akehurst, *Our Lady's Lawsuits*, MRTS 393 (Tempe: ACMRS, 2011).

[41] ¶ 28 **when he had the Last Supper ... rested there** *la ou il fu en sa Ceine ... si se reposad*: John 13:23.

[42] ¶ 28 **Jesus Christ ... mother into his care** *Jesu Crist ... garder sa chere mere*: John 19:26–27.

[43] ¶ 28 **heavenly vision that he showed him** *halt avision ke li mustra*: i.e., the dream of the Apocalypse.

[44] ¶ 28 **The third grace ... pain** *La terce grace ... sanz dolur*: some of this material is found in the *Golden Legend*, 1:50–55, esp. 50.

[45] ¶ 28 **tomb ... manna** *sepulchre ... manna*: the details about John's death and the manna in his tomb are found in "Saint Jean l'Évangéliste" in *Légendier apostolique anglo-normand*, ed. Delbert W. Russell (Paris: Vrin; Montréal: Presses Universitaires de Montréal, 1989), 76, 77.

so much grace on earth, we may know surely that he is very helpful where he is with the Lord God.

[29] This name Mary[46] means Star of the Sea, because sailors, who are very accustomed to traveling by sea, have a star which is situated near the southwest part of the sky, according to which they guide their course. When they see it, they know if they are going too much to the right or the left, or too far ahead or back, or if they are going correctly or wrongly. When they lose this star, because of cloud or storm, then they do not know how they ought to go but are completely lost. This world is just like a great sea full of waves and storms; there is no more stability than at sea, because we are now healthy, now sick, now happy, now sorrowful, now angry, now at peace. On this sea so full of perils, God has provided a clear and bright star issuing forth from himself. It is our Lady, holy Mary, by whose example we ought to guide the entire course of our life, through whose remembrance we ought to avoid all perils, through whose help we ought to come finally to the gate of paradise.

[30] Whatever you may be, man or woman, in or out of religious life, if you feel in peril in this stormy sea, never turn the eyes of your heart from this star in your life. If clouds rise up against you, or great temptations of wind, or you are chased onto the rocks of tribulation, look at the star and call upon Mary. If you are tempted by pride so that you pay too much heed to yourself, look at the star and call upon Mary. If you are tormented with covetousness or envy, look at the star and call upon Mary. If avarice assaults the ship of your heart, look at the star and call upon Mary.[47] If you are sad or grieving, look at the star and call upon Mary. If you are fearful or lost, look at the star and call upon Mary. If you are sometimes too happy or too joyous, so that you cannot recover from foolish error that overcomes your heart, look at the star and call upon Mary. If you are often burdened by your flesh, either asleep or awake, look at the star and call upon Mary.

[31] If you feel inclined to sin, you should do this before you have sinned. But now you have sinned: now you are overcome by temptation, now you have failed in body or in heart or both, which you are accustomed to do at any hour, do not despair. I will tell you still more.

[32] If you should fall into great misdeeds and find your conscience completely filled with filth and dirt, so that you can scarcely tolerate yourself for your horror at the great sin you have committed, then first call with all your heart

---

[46] ¶ 29 **This name of Mary** *Cest non Marie*: this paragraph and the next are based on Bernard of Clairvaux's second Sermon on the Annunciation ("Missus est angelus Gabriel"): Bernard de Clairvaux, *Œuvres complètes: à la louange de la Vierge Marie*, ed. and trans. Marie-Imelda Huille and Joel Regnard, Sources chrétiennes 390 (Paris: Cerf, 1993), 168–70; also *PL* 183. 70.

[47] ¶ 30 **look at the star ... Mary** *esgarder*: the scribe omitted the rest of the phrase, and put "etc.," here and in the next three sentences.

upon the blessed name of sweet Mary together with the blessed title given her by the sailors. And hear what that is: we read that she once appeared to one of her servants when he was at the very point of death, and asked him if he knew her, and he answered, trembling and fearful:

"No, Lady, I do not know you."

Then she said to her brother:[48]

"I am Mary, the mother of mercy."

[33] Great is her name, therefore, but this title is very much sweeter still. You have great strength, glorious Lady, holy Mary, but nothing may be as good to the heart of a wretched sinner as your mercy, when the sinner needs to call upon it.

[34] Adored be your virginity, your humility, your chastity, your honor, and it is right that we should do so. But above all else is your mercy pleasing to us. This we remember most carefully, this we call upon most often; to this do we flee again most confidently just as the nursing child loves none of its mother's parts so much as her breast, for he is better situated there, and most often he finds his comfort there, if he is hungry or thirsty, or if he is angry or hurt: all his refuge is at her breast. Thus we do to you, dear Lady; your children go begging your bread that you give us in every time of need; we have recourse to the breast of your mercy. And why? Because that is where we most often find our comfort.

[35] There is no one, small or great, old or young, who, if he thinks about the great mercy of the sweet Lady, does not often find comfort in it. There is no one who fails to seek her with all his heart. We can put this to the test ourselves, how she rightfully has the name Mother of Mercy.

VI. [36] The two guardians[49] that God has appointed are love and fear. Fear makes us avoid sin; love makes us embrace virtue. Fear warns us to avoid hell; love makes us draw near to heaven. This good fear comes from three things; whoever remembers them well will never be without fear. The first is horror of death that comes at an uncertain hour. The second is the great anguish of the Last Judgment, where nothing but justice will proceed. The third thing is the fire of hell which never goes out.

[37] The other guardian is love, and it also comes from three things: the first that man should keep firmly in mind is how the Lord God created him to participate in his great joy, through both his power and his great knowledge; may his great kindness be praised without end. This is the Holy Trinity, Father, Son, and Holy Spirit. The second thing is the glorious Passion of our Lord, that he suffered to redeem his serfs from punishment. Whoever thinks completely about

---

[48] ¶ 32 **brother** *frere*: i.e., the servant who is dying.

[49] ¶ 36 **two guardians** *dous gardeins*: fear and love are the structuring contrasts of Pseudo-Anselm's "De custodia interioris hominis," ed. F. S. Schmitt and R. W. Southern, *Memorials of St. Anselm* (London: British Academy, 1969), 354–60. I thank Jocelyn Wogan-Browne for this reference.

this sweet thing will not love half-heartedly. The third thing is the goodness of our Lord, which he showed to a sinner who, after baptism, forgot all the great good things that we have listed above. This happens every day, but unless the foolish slave refuses, his Lord forgives him everything; and afterwards he loyally merits the reign of the One about whom these things are recorded, and he should strive hard to have such a good Lord and to love him loyally.

VII. [38] *Come, Creator Spirit, enter the minds of your people, fill with heavenly grace the hearts you have created.*[50] With this prayer to the Holy Spirit (and anyone who does not know it should say seven *Our Fathers* and with them the *Hail Marys*):

Have mercy on me, dear Lord God, Father of spiritual heaven. Through your holy precious Son, protect me from peril and draw me to the salvation by which we have been redeemed by him who is truly the Savior. Call me, Lord, in that conquest that you have accomplished by his voice and by the true holy cross. Jesus Christ, Lord, king of glory, keep in mind and memory this wretched, sinful soul, so that it may exist and live in you. True Savior full of sweetness, extend to me your sweet hands, which you were willing to stretch out on the cross for sinners on Good Friday. Lord, who took all our illness and our pain onto your holy body, and sought them all, and washed them with the holy blood that comes from your right side, wash me, Lord, in that water with which you washed the whole world. Holy Spirit, sweet counselor, sweet light, true sun, I give myself up to you; I count upon you. Sweet light, inspire me and draw me to God the Father through the Son of the Virgin Mary.[51]

---

[50] ¶ 38 **Come... creasti pectora** *Come... hearts you have created*: opening lines of a hymn attributed to Rabanus Maurus used at Vespers, Pentecost, the ordination of priests and the consecration of bishops, and so on. For a complete text and translation, see http://www.preces-latinae.org/thesaurus/Hymni/VeniCreator.html

[51] ¶ 38 **Have mercy... Mary** *Eyez merci... Marie*: the final prayer is cast in rhyming couplets, roughly octosyllabic.

6B. *Meditation on the Cross*, in verse (Dublin, Trinity College, MS 374)

You who look at the image of Jesus Christ, turn your attention to it; put the ear of your heart to it. Pray that God may help you. He is wise who heeds his help—whoever refuses it is foolish. The one who scorns the help of God is most hard of spirit. Know that God will bring him down on the day when he chooses the good, whom he will put on his side, and the wicked [he will put] into the fire that burns eternally.[1] These are the words of salvation that the good Jesus tells us. Whoever wishes to live and reign with him must write them in his heart. (vv. 1–16)

 You who look at my image: I am your God, you are my creature. You must know and understand this, for I am God and you are ash. You can learn a lot from this image. Put your heart to it, and you will do wisely. If your heart listens to me, you must remember that I made you in my image at the very beginning; I created everything for you. There you will see how well I loved you, because you had been delivered to death forever without any reprieve. I came down from heaven, from the bosom of my Father. I became man, which I was not before; perceive my divinity intact.[2] I received your humanity; I became man: it was for you. And I suffered hunger and cold and thirst, all manner of great hardships, as other little children do. I suffered much in my youth to save you: that was my intention. For you I suffered evils enough—reproaches, envy, ignominy—because of your fault and your sin. I was condemned to a very harsh death. Several times, completely naked, I was beaten for you. I shed my blood fully five times because of your sins and your misdeeds. Thorns, cross, nails, and lance I suffered for you without fear, and violent death at the end, in order to release you from the devil. Neither father nor mother would have done it for you, son nor daughter, sister or brother. No man would have done it for another living person, not even the mother for her child. (vv. 17–56)

 Think in your heart how well I loved you, since I redeemed you with my blood. See my hands, see my feet, how they were pierced with iron nails, great

---

[1] 10–12 **on the day ... burns eternally** *al jur ... tutdis art*: i.e., the Last Judgment.

[2] 32–33 **I became man ... perceive my divinity intact**: *Home devinc ... Sauve entendez ma deité*: Jesus was both fully human and fully divine; see "Incarnation," in *ODCC*, 3rd ed. (1997), 525–26.

and sharp; because of you they were struck through the middle. See the blood that gushed forth from them, and also from my side. (vv. 57–64)

Think in your heart how much I loved you, since I redeemed you by means of such a death. Now then, don't you see, dear sweet brother? In order to reconcile you to God my Father, I was hung on this cross, so much did I desire your salvation. (vv. 65–70)

Think in your heart how well I have loved you, since I redeemed you by means of such a death.[3] Then accept, dear sister, the one who dies for you, so that you may not die. So that you would not be disinherited,[4] my flesh was delivered to death. (vv. 71–76)

Think in your heart how well I loved you, since I redeemed you by means of such a death. Now then, don't you see, dear spouse, how painful was my death, which I suffered for your love? For you I became a created being. (vv. 77–82)

Think in your heart how well I loved you, since I redeemed you by means of such a death. Now then, don't you see, dear beloved, how I had great love for you, since I was willing to die like that for you and to suffer such punishment for you? Consider that I tell you, dear, that I was willing to die in such a manner. Sweet beloved, look at me, for I gaze upon you from the cross. So do not disdain to do what I teach you, for certainly anyone who wants to listen to me sincerely can learn. (vv. 83–96)

Indeed, anyone who loves and desires me willingly sees himself in me. Make of me your mirror. You will never find a better one if you know how to admire anything; it will profit you greatly. In me you will find what you need, what you should pursue and what you should abandon. I gave up my own will; I climbed onto the cross for you. My whole body was bound, nailed, and crucified; unto death I remained there, and there I died, there I perished, and may you in turn do likewise. That is my teaching. Love me as I have loved you and do yourself what I have done. Take your cross and follow me;[5] travel the path that I took. Leave behind your own will and you will have the cross in abundance. Bind your body by obedience, crucify it by patience, persevere to the end[6] and you shall reign forever with me. (vv. 95–122)

When Jesus Christ climbed on the cross, he set an example for all his followers that anyone who wishes to follow him and reign with him must rise by means of the cross. In the cross there are many sacraments. It signifies the four elements

---

[3] 71 **heart how well ... redeemed ... death** *quer cum bien ... mort ... rechatai*: the scribe has written "etc" after heart, here and at vv. 78, 83.

[4] 75 **disinherited** *deserité*: because of Adam's sin, humans lost the gifts and privileges to which they had been entitled; cf. above, *Castle of Love* v. 142.

[5] 115 **Take ... follow me** *Pren ... apres mei vien*: cf. Matt. 16:24, Mark 8:34, Luke 9:23.

[6] 121–22 **Persevere to the end ... reign ... me** *Desqu'a la fin parseverez ... mei reignerez*: cf. Matt. 10:22.

from which is made the body of man who was redeemed through the cross. For those who want to know them, the names of the elements are fire, earth, water, and air. Listen to another interpretation, if you wish to hear it. See the cross which is hewn, high and long and deep and wide: the height is hope, the length is perseverance, firm faith is the depth, and the width signifies love. (vv. 123–40)

God! so great is the sacrament of the cross to whoever considers it carefully. The top extends toward heaven, the other end descends to the earth, the two [arms] stretch across the width; in the middle the cross embraces kindly the head of the Savior, and through him includes everybody;[7] whatever they may have done before, he draws them to himself through the cross. I do not know what more to say about the cross except that it binds together heaven and earth. (vv. 141–52)

O glorious, blessed Cross, you were made for our salvation. Above all trees you have won beauty, glory, praise, and esteem. Wise is the one who trusts in you, who adheres to you and binds himself to you. (vv. 153–58)

O fair, sweet mirror, to whom God granted such great honor that you bore the Creator of heaven, and the true lord of earth. You bore the sweetest honey, Jesus Christ, king of heaven.

O beautiful Cross, O sweet friend! On you hung the author of life; on you hung the son of Mary, who governs and guides heaven and earth. On you hung the fairest lily, the beautiful flower of paradise; on you hung the beautiful rose where all sweetness rests. On you hung the great treasure, the fairest golden apple, the fair broom-pod, sweetly scented, sweet and good, for whose seeds both angels and men are grateful. (vv. 159–78)

O beautiful Cross, so sweet and holy from the dear blood that stained you.[8] The coloring was glorious and worthy; God himself was the dyer. You were soaked with the sweet blood and colored purple.[9] Most fair was the color of which God himself was the author. (vv. 179–86)

O Cross! O imperial rod,[10] you are the royal scepter by which the king, who judges everything, consecrated the entire holy Church. Through you it was purified and wed to Jesus Christ. You are my comfort, my joy, and my delight. It is my great solace to hide beneath your arms. Beneath your wings I want to hide; I wish always to cover myself with you. Beneath your shade is my repose; for nothing do I dare part from you, because of the devil and his protectors, and his most wicked snares. Foolish is he who withdraws from you, considering the serpent,

---

[7] **through him . . . includes everybody** *par li tut le mund comprent*: i.e., all humankind is included in, and can benefit from, Christ's suffering on the cross.

[8] 165–80 **O beautiful cross . . . stained you** *O bele croiz . . . fustes esteinte*: many of these images recall those in the sixth-century hymns by Venantius Fortunatus, "Vexilla regis" and "Pange lingua gloriosi proelium certaminis."

[9] 184 **purple** *purpre*: indicates a deep crimson color.

[10] 187 **rod** *verge*: the allusion is to Isa. 11:1.

full of deadly venom: may it not take hold of him. Its attack is most wicked, ugly, dirty, and poisonous. But beneath your wings I have no fear that serpent, lizard, scorpion, dragon, bear, lion, or any other beast may do me harm or molest me. These are the true names of Satan, who brings upon us evil and suffering. I do not know how many names he has, for he harms people however he wants. But may his snares be all undone, and may he be driven out ignominiously by the cross and by the sign that is worthy of all honor. (vv. 187–222)

O beautiful Cross, God does many a fine miracle through your sign. When I see the sign of the cross of Jesus Christ in whom I believe, I ask myself why he had to die upright. My answer to this is that he did nothing without a reason. And since it is appropriate for a combatant to defend himself standing upright, upright he must defend himself, give and take blows. Thus did our sweet Lord, who fought for our love. Upright he proved himself by battle[11] when he brought down the horrible standard.[12] Standing up on the cross he overcame our mortal enemy; he took many blows, but he gave one blow by which he hurled the devil to death. (vv. 223–42)

I will tell you another familiar argument, if it please you. Anyone required to plead for another must stand up to allege. He delivers both his message and his prayer in that way, and bishops and priests are accustomed to do it like that when they say their mass standing up and pray for the people. (vv. 243–52)

Jesus Christ, who was our advocate, did all that. Standing up, he pleaded for us, indeed he helped us greatly by standing. He was the sovereign priest who offered for us the living bread[13]—that was his precious body, which he gave up to death for us. He himself made the sacrifice that saved the entire holy Church. (vv. 253–62)

I will tell you another point, the sweetest I know. Whoever wishes to welcome her good friend must stand up before him, offer kisses and embrace him; thus should loving friends join together. The cross shows this to each one with a mind to it. Now listen to how I understand it, saving a more wholesome understanding. Jesus, our good Lord, shows us so much great love that he is standing before us in order to present a kind and courteous demeanor. He arose before us, and is very happy at our coming. He inclines his head to kiss us and stretches out his arms to embrace us. He presents his whole body to us; he gives himself to whoever wants him. Then there is nothing but joy, nothing but happiness, for God stands up before the sinner. In order to embrace, he extends his arms, and offers his mouth to kiss. Certainly, I don't know what to say here—he humbles himself so much before us! I don't know what to think, and I don't know what to say; nothing could be adequate. Even if our hearts were made of steel, joy could pierce them and soften them to the Lord who is merciful and all kindness. Let us

---

[11] 237 **proved himself by battle** *desreinne*: deraignment: (jur.) proof by battle.
[12] 238 **horrible standard** *orrible enseigne*: i.e., of Satan.
[13] 258 **living bread** *vif pain*: cf. John 6:51.

split our hearts open and receive God, spiritually embrace him, kiss his wounds devoutly so that he may appear to us and reach toward us. Let us weep over his blessed feet, beg mercy for our sins so that he may grant us true pardon by his holy Passion. Whoever wishes truly to adore the cross must meditate in this way. This way, as I understand it, is adequate for ordinary people. Anyone who understands better should do better, and may God give us his grace always. Amen. (vv. 263–308)

6c. *Meditation on the Wounds of Christ* (Lambeth Palace MS 522)

[1]   Whoever loves Jesus Christ loyally is always seeking the things that are most pleasing to him. For this reason, I advise you to take up and practice leading a good life, and the habit will become natural; for what a man or a woman first established and laid down in him- or herself early in life will be the rule of his or her whole life. Begin as you would like to end, for habit is whatever one nourishes, and either vices or virtues grow with the life of man. One can easily practice and shape all things as one wishes, while those things are still tender. New tree shoots, before they are well rooted, can be forced and bent however one wants. For this reason, whatever you think pleasing to God, this you should choose, and follow, and carry out. For the more honorably you are married, the greater your need to consider how to please your spouse. Because of that, you should, above all else, think often of the Passion of Jesus Christ.

[2]   Think how those great iron nails passed through his hands and his feet, and how hard it was to bear hanging by three nails that fastened his feet and hands[1] to the wood of the cross. Think of what anguish Our Lady had in her heart when she saw him hanging all alone and abandoned by his disciples, and that pure blood streaming down from him.

[3]   See yourself reflected often in the cross. Often, wherever you may be, imagine that you see him before you. If your heart troubles you, think of the cross and say one verse[2] before the crucifix; at one of the hands say another; at the wood of the cross, the third; at the nail, the fourth; at the blood, the fifth; the sixth at the anguish that he suffered for you; and do likewise at the other hand and at each of the feet. Say a verse at the side of Jesus Christ, another at the lance; two at the blood and the water that gushed forth; the fifth at the anguish that Our [Lady] felt in her heart. This wound in his side he does not feel, for he is already dying. I know no better meditation than this one. Here lies[3] the perfection of religion, here lies the soul's salvation.

[4]   Imagine that you are holding one of Jesus Christ's feet in your hands, and put one foot and then the other to your eyes and to your face, and kiss them

---

[1]   ¶ 1 **hands** *poinz*: a fist or closed hand.
[2]   ¶ 3 **verse** *vers*: i.e., of a psalm.
[3]   ¶ 3 **Here lies** *Ci git*: the formula is often used on tombstones.

with all your heart, most tenderly. Suck this most sweet glorious blood and stain your whole face and remain there in that intention.[4] Do likewise with the hands of your sweet friend. Then, with the greatest vigor of your soul, embrace that entire glorious body, that fair, sweetest and sweet-smelling flower, that holy virginal flesh conceived, born, and nourished of the holy Blessed Virgin. Embrace and kiss that sweet wound in his side from which your salvation, and all the world's, flowed forth, and thank your Savior. That friend is greatly to be loved, and whoever withholds from him his rightful possession, which is your soul, does great wickedness. And know that if you wrong him, he will avenge himself on you more than he would on a pagan or a Saracen; and that is a rightful judgment because to come to religious life without living religiously is to insult the Lord God, to deceive oneself, and to give joy to the devil.

[5] This day think only that you have lived in a religious order, a life you have spent in holy meditation, without trespassing against your rule. Examine your conscience earnestly, and ask mercy of God for all your sins, and ask that he grant you true pardon, for it is only fitting for the penitent to receive mercy. When you go to bed, think how your most sweet spouse, after suffering great torments, was enclosed in a coffin. Lie down next to him and embrace tightly the tenderness of that most sweet body which was so grievously wounded. Think of the sweet scent that came from it. Blessed are those who are refreshed by his sweet scent. Thus you dwell in Jesus Christ, and when you hear the bells, do not be tardy or negligent, but think how Jesus Christ rose quickly from death in the middle of the night or soon after. Bear him company. Rise together with him. Follow him into the choir. Imagine that the angels are there to receive your suffering and your prayers and your sighs, and to present them to your most loyal spouse, who will reward you very well. Similarly, after your matins, seek your sweet friend and spouse with Mary Magdalen.[5] When you have found him through sweet meditation and tender sighs, enter into his sweet arms; gently find rest. May Jesus Christ in his pity teach you to do his will and grant you eternal life. Amen.

---

[4] ¶ 4 **Imagine that you are holding ... this intention** *Pensez ke vus tenez ... cele volenté*: this passage is reminiscent of the action attributed to Mary in the *Plainte nostre Dame* ("Mary's Lament," in Hunt, "*Cher alme*," 181–97), who kissed the cross where her son's blood ran down it, staining her lips and face red. Cf. C. W. Marx, "The Middle English Verse 'Lamentation of Mary to Saint Bernard' and the 'Quis dabit'," in *Studies in the Vernon Manuscript*, ed. Derek Pearsall (Cambridge: D. S. Brewer, 1990), 137–57.

[5] ¶ 5 **with Mary Magdalen** *ove la Magdalene*: cf. Matt. 28:1, Mark 16:1, Luke 24:10, John 20:1.

6d. *Prayer by the Wounds of Christ*, in Verse (Lambeth Palace MS 522)

Sweet Lord Jesus Christ who, to save us, allowed your holy body to suffer on the cross; for that painful death, dear Lord, I ask that you deign to govern all the senses of my body, so that I have no wish to say—or think, or do—anything that might condemn me. (vv. 1–7)

    Jesus, who allowed your hands to be pierced, keep my heart from foolish desire, my hands from foolish touching, my eyes from foolish glances, my tongue from wicked speech, all my senses and members from evil affliction. (vv. 8–11)

    Jesus, who vanquished the devil and his temptation: Give me the strength to resist the treacherous tempter through the remembrance of your Passion, by often repeating your name, sweet Jesus. Amen. *Our Father. Hail Mary* (vv. 12–15)

6e. *Three prayers by the Crucifixion*, in prose (Lambeth Palace MS 522)

[1] Dear Lord Jesus Christ, who gave your blessed and holy body and your precious blood on the most holy true Cross in order to save the world, and established and stipulated that that same body and sweet blood should be sacrificed in the holy Mass to save us, in this faith I worship your sweet pity, Lord. And so I pray you here, (assisting at Mass), as intently and devotedly as I can, and I know that because of this holy sacrifice you pardon all my sins. And by its holy strength you defend me from all my enemies, spiritual and corporal, and from all their wrongs and from all their wicked ruses and from all their wicked prayers and their ill will, and from the peril of this mortal life, and from sudden death. And by the strength of the Mass, may you lead me to a good end. And so I pray you, sweet Lord, grant at the end that I may receive Holy Communion in proper faith and true recognition. And dear benign Lord Jesus, for the love and holy virtue of Holy Communion, defend my soul, when it leaves this body, from suffering, from torment, and from the cruel enemy from hell. And lead it by your holy angel to your sweet light and your sweet repose. For you alone, Lord, are the true Savior, blessed and glorious, and everywhere all-powerful in this world and in the next, with God the Father and the Holy Spirit for all ages. Amen. *Our Father.*

[2] Dear Lord, sweet fountain of true love and of all sweetness, I offer you this prayer, if you please, for all my friends and my benefactors and my relatives, and all those, N. _____ and N. _____.

[3] Lord Jesus Christ, I worship you there, where you climbed on the Cross; I ask that that Cross may deliver me from the angel who takes vengeance on the wicked. *Our Father. Hail Mary.*

I adore you there, where you were wounded on the Cross; I ask that your wounds may be a remedy to my soul. *Our Father. Hail Mary.*

I adore you dead and buried; I ask that your death may be my life. *Our Father.*

I adore you descending into hell and delivering the wretched; I ask that you never let me enter it. *Our Father. Hail Mary.*

I adore you rising from the dead and sitting at the right [hand] of your Father in heaven. I ask that I may go there, and that you may have mercy on me. *Our Father. Hail Mary.*

I adore you with all my heart and give you thanks and gratitude for your great good deeds, and I myself admit my guilt for my great sins by which I have angered you; I ask, noble Lord, that you be willing to work and to suffer for me, so that I may, through you and with you, be on the straight road to eternal salvation. *Our Father.*

I adore you there, where you will come in the end to judge all the world; I ask you that at that coming you do not judge me solely according to your justice, but that you pardon my sins before I come to judgment.[1] *Savior of the world.*[2] *Our Father.*

---

[1] ¶ 3 **I adore you . . . pardon my sins before I come to judgment** *Je vos aur . . . jugement me pardonez mes pecchez*: for another form of this prayer, see Eamon Duffy, *The Stripping of the Altars: Traditional Religion in England 1400–1580* (New Haven and London: Yale University Press, 1992), 239–40.

[2] ¶ 3 **Savior of the world** *Salvator mundi*: Antiphon from the Office (Hours) of the Holy Cross.

6f. Contemplation on the Passion
(Harley MS 2253)

Here begins the Contemplation of the Passion of Jesus Christ and it begins at Compline[1] because at that hour Judas Iscariot sold him.

When you say Compline, you must think most attentively about how Judas sold Our Lord for thirty pieces of silver[2] and thus at that hour,[3] admit your guilt to God—privately in your heart and orally to a priest if you have the opportunity—for whatever you have done amiss during the day against the commandments of God: for having taken delight in empty trifles, or if you have spoken dishonestly, or looked wantonly with your eyes; and for however you think that you may have sinned against your Creator's will during the day, by any of your five senses. And ask mercy and pardon devoutly and keep the certain hope that you will receive in goodness what you request so that you may be truly repentant and confess well, for, as Our Lord said in the Gospel: "Ask and you shall receive."[4]

Therefore, at this Compline say this: "Sweet Lord Jesus Christ, I give you thanks because, at the hour of Compline, you were betrayed by Judas Iscariot and sold for thirty pieces of silver, and after this Compline you said to three of your disciples, 'watch and pray that you may not fall into temptation.'[5] And then you withdrew somewhat from your disciples, as far as one might throw a stone,[6] and you fell to the ground. And three times you prayed to your Father that the passion that was approaching might pass you by, if possible.[7] And then an angel

---

[1] 254, l. 2 **Compline** *comply*: this is normally the last canonical hour, about 9 p.m. For the equivalence, see William W. Kibler, *An Introduction to Old French* (New York: MLA, 1984), 196.

[2] 254, l. 4 **pieces of silver** *deners*: the normal translation is "penny," but the context clearly alludes to the gospel of Matthew 26:15, "thirty pieces of silver."

[3] 254, l. 4 **that**: MS *tiel* ("such") occurs only three times, and is probably a scribal error for the more frequent "cel" or "icel"; "c" and "t" are easily confused, though clearly distinguished by this scribe.

[4] 256, l. 7 **Ask . . . receive** *Requerez . . . receverez*: Matt. 7:7.

[5] 256, l. 10 **watch . . . temptation** *veilles . . . temptatioun*: Matt. 26:41.

[6] 256, ll. 11–12 **as far . . . a stone** *a la mountance de tant . . . une piere*: Luke 22:41.

[7] 256, ll. 12–14 **your father . . . Passion . . . possible** *ton piere . . . passioun . . . si ce pust estre*: an allusion to Matt. 26:39, 42, and to Mark 14:35. The A-N eschews the metaphorical "chalice" of the gospels for the literal "passion."

appeared and comforted you, and while you were in prayer,[8] you sweated drops of blood in anguish.[9] Meanwhile, your disciples slept,[10] but you alone did not sleep until you died on the cross. Then you slept in the tomb until the day of your resurrection, at which time you awoke."

At Matins,[11] you must think attentively and say this: "I give you thanks, sweet Lord Jesus Christ, because at Matins you were, through the treason of your disciple, arrested for us. Afterwards you were bound, stripped, beaten, struck, scorned, falsely accused, sullied by the foul spittle of the Jews, scorned by their contemptuous words, abandoned by all your disciples, left all alone, denied as lord by your apostle,[12] and all that night vilely and cruelly treated and defiled. For this I give you thanks, most sweet Lord, with all my heart."

At the hour of Prime,[13] say: "I give you thanks, sweet Lord Jesus Christ, for at the hour of Prime you were bound like a thief and led to court before Pilate and given to him to be judged wrongly. And at that[14] hour Judas brought back the thirty coins that he had received for his treason, and then he hanged himself in sorrow and despair.[15] At that[16] hour, most sweet Lord, the Jews accused you to Pilate of three things: first, they claimed falsely that you had forbidden them to pay tribute to Caesar, to whom they were subject;[17] then they claimed falsely that you made yourself king to take Caesar's earthly realm from him.[18] Finally, they accused you of saying what was true — that you were the son of God.[19] At that hour you were sent and presented by Pilate to Herod and you did not say a

---

[8] 256, ll. 14–15 **an angel ... prayer** *un angle ... oreysoun*: Luke 22:43.

[9] 256 l. 15 **sweated drops of blood in anguish** *tu suas d'angoyse goutes de sang*: Luke 22:44.

[10] 256, ll. 15–16 **your disciples slept** *dormirent tes disciples*: Luke 22:45; Matt. 26:40, 43, 45; Mark 14:37, 40, 41.

[11] 256, l. 18 **Matins** *matines*: the first canonical hour, it varies from midnight to dawn.

[12] 256, l. 22 **toun apostle** *de toun apostre*: i.e., Peter; see Matt. 26:69–75; Mark 14:66–72; Luke 22:54–62; John 18:25–27.

[13] 256 l. 25 *Prime primes*: the "first hour" of the day, sunrise, about 6 a.m.

[14] 256 l. 27 **that** *tiel*: see above n. 3.

[15] 256, ll. 27–29 **Judas brought back ... despair** *reporta Judas arere ... deseperaunce*: Matt. 27:3–5.

[16] 256, l. 29 **that** *ytel*: probably scribal for "ycel"; see above n. 3.

[17] 256, ll. 30–31 **forbidden ... subject** *deffendu ... subiectioun eux estoient*: for the accusation of forbidding tribute to Caesar, see Luke 23:2; for the incident that was misconstrued by the accusers, see Matt. 22:21, Mark 12:16–17, and Luke 20:25.

[18] 256, ll. 32–33 **king ... earthly realm** *roy ... regne terrien*: John 19:12

[19] 256 l. 33 **you were the son of God** *tu fuz le fitz Dieu*: Matt. 26:63–64, Mark 14:61–2, and Luke 22:70.

Contemplation on the Passion   *171*

word to him;[20] on account of that they considered you mad and so you were sent back to Pilate."

At the hour of Terce,[21] say: "I give you thanks, sweet Lord Jesus Christ, because at the hour of Terce you so meekly allowed the wicked Jews to cry out against you so hideously 'Crucify him! crucify him!'[22] Then you were led outside while they negotiated your death and plotted the sentence that would destroy you. At that [hour],[23] the wife of Pilate[24] sent word to her lord that he should not have more to do with you, and this was at the instigation of the devil because he wished to disrupt our redemption, for which you deigned to suffer such a harsh passion. At that hour, Pilate washed his hands and wished to have no more to do with you, and in this way he thought to make himself innocent and absolved so that he would not be guilty of your death.[25] At that hour, you were bound naked to a pillar and so beaten with whips that there was no place on your body that was not grievously bloodied.[26] At that hour, they clothed you in a purple cloak and wove a crown of thorns and put it on your head.[27] Then, mocking you, they saluted you and said: 'I hail you, God, King of the Jews' and struck you on the head and spat in your face and, kneeling, they adored you.[28] They took off the purple cloak and put your own clothes on you and pushed you toward the hill of Calvary to hang you on the cross. At that hour, your sweet mother followed you together with other women weeping for you in anguish to whom you turned and asked not to weep for you.[29] These pains and many others you suffered for us between Terce and Midday."

At the hour of Midday,[30] say: "I give you thanks, sweet Lord Jesus Christ, that at the hour of Midday you stretched your blessed body on the cross and

---

[20] 258, ll. 1–2 **sent . . . Herod . . . word to him** *envoyé . . . Herodes . . . yleque*: cf. Luke 23:7–9.

[21] 258, l. 5 **Terce** *tierce*: the "third hour" of the day, about 9 a.m.

[22] 258, ll. 6–7 **Jews . . . crucify him** *Gyus . . . crucifiez le*: Luke 23:21; Mark 15:13–14; John 19:6, 15; Matt. 27:23 has "Let him be crucified."

[23] 258, l. 9 **hour**: after turning to the verso of f. 139, the scribe omitted "houre" but inadvertently repeated "a icele."

[24] 258, l. 9 **the wife of Pilate** *la femme Pilat*: Matt. 27:19.

[25] 258, ll. 12–13 **Pilate washed . . . death** *lava Pilat . . . mort*: Matt. 27:24.

[26] 258, ll. 14–15 **beaten with whips . . . bloodied** *batu de escourges . . . sanglant*: the scourging is alluded to briefly by Matt. 27:26, Mark 15:15, John 19:1. The detail about the extent of his wounds is found in Isa. 1:6 and also in Pseudo-Anselm, *Dialogus beatae Mariae et Anselmi de Passione Domini* (*PL* 159. 271–90), chap. 7, col. 279.

[27] 258, l. 16 **crown of thorns** *coroune d'espynes*: John 19:2; Matt. 27:18.

[28] 258, l. 16–18 **Then mocking . . . adored you** *e en moskaunt . . . te ahorerent*: cf. Mark 15:18–19.

[29] 258, l. 17–18 **not to weep for you** *en moskaunt . . . te ahorerent*: Luke 23:28.

[30] 258, l. 24 **Midday** *mydi*: "the "sixth hour" of the day, about noon, is also known as "sext."

allowed your hands and feet to be pierced so painfully with great nails and attached to the cross, in which there were four kinds of wood;[31] for the upright shaft was of cedar, and the cross-piece was of palm; the upper piece, on which was written in Hebrew, Greek, and Latin 'Jesus the Nazarene, king of the Jews',[32] was of olive, while the lower piece which bore and held up all the others was of cypress.[33] At that hour you asked our very merciful God, your Father, that he should pardon the wicked Jews for your death so cruel.[34] At that hour they divided your clothes, but the tunic remained whole, and so they cast lots to know to whom it should belong.[35] At that hour the passers-by on the road cried out and blasphemed; they insulted and scorned you. At that hour you promised paradise to the thief.[36] At that hour you gave your most holy Mother into the care of Saint John the Evangelist.[37] At that hour the sun became dark and shadowed, and until the ninth hour it lost its brightness."[38]

At the hour of None,[39] say: "I give you thanks, sweet Lord Jesus Christ, that at the hour of None you gave a great cry from the cross where you hung and said in Hebrew 'My God, my God, why have you foresaken me'.[40] You did not say this because you were abandoned by God your Father, for this is not to be believed, but because you saw so few of your believers, of all those for whose redemption and salvation you had suffered and still then suffered so many torments and pains, for in all the world no one could be found who believed firmly in you at that hour except your blessed Mother and a single thief who was hanging near you. For that reason, you, who are the fountain of life, complained that you were thirsty and the miserable Jews gave you vinegar mixed with gall, which you did

---

[31] 258, ll. 27 **four kinds of wood** *quatre manere de fuist*: on the composition of the cross, see *The Golden Legend* (trans. Ryan), chap. 68: "The Finding of the True Cross," 1:278–84.

[32] 258, l. 29 **Jesus . . . Jews** *Ihesu . . . iudeorum*: Luke 23:38; John 19:19–20.

[33] 258 ll. **olive . . . cypress** *olyue . . . cyprés*: on the wood of the cross, see "From Paradise to Golgotha: the Legend of the Wood of the Cross," in Barbara Baert, *A Heritage of Holy Wood: The Legends of the True Cross in Text and Image*, trans. Lee Priedy (Leiden and Boston: Brill, 2004), 288–349, at 302.

[34] 258, ll. 31–33 **pardon . . . cruel** *pardonast . . . cruele*: Luke 23:24.

[35] 258, ll. 32–34 **divided . . . belong** *departirent . . . escheyer*: John 19:23–24.

[36] 260, l. 2 **promised . . . paradise to the thief** *promis . . . al laroun Paradys*: Luke 23:43.

[37] 260, l. 3 **Mother . . . care . . . Evangelist** *mere . . . l'Ewangeliste a garder*: John 19:26.

[38] 260 ll. **sun became . . . brightness** *devynt le solail . . . clareté*: Matt. 27:45; Mark 15:33; Luke 23:44.

[39] 260, l. 6 **None** *nonne*: the "ninth hour" of the day, mid-afternoon, about 3 p.m.

[40] 260, l. 8 **My God . . . forsaken me** *Dieux . . . m'as-tu guerpy*: Matt. 27:46; Mark 15:34.

Contemplation on the Passion   *173*

not wish to drink.[41] At that hour you said 'All is finished'[42] for everything that was to be done before your precious death had been done and accomplished; and then you cried out in a loud voice: 'Into thy hands I commend my spirit.'[43] Thus you gave up your spirit. At that hour the rocks were split and there was a great earthquake and the tombs opened and the bodies of saints came forth, and the veil of the temple was rent.[44] Because of such marvels and many others that happened, the Centurion said (and the just men with him believed him): 'Truly this one was the son of God.'[45] Then the Jews came and broke the legs of the two thieves who were hanging near you on each side, and yours they did not break because they found you dead. At that hour, a knight named Longinus[46] came to pierce your side with a lance and then blood and water came forth to redeem us from the power of the devil and to wash our souls of the filth of sin."

At that hour of Vespers,[47] say: "I give you thanks, sweet Lord Jesus Christ, because you permitted Joseph of Arimathea and Nicodemus,[48] who did not consent to your death, to come at the hour of Vespers, to honor you by removing your most holy body from the cross. With Pilate's permission, they took your body down from the cross and laid it on the ground and anointed it with myrrh and wrapped it in a linen cloth and placed it in a tomb as your holy Mother, grieving for you, looked on."

---

[41] 260, l. 15 **Jews . . . vinegar . . . drink** *Giws . . . eysyl . . . beyvre*: Matt. 27:34.

[42] 260, l. 16 **All is finished** *Tout est acomply*: John 19:30.

[43] 260, ll. 27–28 **Into thy hands . . . my spirit** *In manus tuas . . . spiritum meum*: Luke 23:46.

[44] 260, ll. 19–20 **rocks were split . . . rent** *fendirent les peres . . . fendy parmy*: Matt. 27:51–53, Mark 15:38, Luke 23:51–52.

[45] 260, ll. 21–22 **the Centurion . . . this one was the son of God** *Centurio le fitz Dieu estoit cesti*: Matt. 27:54; Mark 15:39.

[46] 260, l. 25 **Longinus** *Longieus*: in chapter 47 of the *Golden Legend* (trans. Ryan, 1:184), Longinus is identified with the Centurion just mentioned who came to believe in Jesus. See also Rose Jeffries Peebles, "The Legend of Longinus in Ecclesiastical Tradition and in English Literature and its Connection with the Grail" (Ph.D. diss., Bryn Mawr College, 1910; Baltimore: Furst, 1911).

[47] 260, l. 28 **Vespers** *vespres*: nightfall, about 6 p.m.

[48] 260, l. 29 **Joseph . . . Nicodemus** *Josep . . . Nichodemus*: Joseph is mentioned by Matt. 27:57–60, Mark 15:43, and Luke 23:50–55; only John 19:38–39 mentions Nicodemus as well.

Appendix I:
Texts of Unpublished
Passion Meditations and Prayers

6a *Seven-Part Meditation on the Passion* (Dublin, Trinity College, MS 374, ff. 35^{r1}–43^{v1})[1]

Prologue (London, BL, Arundel 288, ff. 3^{v1}–4^{r2})

[1]   Ces oreysons et ces meditacions ke ci siwent sunt prises partye de Seynt Auselyn, [3^{v2}] partye des autres escritz,[2] pur esprendre les corages e les pensers [de celui] ky lit en le amour e en la pour de Dieu e pur se mesmes conoistre; eles ne sunt pas a lire en tumulte mes en quyete, ne mye en corant ne en trespas, mes petit [e petit] od grant demurance e od graunt entente de corage. Ne ne deyt pas mettre entente, cele que ces oreysons dit, k'ele chescone parlise tut outre, mes tant cum il sent ke valer ly puet od l'aye Dieu a esprendre en luy bone talent de orer utant cum il delyte. Ne pestoiest pas ky le comence chescone feys a[l] comencement, mes la u plus ly plairra, kar pur çoe sunt eles departies par letres enluminés, que l'en puisse comencer o finier la ou l'en vodra, e ke l'orison ne puisse torneer a ennui par trop graunt lungur e par sovent rehercier meismes luy, mes que celuy qil lit puisse coiller [4^{r1}] ceo pur quoi eles furent faytes; ceo est pité de corage e talent de Dieu amer, et de sey mesmes conoystre. *Jhesu mitis, Jhesu pie, noli me relinquere.*[3]

I. [2]   Jesu le bon, jo vus vei des oilz de bone creance ke vus m'avez ouvert. Jo vus vei la u vus alez aprés la Ceine od vos disciples al liu de vostre passion. Iloc de vostre [35^{r2}] bon gré estes trahi de vostre disciple meimes, e tut pur moi; de cruels mains pris e retenuz, e estreint de liens, batu des escurges, e feru de

---

[1] Corrections made on the basis of London, BL, Cotton Vitellius F. VII, ff. 147^{r1}–151^{v2}; hereafter *C*.

[2] ¶ 1 partye saint Auselyn . . . escritz: *C reads* partie de seint Augustin partie de seint Anselme partie de seint Bernard partie de seintes escritures.

[3] ¶ 1 Jhesu . . . relinquere: *C om.*

coleies e de palmes, e tut pur moi. Vostre vis est covert des ordes escopies, vestu par eschar de purpre e le ceptre real mis al poin, e fiché de clous, percé de launce, pendu entre les larons, e tut pur mei. Abeveré de fel mellee de eisil, al drein enclinas la teste e rendis l'alme, e tut pur mei. Jesu le bon, tutes ces hontes e tuz ces turmenz vus unt fait mes pecchez e mes mortels plaies ke sereient tut sanz esperance de garison si le precius balme de vostre duz sanc ne fust espandue pur moi, et sur mei. Mes ore est espandu, e sur mes plaies effundu, e la garison de m'alme est ensuie, vostre merci! Desormés sui jo trop maluré si jo par ma folie perde cele saunté ke le filz Deu m'ad si chier achaté.[4]

[3]   Sire Deu del ciel, esgardez vostre duz filz cum il soffri pur moi grant chose! Membre vus, cher Pere, ke c'est pur ki il le sofre e ki c'est ki le sofre—c'est vostre demeine fiz ke [35^{v1}] vus liverastes a mort pur nus, a ki ne poez faillir de nule requeste. Ki est ço pur ki il le soffri? Ço sui jo N._____, plein de pecchez e nepurquant fiant en vostre merci. Vraiment il est filz Deu k'issi vus fu obedient dekes a la mort. Verraiment est il home ki en humaine nature soffre horrible mort cume de la croiz. Sire Pere, gettez vos oilz sur vostre cher filz e veez cum son cors est estenduz en la croiz, e pardonez moi tuz mes pecchez que jo ai de tut mon cors fet. Esgardez les innocentes mains, que unkes ne peccherent, cum eles corent de sanc e pardonez mei les granz mals ke j'ai de mes mains overé. Esgardez cel innocent coste cum il est percé de la cruele point de launce, e lavez moi de la sainte fontaine que en curt. Esgardez icés innocens pez, q'unques mal n'alerent, cum il sunt cruelment des clous fichis; e pardonez mei les malveis pas ke sui alé de mes pez.

[4]   Dunt ne veez vus, cher Pere, cum vostre duz fiz encline son chief e s'alme rend? Sun nu piz enblanchist en la mort, son coste tut est ruge de sanc, les entrailles tutes [35^{v2}] estendues comencent tut a ensechir. Les bels oilz comencent a languir, sun cler vult comence a enpalir, ses braz eslignez devenent tut redz, ses quisses e ses jambes ke melz furent colurez ke marbre comencent a fletrir. Ses piez tresperçues de clous sunt tut arosé del bonuré sanc. Esgardez, Pere glorius, vostre duz engendrure, cum tuz ses menbres li sunt desciré, e aleggent la moi miserie pur ki il sofre tut ceo.

[5]   O duz enfant, le plus duz q'unkes fu nez, que forfeistes vos ke si vilment futes juggé? O amiable bacheler, le plus amiable q'unke fust, que forfeistes vus ke vus si egrementes futes turmentez? Quele ad esté vostre felonie? Quele est vostre cupe? Quele est la achaison de vostre mort? Jeo le sui e mes pecchez! Jo pecchai de ma pulente char: vus puroekes vostre char tormentastes. Jo pecchai par orguil: vus puroekes dekes a la mort vus humiliastes. Jo pecchai par coveitise: vus puroekes la croiz suffristes. Ore poez oir cum merveillos est l'ordre Damnedeu: li mal home [36^{r1}] le fiz Deu le compere. Li peccheur mesfet e li juste en sofre la peine.

---

[4] ¶ 3 Arundel, f. 4^{r2} *adds*: Ceste oreison fet a dire devant la crucifix del muster e sur crucifix peint en livre; *ends here*.

Li serf est cupable e li sires se[5] penist. E pur ço est grant mester ke nus gardum en nus la grace ke Deus nus ad fait, kar tant cum il ad plus soffert, tant serom le plus gref dampnez si nus mescheuns en les pecchesz pur lesqueus le filz Deu suffri amere mort.

[6] O vus maluré, wus doleros, wus forsené, N._____, pur quei est vostre quer si dur ke ne poez entendre cum grant furent ses pechez pur quei le filz Deu meismes estuet si cruele mort soffrir? Kar pensez cum gref furent ces plaies pur ki li estuet le fiz Deu si ameres plaies soffrir. Si ces plaies ne fuissent mortels, e uncore digne de mort pardurable, ja pur lur garison le fiz Deu n'estut cele mort soffrir. Issi puis jeo, par la grandure de ma mescine, entendre la grandure de mes plaies, e nepurquant de cel meismes puis jeo aver bon comencement de bone esperance, kar autresi cum jeo vei d'une part ma maladie si grande k'ele ne poet garir fors par la mort al fiz Deu, autresi puis jo [36^{r2}] ver d'autre part k'ele n'est mie si grande ke ele ne puisse ben garir od si haute medecine cum ele ad overé; kar autrement ne fust pas Jesu sage mire s'il despendist en vein si cheres especes e si precius letuarie, cum son cors e son sanc, s'il ne fut cert ke jeo en puisse garir. Mes ore sunt despendues ces especes en moi. Ore, puis jo garir, si jo voil. Trop sui maluré si jo n'oblie les bons de ma char e les delices de cest secle; e la grossure de mun quer doi jo tut lesser pur aver part en ceste ranceun.

II. [7] Sire Jesu Crist, ore me lessez desputer a vus un poi, e descoverir a vus ceo ke gist a mun quer. Beals duz sire, cele mort ke vus suffristes, vus la suffrites pur moi. Ceo ne poez vus desdire. Vus la suffrites pur moi salver, pur moi deliverer de mort pardurable—ceo ne poez vus desdire—e pur moi mener en vie pardurable. Dunc est vostre mort e vostre passion a moi doné e a mun salu trové.

[8] Veire puet Jesu Crist dire:
"Si vus l'amez, si vus l'ensample de lui sivez e aprés lui vostre vie demenez." Beal sire, e de ceo meismes m'estoet [36^{v1}] vostre aïe aver e vostre grace, kar jeo sui[6] desturbé par mes pechés ke jo ai fet, e par autres dunt jo sui sovent tempté. Mes veramant, vostre misericorde e vostre grace me traient amunt, mes mes pechez me traient aval. Ore i parra lequel veintera, vostre misericorde u mes pechez. Kar saunz dote, jeo ne crei pas ke mes pechez seient plus puissant e plus esforcibles de mei dampner ke vostre misericorde de moi salver. Honi seit ki ço creit! Einz est amu[n]t plus vostre misericorde ke tuz les pechesz del mund, e plus poez vus pardoner en un jur ke jeo ne pus pecher en tute ma vie. E plus volez vus pardoner ke jeo ne voil pecher, kar si jeo ben pens, l'oure e le liu quant jeo unkes fu plus encoragé de pecher, e vus fustes plus prest de moi pardoner e de moi salver.

[9] Veire puet Jesu Crist dire:
"Si jo tros en vus treis choses que jeo demaunt: corage de lesser e de cesser, corage de purement regeir, e corage de fere les amendes." Cher sire, [jeo] tes-

---

[5] ¶ 5 **se** MS: les; *C reads*: li sires est puni.
[6] ¶ 8 **sui**: MS coi; *C* sui.

moine⁷ de vus meismes ke en mun quer veez tutes ces treis choses, ambedeus en volenté e en [36ᵛ²] purpos, tut nel lei jeo si fermement ne si plenerement cum jeo duisse, e de ceo ke faut m'estoet merci crier, e vostre grace demander. Endreit de cesser, vus veiz ben ke jeo voldroi mielz estre mort ke jeo jamés feisse les mals que j'ai fet, e [s'il fuissent a faire, jeo ne les feisse pur tout le monde⁸], si il ceo m'est avis, ne ces ne autres, al curage que jeo ore ai. Endreit de regeir su[i] prest. Jeo ai dit a mun prestre tut le mal ke jeo unkes soi cunter ou retraire de moi meismes, e si jeo plus suisse recorder, plus en direie, en itel corage sui jeo ore, ceo veez vus ben. Endreit des amendes fere, jeo junerai quant jeo averai talent de manger e de beivere. Jo veillerai quant jeo averai talent de dormir. Jeo me taisirai quant jeo averai talent de parler. Jeo serrai en pes quant j'averai talent d'aler de liu en liu. Jeo soffrai disciplin[e]s e travail, e ennuizs, e sur tute ren ma volenté demeine refreindrai pur vostre reverence e pur ceus ke sunt en vostre liu. Si tutes ceste[s] choses ne me po[e]nt sofire pur aver pardun de mes pechez e pur estre sauf, jeo prendrai avant vostre mort, Jesu Crist, que moi est e pur moi sufferte, e parfrai del [37ʳ¹] vostre ceo ke jeo ne puis del mei meimes parfurnir.

[10]   Dunc poet Jesu Crist dire:

"Ore ne vus aseurez mie trop. Uncore n'estes pas eschapé mun jugement, uncore ne savez quel part vus turnerez." Bel sire, de vostre jugement ai jeo veraiment pour, e meins ke jeo ne deusse; ceo conuis jeo ben; meis greinnur est l'amur e la fiance ke j'ai en vostre passion ke n'est la pour de autre part. Kar jeo crei certeinement—lequel que jeo seie en leessce ou en dolur, u en pes u en tristur, ou en tribulacion ou quant jeo sui grevé, ou en bon estat ou en mal estat, ouquel aventure ke m'aveingne—si ceo parfitement eye en remenbrance e en amur vostre croiz e vostre passion, jeo ne purrai mie male voie tenir, ne en ceste vie ne en l'autre.

[11]   Jesu Crist uncore i ad plus, pur quei i[l] m'est avis que vus duissez aver merci de moi. Ke en cel hore bonuree e al point meimes quant vus deviez l'alme rendre en la croiz, vus priastes pur ceus ke vus crucifierent. Saunz dute vus en fustes oïe de cele priere; autrement ne put estre. E ceo conuis jeo ben a tel hore quant vus suffrites [37ʳ²] si haut sacrefise pur nus cum l'alme e le cors al fiz Deu. Kar tut fust lur peché grant, vostre misericorde fu de loinz greignure, e ausi grant cum ele dunc fu, est ele ore. E autresi vertuose est uncore vostre mort cum fu dunc, e mun pecché n'est mie si grant cum fu le lor pur ki vus dunc priastes. Purquei ne serreit autresi ben un pecheur repentant sauf e afiant en la merci Deu cume ceus ke vus crucifierent ki en vus ne crurent, si cum jeo faz.

[12]   Bel sire Jesu Crist, le duz, le gentil, le debonaire, veez mei ci devant vus, mei cheitif od tuz mes pechez, ki unques ne vus crucifiai de ma mein. Tut vus ei jeo asez curcé des males overaines, dites pur moi e pur mes pécchés a vostre cher Pere del ciel ço ke vus deistes pur ceus ke vus crucifierent: "*Pater ignosce illis quia nesciunt quid faciunt*. Bel Pere pardonez lur ço k'il funt, car il ne sevent ke il

---

⁷ ¶ 9 **jeo:** *C:* jeo sire tesmoigne.
⁸ ¶ 9 **et s'il ... monde:** *C;* MS *om.*

funt." Kar c'est la verité quant jeo fizs les pecchez: jeo ne quidai mie qu'il fussent si granz cum puis l'ai aparceu, nent plus que ces ki vus crucifierent seurent qu'il pecchassent tant cum il firent. Par la vertu del sanc que vus espandistes pur moi e par la vertu de [37ᵛ¹] la mort ke vus suffrites pur moi, ensemble od la fiance e l'esperance ke jeo ai en vostre misericorde, tutevois vus met jeo sus ke vus averez merci de mei.

[13] Jesu Crist, je vus vei tut sanglant pur mei, kar al comencement quant vus fuistes circumcis, dunc sanz dute cele partie de vostre cors fu sanglant. Jesu le bon, mult fuistes joefne quant vous primes soffrites peine pur moi; uncore n'euste vus fors huit jurs d'age. Aprés quant vus fuistes batu del escurge, dunc fu vostre dos sanglant. Quant vus futes coruné des espines, dunc fu vostre chief sanglant. Quant vus futes od clous fiché en la croiz, dunc furent vos mains e vos pez sanglantes. E aprés la mort quant vus fuistes fiché de la lance, dunc fu vostre coste sanglant, kar issi furent il cruel ki vus tormenterent que neis aprés vostre mort ne vus esparnierent mie. Les autres parties de vostre cors tutes furent sanglantes, de la suur del sanc que vus suastes quant vus si ententivement orastes enz ke vus fustes pris. Cher Sire, cel sanc dei jeo rendre. Si jeo nel pus rendre par mun sanc espandre pur vus, donez moi tendrur ke jeol vus pusse rendre par mes lermes espandre. Par la ten[37ᵛ²]drur de vostre sanc, traiez hors les lermes de mon quer e de mes oilz ke jeo puisse pur mes pechez doler e plorer.

[14] Des ore parlum un poi plus de cel oraisun ke vus orastes. Le ewangelie me dit que quant vus fustes sur le point d'estre pris, vus eustes grant tristur e grant ennui de corage, e grant pour de la Passion, issi ke de la grant anguisse e de tristur que vus eustes, si issirent de vostre cors ausi cum gutes de sanc gutant en tere. Dunc orastes vus longement e ententivement e deistes a vostre Pere: "*Pater si fieri potest transeat a me calix iste; verumtamen*[9] *non mea voluntas fiat sed tua.*" C'est a dire, bel Pere, s'il poet estre, tresturnez de moi le beverie de ceste Passion que jeo voil beivere. E nequedent c'il estoet ke jol le beive, la vostre volenté voist avant e nent la meie. Bel duz sire Jesu Crist, qu'est iceo que vus dites? Nus lisum de saint Andreu l'apostle quant vit la croiz apparailé a sun hoes qu'il fu si haité e si joius encontre lui ke pur poi ne fust hors de sei[10] meimes de joie. E de grant leesce qu'il out, criad en [38ʳ¹] haut e de loinz: "O precius croiz ke jeo ai tant desiré, e tut jurs vus ai tant amé, e ore plus tard ke ne vaudroie vus ai recoveré, recevez moi od si grant joie cum jeo receif vus, ke jeo puisse venir a lui que par vus me reinst." Jesu le merciable, pius e plein de misericorde, pur quei ne preistes vus a vus meismes si grant force e si grant hardement cum vus donastes a saint Andreu, kar il nel out fors de vostre don, de ki venent tuz bens? Vus lui fuistes Creatur, pur quei ne fustes si hardi cum vostre creatur[e]? Vus li fustes seignur, pur quei ne fustes si hardi cum vostre sergant? Vus li fustes mestre, pur quei ne fustes si estables cum vostre disciple?

---

[9] ¶ 14 **verumtamen**: MS verumptamen.
[10] ¶ 14 **sei**: MS scs; *C* soi.

[15] Uncore ai jeo greingnur merveille de ceo ke dit le ewangeille que la u vus fustes en vostre greignur anguisse, la vint un angele si vus conforta ki conforta autres; ki le messager Deu conforta le filz Deu; la creature conforta le Creatur; li angele conforta le Deu de tuz angeles. Bel sire angele, dunt vus entremeistes vus de lui conforter? Dunt ne seustes vus ben ke ceo fu li soverein confort, sanz ki confort ren [38^{r2}] ne poet valer? Dunt ne seustes vus ben ke ceo fu celui ki par miracle nasqui de la virgine, ke muat l'ewe en vin, ki sanat les leprus e les langurs, ki alat sur la mer, ki les morz resuscitat? C'est icelui ki fist ciel e tere, e tutes choses criat, e tut le mund tent e guverne, sanz ki ne put nule chose durer, enteimes, sire angele, vus meismes ki le confortates.

[16] Mes ore fet a saver pur quei le fiz Deu volt devenir si pourus encontre sa mort qu'il out mester deu confort d'un angele, ki poiet aver plus de duze mil angeles a sei defendere si il volsist. Il le fist pur nus mustrer cum il nus amat e pur quei il nus amat, pur quei il ne voleit mie suffrir sulement al cors, mes ensement a l'alme, anguisse autresi cum il dit: "Frere N._____, vus dussez estre men, kar jeo vus ai achaté tut de mei meismes. Tut vostre cors ai achaté de mun cors, e vostre alme ai achaté de la mei[e] alme. Jeo soffri mort pur vus fere vivere; jeo devinc feble pur vus fere fort; jeo devinc pourus pur vus fere hardi. Jeo devinc triste pur vus fere haité. Jeo soffri anguisse en mei meisme e desconfort pur [38^{v1}] vus fere halegre et conforté."

[17] Cher sire, desoremés ne desperai jeo mie. Jeo chaitif, N. _____, quant jeo sui asailli de temptacion, quant jeo sui feble de corage, ou quant jo sui esmeu de tribulacion ou de maladie, ou de duresce d'ordre ou de autre contrarieté que m'est dute ou de faute, quant vus ki estes nostre soverein refui, nostre soverein confort, deistes e priastes ke vus pussez estre deliverré d'anguosse. Bel duz sire, ceo ke vus priastes, vus le priastes cum si ceo fust de la mei[e] buche e de tels autres cum jeo sui, kar vus ke estes nostre chief, preistes en vus la persone de nos febles membres, autresi cum la geline fet la voiz delie e grele, pur attraire e asembler ses poucins. E quant issi est ke jeo trof en mon sauveur ma voiz, pur quei mei desperei jeo de mun salu? Nenal, bel Sire, mes que jeo die aprés vus ceo ke vus deistes: "*Non mea voluntas sed*[11] *tua fiat.* Nent la meie volunté veaust[12] avant, mes la tue." C'est a dire, nent la volunté d'ome,[13] mes la volenté Deu; nent la volenté de la char, mes la volenté del espirit.

III. [18] Cest non Jesu nus dit autant cum sauveur. Savez cument [38^{v2}] cest non li fu mis. Li ewangele nus dit que kaunt saint Joseph, l'espus nostre dame, aparceut primes qu'ele fu enceinte pur ceo qu'il sout ben que nul autre ne l'aveit adesé, pensa ben que Dampnedeu out comencé aukun grant miracle a overer en lui. Dunt il ne se tint pas digne a ceo veer ne savoir, e pur ceo l'avot privement lessé sanz parlance e sanz apruchance. Tant cum il fu en cel corage li aparust l'an-

---

[11] ¶ 17 sed: MS set.
[12] ¶ 17 veaust: *pres. subj. of* aler. MS neaust. *C illegible.*
[13] ¶ 17 d'ome: MS domei; *C:* d'omne.

Appendix I

gele Dampnedeu e li dist: "Joseph le fiz David, n'eiez nule dute de prendre Marie vostre femme, kar ceo qu'est dedenz lui si est de Dampnedeu e del overaine del Saint Espirit. Ele portera un fiz ke vus apelerez Jesu, e pur ceo avera a non Jesu, kar il salvera sun pople de tuz lur pechez." Boneuré put estre ki de sun pople put estre[14] sauf de ses pechez, e maluré est que de sun pople n'est par aukun mortel peché.[15] E cest non Jesu trovum en un livere Salomon k'est apele *Cantica Canticorum*, ke l'espuse Dampnedeu dit a sun espus (c'est sainte esglise a Jesu Crist) e quei dit ele: "*Oleum effusum nomen tuum.* Vostre non est cum oile k'est es[39r1] pandue." Oiez pur quei la comparison est fete entre le oile e nostre espus. En l'oile i a treis maneres de buntez, kar il est bon a lumere pur arder cler; il est bon as viandes pur els savurrer; il est bon a uinnement pur dolurs asuager. Tutes ces treis choses si trovum el non Jesu: Par la lumere de cest non est tut le mund aluminé e mis hors de tenebrurs e de mescreance. Par la lumere de cest non est chescun home ki a Deu se torne mis hors de peché en la clarté de soi meismes conustre e de sei meismes amender. Par la poesté de cest non eimes nus confortez e refet de corage al servise e a l'amur Deu. N'ad en tut le munde rens ke tant norist nostre esperit cum cest non, Jesu: Quant nus en pensum enterement par la duçur de cest non, nus delitent les bens e assavoreunt les mals ke nus soffrum pur Deu. Autresi cum l'oile assavore tutes viandes, si l'estrif[16] n'i ad ren de savor si jeo n'oi soner le non Jesu. Jesus est mel en la buche, en l'oreille melodie, al quer leesce sanz mesure. C'est a dire, duce chose est cum mel si vus meismes parlez de Jesu[17]; si vus en oez autre parler, il [39r2] est mult duz. E si vus pensez de lui sovent, uncore ad el nom Jesu mescine mult ateingnaunte. Si oez quel. Qui[c]unkes[18] est triste ou desconforté, ou ki[c]unkes seit chaet en crime, ou ki comence a desesperer de son peché qu'est si grant ke Deu nel puisse ou nel voile pardoner, ki[c]unkes lest cure[19] de peché en peché pur ceo k'il quide ke Deu n'eit cure de lui, ou ki[c]unkes est trové en tel maluré point: vienge lui en memorie le salvable non al merciable Jesu, e del quor li saudera en la buche si k'il l'apele devotement. Esté vus, lui n'estrat sudeinement une clarté al corage issi k'il comencera erraument a resperrer en vie, ke einz fu turné tut vers la mort.

[19] Ja nul home en tut le mund en ki alme pust unkes arester duresce de quor, ne rancor de corage, ne langur de tristesce, aprés ceo eust une fiez apellé de quer le succurable non Jesu. E si il i eust defaute de lermes k'il ne peust pur ses pechez plorer, si tost cum il apelast le non Jesu, ke ne li correint dunc les lermes

---

[14] ¶ 18 **estre**: MS *adds* pur estre; *cf. C*: poeple puit estre lavez de.
[15] ¶ 18 **Boneuré ... peché**: cf. *C* Benurez puit estre de son poeple puit estre [la]vez de ses pecchez. Et malu[ré] est qi de son poeple n'aist pas [une] tele pecché.
[16] ¶ 18 **estrif**: MS escrif; *cf. C* estriver.
[17] ¶ 18 **Jesu**: MS: il est plus diz ke nul mel *expunctuated after this word*.
[18] ¶ 18 **Quicunkes**: MS Qui unkes, *here and in the following instances*; *C* Qiqe unqes.
[19] ¶ 18 **cure** = coure, *to run*.

plus doucement[20] e plus plenerement k'il einz ne firent. Ou s'il fust esgarré de chose que il dust fere, si tost cum [39^v1] il nomast le non Jesu, dunc fust cert dunt avant duta. Ou s'il fust en adverseté tut alassé u tut pres de recreir, dunc li vendreit force, aïe e confort, si tost cum il apelast le non Jesu. Tutes ces choses ke j'ai aconté sunt les maladies de vos almes, e Jesu est la veraie mescine e la ren del mund ke plus vaut a refrener orguil e asuager envie, a restreindre lecherie, a temprer avarice, a tuz mals e tutes malices e vilanies enchacer, en le non Jesu. Si vus dirrai pur quei.

[20]   Quant jeo met devant moi le non Jesu, jeo voi devant mei un home deboneire e amiable e pius e plein de misericorde, e si plein de tute seinteté e tut honesté cum unkes home poet estre. Celui meismes pense jeo k'il est tut pussant, qu'il me put salver e conforter par sa aïe. Tutes cestes choses me purporte le non Jesu quant jeo l'oï nomer. Dunc me prendrai jeo al essample del home une part e al aïe de Deu d'autre part. L'un, autresi cum ceo fussent especez dunt jeo vol fere un letuarie; l'autre, ausi cum ceo fust le anguissement dunt jeo dei anguisser. [39^v2] De ces dous choses me doi jeo fere un letuarie si precius e si salvable que nul mire del munde puisse si precius fere. Ceo letuarie, ke si est suffisant a garri[r] tutes les plaies e tutes les maladies de m'alme, ai jo estu en cel vessel de non Jesu. Cest letuarie dei jo porter tut dis en ma main ou en mun sein. C'est a dire ke tutes mes overaines e tuz mes pensers deivent estre menés e guiez aprés le non Jesu. C'est aprés la essample de mun salveur. En cest non ad m'alme dunt ele puisse[21] amender de peché si ele est en peché.

[21]   L'em sout mettre en[22] bref ki ces mariners e ces pelrins porteient entur eus uns nons ke l'em apele le haut non Dampnedeu, que nul ne deit nomer fors en peril de mort. Ceo fet l'em entendre a ceste simple gent. Sachez de fin ke c'est encontre Deu e encuntre sainte creance,[23] kar nul non del mund n'est si haut cum le non Jesu. Ceo poez saver par la parole seint Pol ke dit: "*Christus factus est pro nobis obediens usque ad mortem, mortem autem crucis propter quod et deus* [40^r1] *exaltavit illum, et donavit illi nomen quod est super omne nomen ut in nomine Jesu*[24] *omne genu flectetur, celestium, terrestrium*[25] *et infernorum.*" C'est a dire, Jesu Crist fu obedient deskes a la mort en la croiz. E pur ceo l'ad Deus eshalcé, si li ad doné un non qu'est sur tuz non. C'est le non Jesu ke deit estre ahurez de quantke ad en ciel, e en terre, e enfer. Ço ne dist il mie de *Agla,* ne de *Eloy,* ne de *Adonay,* ne de nul autre non fors sul de Jesu. Cest non deit l'em apeler en peril de mort, ne mie sulement en ço, mes en tutes bosoignes.

---

[20] ¶ 19 **doucement**: MS deutant; *C* doucement.
[21] ¶ 20 *C adds* garder de pecchez dunt ele puisse.
[22] ¶ 21 **en** *C*; MS un.
[23] ¶ 21 Lambeth Palace, 182 [*L*], *begins here* (f. 185A).
[24] ¶ 21 **Jesu**: MS Jehum.
[25] ¶ 21 **terrestrium**: MS terrestium.

IV. [22]   Aprés les cinc *pater noster* ke vus dites en l'onor de[s] cinc plaies que nostre seignur soffri, dites ço: Jesu Crist, ke soffristes ke l'em vus lia, que l'em vus flagella, ke l'em vus crucifia, ke l'em vus ficha des clous par mi les mains e les pez, ke l'em vus ficha la lance el coste si que le sanc en issit, a la fin la teste enclinastes e l'alme rendistes, pur cele misericorde e pur cel pité que vos volez tant suffrir pur moi, e neent a enviz mes de vostre bon gré si cum vostre grant charité vus amena pur moi a la mort, vostre grant merci! [40r2] Ne soffrez pas que jo chaitif, jo dolerus N._____, par le men forfet e par le men peché, perde vostre grace e vostre benfet. Ne soffrez ke jeo, par ma folie, perde le pru de cele Passion e le frut de celes plaies. Jeo conuis e ben enteng, e cert sui e neent en dute ke jo sui ben digne, e ben l'ai deservi, neent sulement de perdre le ben fait de cele mort e de cele Passion ke vus soffrites pur moi. Ne me seit nent sulement turné a pru, mes enteimes qu'ele me soit turné a damage e a torment[26] e a cresement de dampnacion e de perdicion. Tut ço ai jo hui deservi, quant vus cestes graces m'avez fet, e jo l'ai si despit e mis a nonchaler. Mes merci vus cri, bel Sire, que dunc fustes pius e uncore estes, que dunc fustes merciables e uncore estes, que dunc aviez cure de moi e uncore avez, par la force de ses cinc plaies, restreignez e guvernez e liez en amur e en la pour de vus les cinc sens de mun cors. C'est a dire mes oilz, mes orailles, mes narines, ma buche, mes mains e mes piez; ne soffrez k'autre servent si vus non. Si me done signe de la seinte croiz en corage qu'ele me seit tut dis armeure [40v1] e defense encontre le diable, e encontre ses engins e encontre ses assauz, qu'il n'eit en mei nule poesté, ne jo en nule ren a lui consente.

[23]   Pensez, pensez, frere N._____, e sovent pensez e repensez, cum vus puissez rendre a Jesu Crist les peines k'il a pur vus soffertes, kar si vus n'i metez peine de li rendre dunc estes vus cupable de deus choses, des pechez que vus avez fet que ne sunt pas pardonez, e de la mort Jesu Crist ke vus li feistes perdere quant a vus, quant ele ne vus turne a prou. Si cum il avoit en pensé quant il la soffrit, grant chose fit pur vus e grant chose dona pur vus, mes tut avez prest e ben l'avez entamé ço qu'il vus demande puroek. Kar il ne vus demande hel en tut le munde fors que vus ne li toillez son dreit; e que vus son serf a autre seignur ne liverez son dreit (c'est vostre alme son serf; c'est vostre cors son dreit). C'est vostre alme quant il mist la sue alme pur lui; son serf fist il vostre cors quant il pur li a la mort livera son cors. Ore pernez garde ke cest qu'il demande de vostre esperit, e quei de vostre cors. Dunt ambedous deivent estre ses serfs par dreit. Amez lui de tut vostre quer, si li avez rendu ço qu'il vus demande [40v2] de vostre esperit. Dunez lui tut vus membres a lui servir, si li avez rendu ço qu'il vus demande de vostre cors. Ses boneurez oilz en oscurerent en la mort pur ço que les voz oilz se dussent tresturner de chescune vanité veer. Ses sewfs orailles furent overtes as escharnissantes e ameres paroles pur ço que le voz surdes orailles dussent estre closes al udiuesce e a la vanité de cest secle esculter. Sa duce buche fu enbeiveré

---

[26] ¶ 22 **torment**: *C*; MS aortement.

del amer fel e de eisil pur ço ke vostre buche mençoingere se dust auser de verité parler. Ses nectes mains furent estendues en la croiz pur ço ke voz ordes mains dussent estre overtes a fere bones overaines. Ses innocenz piez furent fichés des clous pur ço ke vusz maveis piez se dussent acustumer a dreite voie aler. E ke vus dirai jeo plus? Tut son cors suffri les anguisses de la mort pur ço ke tut nostre purri cors dust devenir son membre.

[24] Ces sunt les choses ke nostre seignur pleint en vus pur quei il vus achata e quei il demande de vostre.[27] Il ad mis vostre cors que vus poez deservir de lui, lequel que vus voldrés, ou turment ou joie. Si vus estes mauves[28] [41r1] sergant, od les malignes esperiz senterez sun corouz[29] sanz fin. S'il vus trove leal sergant, od ses angeles e od ses enfanz esjoierez en la joie ke ja ne faudera. *Quod ipse prestare dignetur qui vivit et regnat per omnia secula seculorum amen.*[30]

V. [25]   Quant vus veez le crucifix devant vus, ou a muster ou en vostre livere paint, e vus veez Jesu enmi liu e la Marie d'une part e le Johan de l'autre part, dunc deve[z v]us[31] purpenser ke Deu vus ad purveu autresi cum ces seient treis dignetez par quei vus puissez de ben en melz monter, e aprocer en vostre corage a vostre Pere del ciel. Li primer degré si est saint Johan l'apostle, par ki vus devez regarder a la Dame qu'il out en sa garde, cum son chambreleng e cum son demeine sergant,[32] e ententivement requerez saint Johan pur cele duçur k'il out de la compaignie la Dame quant l'une fu comandé a l'autre, k'il vus seit plus prest a voz bosoignez.

[26]   Quant vus estes aukes aseuré par la fiance ke vus avez as merites saint Johan, dunc alez deskes a la Dame e chaez lui as piez de quer e de bone volunté. Requerez la Da[41r2]me pur cele dulçor qu'ele senti en sei meisme quant ele out le fiz Deu en son ventre, e pur icele pité qu'ele out quant ele le vit primes turmenté e crucifié, e pur cele joie qu'ele out autrefiez quant ele le vit relevé de mort, e pur cele joie qu'ele out quant ele le vit monter al ciel, e pur cele joie qu'ele ad ore de lui e ovec lui est en son regne sanz fin, k'ele vus seit en aïe envers son fiz, que nule requeste ne li poet escondire; qu'il, par les merites de sa mere, oïe voz preeres, que par voz merites meismes ne sunt pas dignes estre oïes. Ben reprovez a la sainte Dame ke pur vus e pur achaison de voz pecchez li est avenu si grant honur cum ele ad. Kar pur les voz e les autri pechez garir, prist le fiz Deu de lui char e sanc, e pur ceo nomement l'ad enhaucé e fet dame de quantqu'il ad en ciel e en tere e e[n] enfern, pur estre preste a succure nus e tuz autres pecheurs.

---

[27] ¶ 24 **de vostre:** *confirmed by L, but the sense is* "of you."
[28] ¶ 24 **mauves:** MS: mau ves; *L*: mauveiz.
[29] ¶ 24 **corouz:** *C*; MS: cors.
[30] ¶ 24 *C ends here.*
[31] ¶ 25 **deve[z v]us:** MS: deveus; *also L.*
[32] ¶ 25 **son chambreleng . . . sergant:** i.e., John is the chamberlain and servant of Jesus Christ.

[27]   Quant vus avez si desputé a la Dame, e vus l'avez si estreit mené que vus est avis en vostre corage qu'ele ne vus pusse failler de nule requeste, dunc alez avant surement desques Jesu le pendu, si le seïssez par [41^{v1}] le pé si vus le poez ateindre pur la pesauntime de voz pechez, que s'il vus traient aval recevez les mult ententivement; e leschez, si vus poez, icel boneuré sanc. E pur l'amur de sa duce mere, li priez qu'il vus acorde a son cher Pere del ciel, de ki vus estes si durement desacordé, ke par vus meismes sanz autre aïe ne poez jammés estre acordé. Issi poez aver grant aseurté en vus e a tuz autres pecheurs, quant il veit ke dous si haut messagers apreer pur lui, e dous si bons avocaz aplaider pur lui, cum est le Fiz devant le Pere e devant le Fiz la mere. Le Fiz desnue son coste e mustre a son Pere ses plaies, ausi cum se il deïst: "Bel Pere, veez ci les plaies ke jo suffri par vostre comandement. Aiez merci de ces chaitifs pur qui vos les me feïstes soffrir." La mere desnue son piz e mustre a son Fiz ses mameles ausi cum se ele li deïst: "Bel Sire, veez ci les mameles que vus aleistates. Jeo vus pri cume seignur e vus command cum fiz, ke vus unkes ne cessez de prier pur ces chaitis ki unt sur mei lur fiance." Ici ne poet estre nul escundit, que nostre bosoigne ne seit tute fete. Si nostre maluré vie ne desturbe, tutes ses choses [41^{v2}] nus purportent ces treis ymagines qui ben en pense.

[28]   Cest non Johan vus dit autretant cum la grace Deu, ou ki la grace Deu est. Oiez que li fist Dampnedeu. La primere grace fu qu'il apelat a sei quant il fu aparilé a femme prendre, e si garda sa chasteté. La secunde grace fu k'il de commun nombre des autres disciples le fist son apostle, e ne mie sulement apostle pur la ewangelie precher, mes ensement ewangeliste pur ewangelie escrivere. La terce grace fu ke la ou il fu en sa Ceine od ses autres disciples sur son piz le fist mettre si se reposad e li aprist sa doctrine k'il pus nus enseignat. La quarte grace fu que quant Jesu Crist fu en la croiz sur la mort en son liu le mist pur garder sa chere mere. La quinte grace fu que la ou il fu en exil la le conforta par mult haut avision ki li mustra. La sime grace fu que quant il fu getté en un vessel pleine de oile buillant sans dolur e grevance e anguisse li deliverat. La settime grace fu ke quant dust de cest secle partir, Jesu Crist meismes vint pur li e sa mort li dona sanz dolur, e de son sepulcre [42^{r1}] ist uncore chescun an le jor de la feste une viande qu'est apelé manna. E quant il out taunt de grace en tere, ben pout um saver que mult est succurrable la ou il est od Damnedeu.

[29]   Cest non Marie vus dit autretant cum esteile de mer, kar les marine[r]s ke mult sunt acustumé d'aler par mer, il unt une esteile que set pres al suthwest del ciel aprés laquele il guient tut lur curs. Quant il la veent, si sevent il s'il vont trop a destre ou a senestre ou trop avant ou arere, ou s'il vont ben ou malement. Quant il ceste esteile perdent ou par niule ou par tempeste, dunc ne sevent coment il deivent aler, enz sunt tuz esgarriz. Tut cest mund est autresi cum ceo fust une grant mer pleines des undees e des tempestes, n'i ad ren d'estableté nent plus k'en la mer, kar ore eimes nus sains, ore malades, ore haité, ore dolent, ore curcé, ore apaee. Sur ceste mer qu'est si plaine de perilz nus ad Deu purveu une esteile bele e clere de lui meismes issante. C'est nostre dame seinte Marie par ki

essample [42r2] nus devum guier tut le curs de nostre vie, par ki remembrance nus devum eschure tuz perilz, par ki aïe nus devum cesser al porte de paraïs.

[30] Quelkeunkes seez, home ou femme, ou en religion ou hors de religion, ke vus vus sentez en ceste tempestiuose mer e en perilz, ne tresturnez unkes les oilz de vostre corage de cest' esteile en vostre vie. Si nues levent encontre vus, ou grant temptacions de vent, ou vus estes chacé sur roches de tribulacion, esgardez l'esteille e apelez Marie. Si vus estes tempté de orguil ke vus tenez trop grant plait de vus meismes, esgardez l'esteille, e apelez Marie. Si vus estes travaillé de coveitise ou d'envie, esgardez l'esteille e apelez Marie. Si vus estes travaillé de detraccion, regardez l'esteile si apelez Marie. Si avarice assaut la nef de vostre corage, regardez [l'esteile si apelez Marie].[33] Si vus estes tristes ou dolenz, regardez [l'esteile si apelez Marie]. Si vus estes pourus ou esgarrez regardez [l'esteile si apelez Marie]. Si vus estes a la fiez trop haité ou trop joius, si ke vus ne vus pussez a par meismes reprendre de fol errur ke vus surmonte le corage, esgardez l'esteile e apelez Marie. [42v1] Si vus estes suvent grevé de vostre char ou en dormant ou en veillant, esgarder [l'esteile si apelez Marie].[34]

[31] Issi devez vus fere si talent vus prent de pecher, ainz ke vus aiez peché. Mes ore avez peché: ore estes vencu de la temptacion, ore estes chaet de cors ou de corage ou de ambdous, quei devez dunc fere nul hore, ne seez tristes de deseperance plus vus dirai uncore.

[32] Si vus chaeez en grant crimes e vus trovissez vostre conscience tute pleine d'ordure e de soillure, si ke ne puissez a peine soffrir vus meismes pur la grant hidur que vus avez pur le grant peché qu'avez fet, dunc a primes apelez de tut vostre quer le beneit non de la duce Marie ensemblement od le benuré surnon ke le[s] merine[r]s i mist. Si oez quei il est. Nus lisum qu'ele aparust une fiez a un son sergant, la ou il fu al drein point de la mort e li demanda s'il la conuist, e il respondi tut en tremblant e pourus: "Nai, Dame, jo ne vus conus pas." Dunc dist ele a son frere: "Ço sui jeo Marie, mere de misericorde."

[33] Mult est dunc son non, mes mult plus est duz uncore icest surnon. Mult i ad vertu en vus, gloriuse dame seinte Marie, mes nule ne seit [42v2] si ben al quer del chaitif pecheur cum vostre misericorde, quant il la deit nomer.

[34] Auré vostre virginité, vostre humilité, vostre chasteté, vostre digneté e ben le devum fere que raison est que nus lc façum. Mes sur tuz nus asavore vostre misercorde. Cest recordum nus plus tendrement, cest apelum nus plus sovent, a ceste refuium nus plus surement, ausi cum l'enfaunt leitaunt de tuz les membres sa mere n'aime il nul tant cum il fet la mamele, kar plus i est aus e plus sovent i trove son confort s'il ad faim ou s'il ad sei, s'il est corucé ou blescé, a la mamele est tut son refui. Issi le fesum nus chere Dame a vus; voz[35] enfanz vont mendianz vos

---

[33] ¶ 30 **l'esteile si apelez Marie:** *here and in following instances,* MS et cetera.
[34] ¶ 30 **l'esteile si apelez Marie:** MS *om.*
[35] ¶ 34 **vos:** MS noz.

painz que ranz en tut noz bosoignes, recurum a la mamele de vostre misericorde. E pur quei? Car la trovum nus plus sovent nostre confort.

[35]   I[l] n'i ad un sul, ne petit ne grant ne veil ne jofne, s'il ben se purpense qu'il en la grant misericorde de la duce dame n'eit sovent trové son confort. Nul n'est ke faille que de tut sun quer la voille requere. Issi povum nus en nus meismes esprover: cum a bon dreit ad a non Mere de Misericorde.

VI. [36]   Ses sunt les dous gardeins que [43^{r1}] Deus ad mis, c'est amur e pour. Pour fet eschure peché, amur fet embracer vertu. Pour amoneste de enfern esloingner. Amur fet al ciel aprocer. Ceste bone pour vient de treis choses. Ki ben en memorie les ad, ja sanz pour ne serat. La primere est hidur de mort que vient a hure nent certaine. La secunde est la grant destresce del grant jugement, ou ren nule si dreit non ne irra avant. La terce chose est le feu d'enfern que jamais n'esteindera.

[37]   L'autre gardein est amur, si vient ausi de treis choses. C'est la primere ke home eit en ferme memorie coment Dampnedeu le cria pur estre parcener de sa grant joie, e par sa pussance e son grant saver e sa grant debonerté sanz fin loer. C'est la sainte Trinité, Pere e Fiz e Sainte Esperit. La secunde chose est la gloriose Passion nostre seignur qu'il soffri pur ces serfs de peine achater. Ki ceste duce chose parfitement volt penser ne porra feintement amer. La terce chose est la bonté nostre seignur k'il ad mustré aprés bapteisme a pecheur ki tut ad oblié les dous granz bens qu'avant avom nomé. Icest avent [43^{r2}] chescun jur, mes ke le fol serf ait refusé son seignur tut li pardone; si aprés lealment desert le regne de Celui dunt ces choses furent recordez, e mult se deit pener de si bon seignur aver e lealment amer.

VII. [38]   *Veni creator spiritus mentes tuorum visita imple superna gratia que tu creasti pectora.* Od le orasion del Saint Esperit, (e ki ço ne seet, die set *Pater Noster* od les *Ave Maria*):

> Eyez merci de mei, bel sire Deus,
> Pere del ciel esperitels,
> Par vostre saint precius Fiz,
> Defendez moi de perilz
> E traiez a la salveté
> Par quei nus sumus rechaté
> Par lui ke veirs salveres est.
> M'apellez, Sire, en cel conquest
> Ke vus faites par sa voiz
> E par la sainte verai croiz.
> Jesu Crist, sire rei de glorie,
> Aiez en sen e en memorie
> Ceste alme pecherif chaitive,
> K'en vus seit e en vus vive.
> Verrei Salvere de duçur plains,

Tendez a moi voz duces mains,
Ke vus plot en la croiz estendre
Pur pecheurs le grant divendre.[36]
Sire, ke tutes noz langurs
E noz pechez e noz dolurs
Preïstes sur vostre saint cors,
E tutes le[s] perchastes hors,
E lavastes de vostre sanc
Ke vient de vostre destre flanc,
Lavez mei, Sire, de [43ᵛ¹] icel' unde
Dunt vus lavastes tut le munde.
Saint Espirit, duz Conseil,
Duz lumere, verrai solail,
A vus me rend, a vus me ottrei.
Duce lumere, enluminez mei,
E mei trahiez a Deu le Pere
Par le Fiz de la Virgine Marie.

---

[36] ¶ 38 **divendre:** MS *sic for* vendredi.

Appendix I 189

6b *Meditation on the Cross*, in verse (Dublin, Trin. Coll. 374, ff. 67ʳ¹–69ᵛ¹)[37]

[67ʳ¹] Tu ki esgardes la figure
De Jesu Crist, met i ta cure;
De tun quer i met le oraille.
Priet ke Deu te conseille.   4
Sages est que son conseil out;
— Ki le refuse fet ke sot.
Trop est de dur esperit
Ki le conseil Deu despit.   8
Sachez ke Deu le despirat
Al jur quant il eslirrat
Les bons qu'il mettrat en sa part,
Les maus al feu que tutdis art.   12
Ces sunt les paroles de salu
Ke nus dit le bon Jesu.
En son quer les deit escrivere
Ki vot od lui regner e vivere.   16
Tu ki esgardes ma figure,
Jeo sui ti deus, tu ma faiture.
Ceo deis tu saver e entendre,
[67ʳ²] Ke jeo sui Deus e tu es cendre.   20
Mult poez aprendre en cest ymage.
Met i tun quer, si fras ke sage.
Trestut al comencement,
Si tun quer a mei entent,   24
Venir te deit en remembrance
Ke jeo te fis a ma semblance;
Tute ren pur tei criai.
La porras veer cum ben t'amai,   28
Pur ceo que esteies liveré a mort
A tutdis sanz nul resort.
Del ciel descendi del sein mun Pere.
Home devinc, ceo ke einz ne ere;   32
Sauve entendez ma deïté.
Receu jo ta humanité;
Home devinc: ceo fu pur tei.
E suffri faim e freit e seif,   36
De tutes maneres meseises grant,
Cum funt li autres petiz enfanz.

---

[37] *Corrections made on the basis of* Cambridge, Emmanuel Coll. 106, ff. 36ʳ-37ʳ [*E*].

Mult suffri en ma jovente
Pur tei salver: ço fu ma entente.   40
Pur tei suffri [jeo] maus assez
—Reproces, enviz e viltéz.
Pur ta cupe e tun peché
A mult vil mort fu jugé.   44
Plusurs feiz, trestut nu,
Cruelement pur tei batu.
Mun sanc espandi ben cink feiz
Pur tes pechez e tes mesfaiz.   48
Espines, crois, clous e lance.
[67^{v1}] Pur tei suffri sanz dotance,
E dure mort al paraler,
Pur tei del diable deliverer.   52
Nel feist pur tei pere ne mere,
Fiz ne fille, soer ne frere.
Nel feist home pur autre vivant,
Neis la mere pur sun enfant.   56
Pens en tun quer cum ben t'amai,
Ke de mun sanc te rechatai.
Veez mes poinz, veez mes pez,
Cum il furent trespercez   60
Des clous de^{38} fer gros e aguz;
Pur te[i] furent par mi feruz.
Veez le sanc ke en issi,
E de mun coste autresi.   64
Pens en ton quor cum ben t'amai.
Ke par tele mort te rechatai.
Dunt ne voies tu, bel duz frere?
Pur tei acorder a Deu mun Pere,   68
Fui en ceste croiz pendu,
Tant desirai le ton salu.
Pens en ton quer [cum ben t'amai,
Ke par tele mort te rechatai.^{39}]   72
Dunt pernez, bele soer,
Ke tu ne morges, ke pur tei moer.
Ke tu ne fuses deserité
Fu ma char a mort liveré.   76
Pens en tun quer [cum ben t'amai,
Ke par tele mort te rechatai.]

---

[38] 62 MS n *expunctuated*.
[39] 71, 77, 83: MS Pens en ton quer et cetera.

Dunt ne veis tu, chere espuse,
Cume ma mort fu doleruse   80
Ke jeo suffri pur tu[n] amur?
[67D] Pur tei devinc jeo creatur.
Pens en ton quer [cum ben t'amai,
Ke par tele mort te rechatai.]   84
Dunt ne veis tu, duce amie,
Cum oi vers tei grant drurie,
Ke issi volai pur tei morir
E teles peines pur tei suffrir?   88
Veez coment jeo te di, chere,
Que voleie morir en tele manere.
Duce ami[e], esgardez moi,
Kar de la croiz esgard jeo tei.   92
Si⁴⁰ nel tenez pas en desdeing
De fere ceo ke jeo te enseing,
Car ci poet chescun aprendre
Ke a mei de quer ore volt entendre.   96
Kar cil ke me aime e desire
Volenters en moi se esmire.
De moi fai ton mirur.
James ne troveras nul meillur   100
Si tu ses ren esmirer;
Mult vus porra profiter.
En mei troveras dunt as mester,
Quei deveras siwer e quei lesser.   104
Ma propre volenté lessai;
En la croiz pur tei montai.
Tut mun cors [i] fu lié,
Cloufiché e crucifié;   108
Desques a la mort i demorai,
Illoec morui, illoec finai,
E tu refaces ensement.
C'est le men enseignement.   112
[68ʳ¹] Amez moi cum jeo t'amai,
E ço ke jeo fis ceo meismes fai.
Pren ta croiz, aprés mei vien;
Le chimin ke jeo tinc, si ten.   116
Lessez ta propre volenté
Si averas croiz a grant plenté.

---

⁴⁰ 93 **Si**: MS Sil.

Liez tun cors par obedience
Crucifiez par pacience, 120
Desqu'a la fin parseverez
E sanz fin od mei regnerez.
Quant Jesu Crist a la crois munta,
Essample a tuz sens dona 124
Que par la croiz estoet munter
Ki li volt siwere e od lui regner.
En la croiz ad multz sacremenz.
Ele signefie quatre elemenz 128
Dunt le cors de l'ome est fet,
Ki par la croiz reint esteit.
Les nuns des elemenz ke veut saver:
Ceo sunt feu, terre, ewe e eyr. 132
Oiez autre entendement
Si del oier avez talent.
Veez la croiz qu'est quarré,
Haut e longe, parfund e lee: 136
La hautur est esperance,
La lungure perseverance,
Ferme fei est la parfundur,
La leesce signifie amur. 140
Deu! tant est grant le sacrement
De la croiz, ki garde en prent.
[68^{r2}] Le chief vers le ciel se estent,
L'autre vers la tere descend, 144
Les deus estendent en laur;
Enmi la teste del salveur
La croiz embrace ducement,
E par li tut le mund comprent; 148
Quanque qu'il aveit avant fet,
Par la croiz a sei attret.
Ne sai ke plus de la croiz die,
Fors ciel e tere ensemble lie. 152
O gloriose Croiz beneite,
Pur nostre salu futes fete.
Sur tuz arbres avez conquis
Beuté, glorie, loenge e pris. 156
Sages est qu'en vus s'afie,
K'a vus se prent e a vus se lie.
O bele duce esmirur,
A ki Deu fist si grant honur 160
Ke vus portastes le Creatur

Appendix I

De ciel, e terre dreit seigneur.
Vus portastes le tresduz miel,
Jesu Crist, le rei del ciel.   164
O bele Croiz, o duce amie!
En vus pendi le actur de vie;
En vus pendi le fiz Marie
Ke ciel e tere governe e guie.   168
En vus pendi le tres beus lis,
La bele flour de paraïs;
En vus pendi la bele rose
Ou tute duçur se repose.   172
[68^{v1}] En vus pendi le grant tresor,
La tresbele pome d'or,
La bele pome de genette,
Seuf olante, duce e nette,   176
Des greins de cele bele pome
L'unt recreiz e angele e home.
O bele Cruiz, tant duce e sainte
Del duz sanc ke fustes esteinte.   180
La teinture fu gloruse e chere;
Deu meismes en fu tenturere.
Del duz sanc fuistes arosee
E tut en purpre[41] culuree.   184
Mult fu bele la colur
Dunt Deu maismes en fu auctur.
O Croiz! O verge emperial,
Vus estes le ceptre real   188
Par ki le rei, ke tut justise,
Dedia tute sainte eglise.
Pur vus fu reconcilié
E a Jesu Crist espusé.   192
Vus estes le men confort,
La moie joie, e mun desport.
C'est le men granz solaz
De tapir par desuz voz braz.   196
Desus voz eles voil tapir;
De vus me voil jeo tutdis coverir.
Desuz vostre umbre est mon repos,
De vus partir pur ren nen n'os,   200
Pur le diable e ses awouez,

---

[41] 184 **purpre**: MS propre; *Purple was the name used for deep crimson, like dried blood.*

E ses[42] engins tant malurez.
[68ᵛ²] Fous est ki de vus s'esloigne,
Pur la serpente k'ele nel poigne, 204
Ki est de mortel venin plein.
Le soen acost est mult vilein,
E malveis e perillus,
Led e ord, e venimus. 208
Mes desuz vos eles n'ai jeo garde
De serpent ne de lesarde,
De scorpion ne de dragun,
Ne de urs, ne de leon, 212
Ne de nul autre beste
Ke mal me face ne moleste.
Ces sunt les propre nuns Sathan,
Ke tant nus quert e mal e han. 216
De ses nuns ne sai le numbre,
Car en nul maneres la gent encumbre.
Mes ses engins trestut deface,
E lui otut vilment en chace 220
Par la croiz e par la signe
Ke de tute honur est digne.
O bel Croiz, maint bon miracle
Fet Deu par vostre signacle. 224
Quant jeo le signacle vei
De Jesu Crist en ki jeo crei,
Mult merveil ke ceo dut
Pur quei en estant morust. 228
A ceo respont ci ma raison
Que ren ne fist sanz achaison.
E ke ceo afert a combatant
Que il se defende en estant, 232
[69ʳ¹] En estant se deit defendre,
Coups doner, e autres prendre.
Issi fist nostre duz seignur,
Ke se combati pur nostre amur. 236
En estant fist sa desreinne
Kant il venqui l'orrible enseigne.
En croiz en estant venqui
Nostre mortel enemi; 240
Mult coups receust, mes un dona

---

[42] 202 **ses** MS sens.

Dunt le diable a mort rua.
Un[e] autre raison mult usee
Vus dirrai, s'il vus agree. 244
Ki pur autre deit pleder
En estant deit aleger.
E message e priere
Fet l'en en itele manere, 248
E li esvesque e li pruvere
En tele manere soleient fere,
Ke en estant lur messe dient
Quant il pur le pople prient. 252
Jesu Crist tut ceo fesoit
Ki nostre avocat estoit.
En estant pur[43] nus plaida,
Kar del ester mult nus aida. 256
Il fu le prestre soverein
Ki pur nus offri le vif pain
—Ceo fu son cors precius
K'il dona al mort pur nus. 260
Il meismes fist le sacrefise
Ke salva tute seinte eglise.
[69r2] Un[e] autre raison vus dirrai,
La plus duce ke jo sai. 264
Ki volt sun ami wolcummer
Si deit encontre lui ester,
Offrir beisers, e acoler;
Si deivent amis asembler. 268
La croiz tut ceo represente
A chescun ki i met sa entente.
Oiez ore cum jeo l'entent;
Salve plus sain entendement. 272
Jesu nostre bone seignur
Tant nus mustre grant amur
Ke encontre nus est en estant
Pur fere duz e bel semblant. 276
Encuntre nus est adrescé,
De nostre venue est tut lee.
Ses braz estent pur embracer,
Son chef encline pur nus baiser, 280
Trestut son cors nus abaundone,

---

[43] 255 MS u *expunctuated after* p *with superscript abbreviation sign.*

A quicunkes volt sei meimes done.
Dunt n'a ci joie, n'ad ci leesce,
Ke Deu contre pecheur se dresce. 284
Pur acoler ses braz estent,
E pur baiser sa buche tent.
Certes isci ne sai jo ke die,
Ke vers nus tant s'umilie. 288
Ne sa[i] ke penser, ne sa[i] ke dire;
Ren ke puisse a ceo suffire.
Si nus quers fussent d'ascer,
Joie les pust trespercer, 292
[69^{vl}] Enmoillir vers cel seignur
Ki tant est pie e tut duçur.
Fendom nos quers, Deu recevom,
Espiritalment le enbraçom, 296
Baisom les plaies devotement
K'il nus mustre e vers nus tent.
Plorum sur les beneiz pez,
Crium merci de noz pechez 300
K'il nus face verrai pardon
Par sa seinte Passion.
En tele manere deit penser
Ki veut la croiz ben ahurer. 304
Ceste manere, cum jeo l'entent,
Put suffire a simple gent.
Ki meuz entent, e meuz face,
E Deu nus doint tuz jurs sa grace. Amen. 308

Variants from MS E:

18) sui d. 20) j. fu. 21) a. a c. 22) Mettez t. q. si frez com s. 30) s. nulle r. 32) Et h. d. pur vous en terre 33) Saunc e. 34) Resceivre la tue h. 36) s. freit et feim 37) Et mout m. 38) a. joevens e. 42) Que r. en graunt v. 45) P. f. fu fait tu n. 46) P. t. c. fu b. 47) s. b. 48) t. maveitez 51) al apparailler 53) N. freit 55) N. freit p. toi nulle h. v 56) Ne l. 57) Pensez 58) Quant par tiel mort t. r. 59–84) *om.* 85) Ne vous ne veez ta chere a. 86) Que ad v. vous 87) i. voleit 88) Et tele peine 89) V. bien com j. 90) Q. m. volei; *adds* Puis en ton queor que te plasmai Et de moun cher sanc que te rechatai 91) e. a m. 92) c. regarda t. 93) Si nel tienge p. a d. 95–96) *replaces with*: Car issi pendi jeo pur toi Si tu veus entendre a moi 97) Cil qui mei eime et mei d. 98) m. se mire 99) f. dunc esmirour 100) Car ja ne t. m. 101) Si tu toi veus issi mirer 102) M. i purras 103) En moi pense si te voille moustrer 104) d. faire 107) c. i fust l. 108) Od clous fiché 111) Et tu si faceez e. 112) Ceo est 114) Ceo que jeo te fis cil m. 116) Al c. que t. ce le t. 117–18) *om.* 120) Toi c. 122) *ends*

6c *Meditation on the Wounds of Christ*
(Lambeth Palace, MS 522, f. 59ᵛ-62ʳ)

[1] [59v] Ki leaument eyme Jesu Crist est tuit dis enquerant les choses ke meuz lui sunt plesant. Por ceo vos lou jeo, comencez e ausez vos de bien vivre, kar l'usage vos turnera cum a nature, kar ce ke home ou femme primes establist e a furmé en sei en sa primere conversatiun, si serra come reule de tuitte sa vie. Tiele comencez a estre come vus vodrez finir, kar custume est quel ke l'em nurrit; vices[44] ou vertuz si crescent o vie de home. Tuittes choses poet hum legerement auser e furmer a ceo ke l'em voet, tant come [60ʳ] eles sunt tendres. Noveles plançouns de arbres eynz ke eles seient bien esracinez poet em traire e faire encliner quele part ke l'em veut. Por ceo,[45] ceo ke vous quidez ke a Deu pleise, ceo eslisez, ceo siwez, ceo facez. Kar tant cum plus hautement estes mariee, tant avez greignur mester de estudier coment vos puissez plaire a vostre espus. Por ceo, sur tuitte rien ausez vus de penser de la Passiun Jesu Crist.

[2] Pensez cum ces gros clous de fer li passerent parmi les mains e les piez, e come ceo fu dur de suffrir de pendre par treis clous ke lui estreindrent les piez e poinz al fust. Pensez quel anguisse nostre Dame avoit [60ᵛ] al quer kant ele le vist tuit sul pendre, e de suens deguerpi, e isel virginel sanc ke il de lui prist jus raer.

[3] Esmirez vos sovent en la croiz; sovent, ou ke vus seez,[46] pensez ke vus le veez devant vos. E si vostre corage vus truble, pensez de la croiz e al crucifix metez un vers, a une des mains un altre, al fust le tierz, al clou le quart, al sanc le quint, le sisme a l'anguisse ke il suffri por vus, e tuit altresi a l'altre main e a chescun des piez. Al coste Jesu Crist metez un vers, un altre al gleive, dous al sanc e a l'ewe ke en issirent, le quint a l'anguisse ke nostre [Dame] senti al quer. Cele playe del coste ne [61ʳ] senti il pas ka[r] ja devie. Meillure meditaciun de ceste ne sai nule. Ici git la perfectiun de religiun; ici git le salu de l'alme.

[4] Pensez ke vus tenez un des piez Jesu Crist entre voz mayens, si metez l'un pié e puis l'autre a voz euz, e a vostre face l'un pié e l'autre, si les beysez de tuit vostre quer, tresducement. Suchez cel tresduz glorius sanc, si en teignez tote vostre face e bien i demorez od cele volenté. Autresi faites des mayens vostre duz ami. Puis enbracez od tresgrant vigur de alme trestut icel glorius cors, cele bele tresduce flur suef odorant, cele seynte virginele char de la seynte Virgine conceue, nee e nurrie. Enbracez e [61ᵛ] beisez cele duce plaie del coste par unt vostre e le salu de tuit le mund issi. Si merciez vostre sauvere. Mult fait cel ami a amer, e grant felonie fait ke sun dreit lui detient, c'est vostre alme, e sachez si lui faites tort, il se vengera plus de vos ke il freit de paen ou de Sarasin, e ce est par dreit

---

[44] MS vices *expunctuated before this word at beginning of line.*
[45] MS hole after this word.
[46] MS hole after this word.

jugement, kar venir en religiun sanz religiusement vivre,[47] si est escharnir Dampnedeu, sei meismes desceivre, faire joie al diable.

[5] Icel jur quidez sulement ke vus eez en religiun vesqui, ke vus issi avez despendu en seynte meditaciun, sanz trespas de vostre ordre. Estreitement cerchez vostre conscience, e de tuz voz trespas criez a Deu [62^r] merci, si le requerez k'il vos face verai pardun, kar del repentant ne siet il for[s] merci aver. Quant vos chochez, pensez cum vostre tresduz espus aprés grant travaus suffri ke l'em le enclost en un sarcu. Cochez vos delez lui, si le enbracez bien estreitement, tendrur de icel tres duz cors ke si estreitement esteit plaé. Pensez de la tresduz odur ke en issi. Bonurez sunt ke de duz odur de lui sunt refez. Issi vos reposez en Jesu Crist e quant orrez les seyns, ne seez pas tardivant, ne ne negligent, mes pensez cum Jesu Crist leva ignelment de mort entur la mie nuit ou tost aprés. Portez le compaignie. Levez ensemble[62^v]ment ove li. Siwez le deskes en quer.[48] Pensez ke la sunt les angles por receivre vostre travail e voz oreisons e voz suspirs, por presenter a vostre tresleal espus ki tresbien le vos merrira. Ensement aprés voz matynes querez ove la Magdelene vostre duz ami e espus. Quant l'averez trové par duce meditation e duz suspirs, entrez en ces duz braz ducement vos reposez. Jesu Crist por sa pité vos aprenge de faire sa volenté e vos doint la vie pardurable. Amen.[49]

---

[47] MS: vi *expunctuated before* vivre.

[48] quer = choeur

[49] At the bottom of the page, below the prayer, is a miniature showing a Dominican friar raising a white cross, with a hooded figure in black at his feet, addressing a group of five people kneeling; at right, outside the miniature is an angel with colored wings seated on a rock and playing a harp.

6d *Prayer by the Wounds of Christ,* in verse (Lambeth Palace, 522, f. 83[r-v])[50]

Duz sire Jesu Crist ke por nus sauver[51]
Suffristes vostre seint cors en la croiz pener;
Por cele mort penuse, beau sire, vus requer
Ke tuz les sens de mun cors deignez governer,   4
Ke jeo n'ai volenté de dire ne penser
Ne de faire, chose ke me deyve dampner.
Jesu ke suffristis voz meyns trespercer,   8
Gardez mun quer de fol desir, mes mains de fol tucher,
Mes oilz de fole regardure, ma lange de mal parler,
Tuz mes sens e membres de mal encumbrer.
Jesu ke venquistes le diable e sa temptatiun,   12
Donez moy force de rester encontre le temptur felun
Par le remembrance de vostre passiun,
Par sovent rehercer, duz Jesu, vostre nun. Amen. *Pater Noster. Ave Maria.*

---

[50] Repeated at ff. 200[v]-201[r] with no significant variants.
[51] To the right of the first two lines is a miniature of a crucified Christ with a Benedictine monk prostrate at the foot of the cross.

6e *Three Prose Prayers by the Crucifixion*
(Lambeth Palace, MS 522, ff. 196ᵛ-199ʳ)

(1)   [52]Beau sire Jesu Crist, ke le vostre beneit e seyntime cors e vostre precius sanc donastes en la seintisme verraye croix por le mund sauver, e avez establi e doné ke isel meime cors e isel duz sanc seit sacrifié [197ʳ] en la seynte Messe por nos sauver, en iceste fei aur jeo la vostre duze pité, Sire. E si vos pri issi ententivement e devotement cum jeo puis, e sai ke vos por iceste seynte sacrifise me pardonez tuz mes pechez. E par sa[53] seynte vertu me defendez de tuz mes enemis espiritels e corporels, e de tuz lur contrairies e de tuz lur maus engins, e de tuitte lur male preere e de tuitte lur male volenté, e de peril de ceste mortele vie, e de la mort subite. E par sa vertu me conduiez a bone fin. E si vos pri, duz Sire, donez mei en la fin la seynte Communiun en dreite fei, verreie reconissance [197ᵛ] receivre. E beau sire benigne Jesu, por la sue amur e por la seynte vertu, defendez m'alme idunc a le issir de cest cors de peine, e de anguisse, e del cruel enemi de enfern. E si la conduez par vostre seynt angle a vostre duce lumere e a vostre suef repos, kar vos, sire, estes sols veirs sauvere beneiz e glorius. E partuit trestuit puissant en icest siecle e en l'autre od Deu le Pere e od le Seynt Espirit *in secula seculorum. Amen. Pater noster.*

(2)   Beau sire, duz fontaine de veir amur e de tute duceur, iceste priere vos offre jeo, si vus plaist, por tuz mes amis e mes bienfetors e mes apartenanz, e por [198ʳ] tuz ices e celes N _____ e N _____.

(3)   Sire Jesu Crist, jeo vos aur la ou vos muntiez en la croyz; requer vos ke cele croyz me puisse delivrer del angle ke prent venjance de mesfesanz. *Pater. Ave.*

Jeo vos aur la u vos fuistes plaé en la croiz; requer vos ke vos plaies seyent remedie a ma alme. *Pater noster. Ave.*

Jeo vos aur mort e enseveli; requer vos ke vostre mort puisse estre ma vie. *Pater noster.*

Jeo vos aur descendant en enfern delivrant les cheitifs; requer vos ke james ne me lessez entrer. *Pater noster. Ave.*

Jeo vos aur relevant de mort [198ᵛ] e seant au destre vostre Pere del cel; requer vos ke vos i voie[54], aez de mei merci. *Pater noster. Ave.*

Jeo vos aur de tuit mun quer e gre, e graces vos rend por voz granz bienfez, e mei meymes rend jeo culpable de mes granz pechez, dunt jeo vos curucé ai; requer vos, deboneire Seignur, ke tant voliez overer e suff[r]ir por moi, ke jeo puisse par vos e od vos estre en dreite veie de salu pardurable. *Pater.*

---

[52] To the left of the beginning of the prayer is a miniature on a gold ground, with a monk in black kneeling before the crucified Christ.

[53] The possessive adjective here and in the next sentences refers to the sacrifice of the Mass.

[54] MS. iboie

Jeo vos aur la u vos vendrez a la fin por juger tuit le mund; requer vos ke a sel aveinement ne me jugez pas solum vostre justise sule, mes einz ke vienge al jugement me pardonez mes [199ʳ] pecchez. *Salvator mundi. Pater.*

Appendix II:
Original Text Extracts

1a *Le Chasteau d'Amour*,[1] vv. 571-628: the castle

En beau lu fei il veraiement,
La ou Deu de ciel descent
En un chastel bel e grant,
Bien fermé e avenant,   572
Kar c'est le chastel de amur,
De tuz solaz, de tuz sucur.
En la marche est assis,
N'ad regard de ses enemis.   576
E si vus dirrai pur quel chose
La tur est si bien enclose
De fossez parfunt e haut,
Ne ad regard de nul assaut,   580
Kar ele est si haute assise,
Sur une roche dure e bise
E bien poli de ci k'aval,
Ou habiter ne poet nul mal.   584
Ne engin ne i poet geter
Rien ki li peüst grever.
Environ ad quatre tureles,
En tut le mund n'i ad si beles.   588
Pus i ad treis bailles en tur
De fort mur e de bel atur,
Cum vus deviser le orrez,
De beauté i ad plus assez   592
Ke lange ne peüst descrire,
Cuer penser ne buche dire.
Sur roche naive sunt fermez,

---

[1] I have made slight emendations and changes of punctuation to Murray's text to facilitate comprehension.

Enclos de mult parfond fossez   596
E atornez de kerneaus,
Bien poliz e bons et beaus.
Barbecanes i ad set
Ki par bon engin sunt fet.   600
Chescune ad e porte e tur
Ou ja ne i faudra sucur,
Ne ja n'i avera ennui
Ki la vient quere refui.   604
Le chastel est bel e bon.
Dehors depeint environ
De treis colurs diversement.
E si est vert le fundement,   608
Ki a la roche se joint.
De grant duçur ne i faut point,
Kar bien di ke duce verdur
Ne pert jamés sa colur.   612
La colur ki est en mi liu
Si est inde e si est bliu,
Ki meine colur est nomee,
De beauté est enluminee.   616
La tierce colur par en som
Les kerneaus covre environ.
Plus est vermeille ke n'est rose
E piert une ardante chose.   620
Tant reflambeie environ
Ke tut covere le dongon
Jamés ne i vient male oree,
Mes de duçur i ad plenté.   624
Dedens est li chasteus blans.
Plus ke neif ki seit negans;
Ke gette si grand clarté
De lung la tur e de lé.   628

1b *Chasteau d'amour*, vv. 659-716: the allegory

Ce est le chastel de delit
E de solaz e de respit,   660
De esperance e de amur,
E de refui e de duçur.
Ce est le cors de la pucele.
Onkes autre ne ot fors cele,   664
Ki de tant vertu fust garnie,

Cum la duce Virgine Marie.
Assise nus est en la marche,
Si ele nus est escu e targe, 668
Encontre tuz nos enemis,
Ki nus aguaitent tut dis.
La roche k'est si bien polie,
C'est le cuer la duce Marie, 672
Ki onkes en mal ne mollist,
Mes a Deu servir se prist,
E sa seinte virginité
Gardat en humilité. 676
Le fundement ki est nomez,
Ki a la roche est fermez,
Ki est depeint a colur,
E de si tres bele verdur, 680
Ce est la fei de la Virgine
Ki sun seint cuer enlumine.
La verdur ki tant est bele,
Sa fei tut tens renovele, 684
Kar fei est apertement
De tutes vertuz fundement.
E puis est la meine colur
E de beauté e de duçur. 688
Ce est la signefiance,
Ke od tendrur en esperance
Servi tut tens sun seignur
En humbleté e en duçur. 692
E la colur par en som
Ki covere tut environ,
C'est cele ki tant est vermeille:
N'i ad nule ki tant vaille; 696
E c'est la seinte charité,
Dunt ele est enluminee
E esprise del feu d'amur
De servir Deu sun Creatur. 700
Les quatre tureles en haut
Ki gardent la tur de assaut,
Ou habiter ne poet nus mals
Sunt quatre vertuz kardinals. 704
Ce est Force e Temperance,
E si rest Justice e Prudence.
As quatre portes sunt porter,
Ke rien ne puet fors bien entrer. 708

Les treis bailles du chastel
Ki ovrees sunt au karnel
E k'acompassent environ
E si defendent le dongon. 712
Cele a le plus haut estage
Signefie sun pucelage
K'onkes de rien ne fu blesmie
Tant fu de grace replenie. 716

1c *Le Chasteau d'amour*, vv. 1003-1089: the temptation of Jesus

Ore oiez deboneirement
E je vus dirrai bien coment, 1004
Kant Jhesus en le mund fu nez,
Del diable fu tant celez
Ke il ne sout de sun venir,
Mes quidout par tut seignurir, 1008
Cum il enceis fet aveit,
Mes sun poër li est toleit.
Mult bien le vit home en terre,
Mes il ne sout de quel affere, 1012
Home vint en terre nestre,
E tuz jurs sanz peché estre.
En merveillant dist: "Ki es tu?
Es tu donke le fiz Deu? 1016
Tut icest mund te voil doner
Si tu me veus aorer."
E Jhesu dist: "Va, Sathanas;
Tun Seigneur Deu ne tempteras." 1020
E cil dist donc: "Ke veus tu fere?
Princes su de ceste terre.
Long tens ai eü la seisine
Par le grant a le rei hautime, 1024
Fors sul ke tun conseil ne vei
Ne jo ne conuis tun secrei.
Mult i averez ore a fere,
Se de mei volez rien conquere. 1028
E se de tei puissance n'eie
Me quidez vus tolir ma preie?
Nai; le covenant est fermez,
En la curt Deu cirographez, 1032
Ke s'il le comand Deu passat,

Od mei tut tens demorast,
E morreit en fin de mort
E Deus ne veut fere nul tort, 1036
Mes bien tiendra le covenant
Ki en sa curt fu fet avant."
Dont respundi li duz Jhesu:
"Li covenanz fu bien tenu, 1040
Meis tu primes le enfreinsistes,
Kant en traïson li desistes:
'Tu ne murras pas pur tant
Einz serez cum Deu sachant.' 1044
De le fet fustes acheson.
Ores esgardez donc reson.
Veus tu del covenant joïr
Kant covenant ne veus tenir?" 1048
—"O! dist li diables, traï su,
Kant en pleidant su vencu."
E dist, "Dunt te vient teu poer
Teu vertu e teu saver 1052
Ke a mei osiez enprendre
A desputer e reson rendre?
Tut ai perdu en pleidant,
Mes ne demurrai mie atant, 1056
Tute feiz a il forfet,
Si ke il en ma prison est,
Ne sanz redemption pur li
Ne serai a tort desseisi." 1060
Dunc dist Jhesu li Rei verrai,
"Pur li redemption ferai."
E dist li diables: "Quel reson
Frez vus pur raindre cel prison? 1064
Si tu le vues achater,
Il te costera mult chier."
—Et cum chier?"—"Mes tant cum il vaut,
Einz ke il de ma prison aut." 1068
Donc dist li duz Jhesu beneit:
"Kar iceo est bien reson e dreit,
Encontre dreit ne voil je mie
Tolir tei rien par mestrie. 1072
Fai le me donc volontiers;
K'est iceo donc ke tu quiers?"
—"Je te le dirrai bien sanz faille.
Rendez mei donc ki tant vaille, 1076

Cum fet ore tut le mund
Et kant k'aprés tuz jurs vendrunt."
—"Volontiers tut iceo ferei,
Kar mieuz vaut mun petit dei   1080
Ke tels cent mil mundes ne funt
Od tute la gent ki i sunt."
Li diable dist par fierté:
"Bien vei ke cest est verité,   1084
Kar tut le mund puis justiser,
Mes tei ne puis rien aprismer.
E vues tu donc tun dei doner
Pur si vil merz achater?"   1088
—"Nai, fet il, mes tut mun cors."
—"Ainz ke eies le prison hors
Il te coviendra mult plus fere
Suffrir tant de maus e contrere.   1092
Si amender vues sun tort,
Il te estuet suffrir la mort,
Od tant de peine e tant dolurs,
Si cum il fereit a tuz jurs,   1096
Se il fust od mei manant
E en enfern demurant."
Adonc respont li duz Jhesu:
"Kant ke as dit tut iert tenu,   1100
Kar Verité le devise
E pus le ad jugé Justise.
Plus ferai ke dit ne avez.
Si iert li serfs deliverez."   1104

2 *"Jesus" from* **Suidas: p. 612, lines 5-22**[2]

". . . Quant li provoires oïrent ceste parole il furent mult esbaïz e manderent venir matrones e norrices por encerthier e prover si Marie estoit virge. Il furent certein de la virginité e furent mult esbahi e prierent Marie ke ele lour deist priveement ki estoit pere Jesu ke il puissent en livre escrivre la verité.

    Marie lor respondi ke ele li avoit enfaunté, e ke il ne avoit nul pere, e ke ele avoit oï ke li angle luy apela le fiz Deu, e ke ele estoit virge e non pas corrumpue.

    Quant luy provoires oïrent ce, il aporteyent se livre e escriveyent: a tel jor morust tel prestre, fiz de tel pere e de tele mere, e par concord e eleccion est fait

---

[2] I have normalized the use of i/j and u/v, as well as added punctuation.

prestre, Jesus filius Dei viventis et Marie virginis. E cest livre est gardé en le temple o grant reverence, e cest secrez ne est pas seu de tuz. Mes a moi est revelé car je sui mestre e princes de nostre gent. E nus ne garantissum mie soulement par la ley ke Jesu Crist ki est aoré de vos crestiens ki il seit fiz Deu ki vint por le salu del munde en terre, mes por la inscription du livre ki est sauvé.

Mes en aprés la passion, quant nos auncessors virent ke il eurent condempné e crucifié le fiz Deu, il emblerent fausement le livre e le reposirent en Tyberiade."

Quant li crestien oï ces paroles il fu mult liez e mercia nostre Synur; e voleit tantost aler recounter cestes paroles al empereour ke il enveiast a Tyberyaden e recoverast le livre por le redargucion de infidelitate Judeorum.

3 *Les Enfaunces Jesu Crist*, vv. 1101-56: the children in the oven

De Jerico est pus alé	
Tut pa[r] sei, en verité,	
Jesu tut plein de bonté.	
Si ad lé Gius demandé	1104
U les enfans esteient mis	
Ke esteient du païs	
U il soleit güer jadis.	
Il li distrent: "Beus amis,	1108
Nus ne savoms u i[l] sunt	
Ne u veir trové serrunt."	
E sachét k'il mesfunt,	
Kar mut cher l'achaterunt.	1112
Tuz lé Gius, petiz e granz,	
Urent mis tuz lur enfanz	
En un furneis ben tenanz,	
K'il ne fusent pas alanz	1116
Ove Jesu, cum il soleient,	
Ça ne la, kar il doteient	
Sa manere, e parleient	
Mal de li, cum il poeient.	1120
Jesu sout lur mavestez,	
E cum il furent enfermez.	
Il lur pria par amistez	
K'il fusent dunc mustrez.	1124
Il dist k'il vout o eus aler	
E boneirement o eus jüer.	
E ceus comencerent a jurer	
Ke nuil ne les vist dés her.	1128

Jesu dunc s'en est alé
A furneis tut de gré;
As Gius ad dunc demandé:
"E ki sunt ci enfermé?"   1132
Les Gius firent serement
Ke pors furent verrément.
Jesu dist dunc a cele gent:
"E pors serrunt certeinement."   1136
Ausitost cum ço disoit,
Checun dunc pors esteit,
E cume porc checun mangoit
E ausi tut dis groinoit.   1140
Kant Jesus esteit alez,
Les forneis sun[t] debarrez,
E ceus ke furent leinz botez
Tuz furent pors en veritez.   1144
Kant il vindrent trestuz hors,
E lé Gius lur virent pors,
Tuz ce tindrent cume mors;
Honiz se tindrent de lur cors.   1148
Tut dis pus ça en arere
Lé Gius tindrent come frere
Checun porc en sa manere,
Si esteit miracle fere.   1152
Pus cel' hure ne manga
Unc nul Giu, ne les assa,
Ne jamés pur veir ne fra,
Kar la lei defendu l'a.   1156

4 *La Vengeance de Nostre Seigneur*, lines 173-204: punishment of the Jews, and cure of the Emperor

". . . Dunc avint que Deu fud irrez pur sun fiz qu'il l'i orent mort en tere. Si envead sun angle a Titum e a Vaspasianum ne mie a nus kar nus n'erium nient digne e pecheur, sis aspirat e fist aler en la tere de Jerusalem. Quant il vindrent, si pristrent treis reis e jujerent coment il deveient murir. Et jo oï ben dire coment il en errerent. Quant il les orent pris, Vaspasianus dist:

    'Que ferum nus de eus?'
Titus respondi:
    'Il pristrent Nostre Seigneur sil lierent. Nus prendrum euls si lierum.'
E sil firent. Vaspasianus dist:
    'Que iert pus de euls?'
Titus respondi:

'Il flaierent Nostre Seigneur e laidengerent. E nus flaelerum euls e ledengerum.'

E il si firent. Vaspasianus dist:

'Que iert puls [= pus] de euls?'

Titus respondi:

'Il pendirent Nostre Seigneur en vert fust e ferirent de launce. Nus penderum euls en sech fust e ferrum de lances.'

Et issi le unt fet. Vespasianus dist:

'Que iert pus de euls qui remeinderunt?'

Titus respondi:

'Il pristrent la vesture Nostre Seignur si la deviserent encuntre en quatre parties. Nus deviserum euls ensement en quatre parties, la une en averai jo e tu l'autre; e mi huem la tierce e li tuen la quarte.'

E issi furent departiz. Vaspasianus dist:

'Que ferum pus de euls?'

Titus respondi:

'Il vendirent Nostre Seignur pur trente deners. E nus les vendrum, si durrum trente pur un denier.'

E issi fud fait. Pus firent quere u il trover[ei]ent le vult Nostre Seinnur, sil truverent od une femme, Veronice par nun, ki l'aveit. E si mistrent Pilate en un escrin de fer sil me unt livered. Jo ai ici e lui el vult e la femme."

Dunc dist Tyberius:

"Descovre le vult sil verrai e aurrai, kar mulz avoegles e leprus e clops e muz e surz unt en lui grant fiance."

Dunc le desa[n]volupat Velosianus. Cum Tyberius le vit, si l'aurat. Cum il le oud veüd e aured, la lepre li chaïd e sa charn fud saine e si nette cume la charn de un petit enfant. E tut li autre enfermetés ki iluec esteient furent sanez od lui. Dunc enclinat Tyberius sun chef e flechit ses genuilz e menbrat lui de ceste parole:

"O tu, Crist, beneïz est li ventres ki te portat, e les mameles que tu alaitas sunt beneïtes, e icil sunt beneïz ki owent ta parole e puis si la gardent."

Dunc adreçat les oilz vers le ciel e plurat de sun quor e de ces oilz e dist a Nostre Sire par privé voiz:

"Deus, Sire del ciel e de terre, ne me laisses murir mais conforte mei, kar jo m'afi mult en tun nun."

5 *Little St. Hugh of Lincoln*, vv. 104-119: the crucifixion of Hugh[3]

L'enfant delié mult tost fu
Et sur la croiz mult tost pendu,
Vilement, cum Jhésu fu,
Qui murust pur nostre pru.

Ore oez grant pru u dolur.
Deu merci! cum ont poür
Li juven enfant a cel ure
Quant la croiz i fu mis sure.

Ses braz furent estendu
Sur la croiz si lié cum il fu,
Et percé furent par mainz de Ju
Ses pez, ces meinz, des clous agu.

Issi furent atachez
De cel enfant meinz et pez
A la croiz, cum vus oez,
Et tut vif sur la croiz crucifiez.

6f *La Contemplacioun de la Passioun*, (London, BL, Harley MS 2253), 254-56

Ici comence contemplacioun de la passioun Jhesu Crist e comence a comply pur ce que a cel oure Judas Scarioth ly vendy.

Quant vus dites comply, pensir devez mout ententivement coment Judas vendy Nostre Seigneur pur .xxx. deners e pur ce a tiel oure vus rendez coupable a Dieu priveement en vostre cuer e a prestre de bouche, si vus le poez avoir, de quanque vus avez le jour mesfait encountre les comaundementz Dieu. E de ce qe vus avetz en delit, en vanités e si vus eiez malement ou deshonestement parlé ou de vos yeux folement regardé e de quanqe vos quidez le jour par nul de vos synk sentz encountre la volenté de vostre Creatour avoir pecchié, si en requerez devoutement merci e pardoun, e certeyne esperance eyez que vus averez ce que vus dreitement requerez en bounté, eynssi qe vus soiez verroiement repentant e bien confés, quar ce dit Nostre Seigneur en le Ewangelye: "Requerez e vus receverez." Dites donque a cest comply einsi:

---

[3] After checking Paris, BnF, fr. 902, I have modified some of the readings of Michel's edition.

Appendix II

"Douz Sire, Jhesu Crist, je te renk graces qe a oure de comply estoiez trahy de Judas Scarioth, e vendy pur .xxx. deners. Et aprés cest comply tu dys a trois de tes deciples, 'Veillés e horez que vus ne entrez en temptatioun' e pus t'en alas tu un poy de tes deciples a la mountaunce de tant come um porroit rochier une piere e te cochas a la terre e prias trois foiz ton piere que cele passioun qu'adonque te fust en venant passast outre de toy, si ce pust estre, e donque apparust un aungle a toi e te counforta, e tant come tu fus en t'oreysoun, tu suas d'angoyse goutes de sang e dementiers dormirent tes desciples, mes tu soul ne dormys point jesque ataunt qe tu moruz en la Croys, e pus dormys el sepulcre jesqe au jour de ta resurexioun, e adonqe eveillas."

Index of Proper Names

References for poetic texts (**1**),[1] (**3**), (**5**) (**6b**), (**6d**) are to verses; for published prose texts, to lines (**4**), or to page numbers followed by the line on the page (**2**), (**6f**); for the prose texts edited here (**6a**), (**6c**), (**6e**) to numbered paragraphs.

Aaron, Old Testament priest: (**1**) 829
Abraham, the Patriarch: (**1**), 499, (**3**) 611, 617, 631
Abstinence (*abstinence*), one of the seven virtues: (**1**) 738
Adam, the first man: (**1**) 31, 59, 74, 112, 131, *etc.*
Adonay, name of God: (**6a**) 21
Agla, name of God: (**6a**) 21
Almighty (*Tut puissant*), i.e. God: (**1**) 852, 1690
Andrew (*saint Andreu*), apostle: (**6a**) 14
Anger (*ire*), a deadly sin: (**1**) 743
Annas, a Jewish priest (*Anne*): (**3**) 486
Anselm, Archbishop of Canterbury (*seynt Auselyn*): (**6a**) 1
Aquitaine, Roman province in SW France: (**4**) 2
Archelaus, son of Herod and (here) father of Pilate: (**4**) 57, 156
Archeteclin (*Architriclin, Archeteclin, Archeticlin*), the bridegroom at the marriage feast (of Cana): (**1**) 1247, 1251; (**3**) 1820, 1857
Augustine (*Augustin*), saint and Father of the Church: (**1**) 1389
Avarice (*avarice*), a deadly sin: (**1**) 741

Bethlehem (*Bedlëem, Bethleem, Betheleem*), birthplace of Jesus: (**3**) 61, 129, 1717; (**4**) 47
Bordeaux (*Bordele*), city in Aquitaine: (**4**) 2

Caesar (*Roy Cesar, Cesar*): (**6f**) 256: 31, 32
Caesar Augustus (*Augustus Cesar*), the first Roman emperor: (**1**) 861
Caiphas (*Caÿpham*), the high priest: (**4**) 156
Calvary (*Calvarye*): (**6f**) 258: 20
Cana (*Kane*), the site of the marriage feast: (**1**) 1246
Canwick (*Canevic*), a hill to the south of Lincoln: (**5**) 365
Capharnaum (*Capharnaun*) (**3**) 1655
Chaim (*Agon, Agim*), killer of Hugh: (**5**) 84, 94, 121, 124, 324
Charity (*charité*), one of the seven virtues: (**1**) 737
Chastity (*chasteté*), one of the seven virtues: (**1**) 740
Christ (*Crist*): (**4**) 46, 73, 78, 80, *etc.*
Counselor (*Conseillere*), i.e. Jesus Christ: (**1**) Prol., 513, 880, 900, 909, 1207
Creator (*Creatur, nature naturante, Creatour*), i.e. God: (**1**) 700, 867, 1654; (**6b**) 161; (**6f**) 256: 3

---

[1] Names in the Latin prose prologue are indicated with "Prol."

Damascus (*Damasche*), where Pilate was imprisoned: (4) 88, 157
Daniel, the prophet: (1) 503; (4) 207
David (*David, Davi, Davit*), the prophet and psalmist: (1) 505; (3) 1642; (4) 205; (6a) 18
Dernestal (*Dernestal, Desternal*), the Jewish quarter of Lincoln: (5) 6, 199, 229

Edward, St., the Confessor and favorite saint of Henry III: (5) 62
Egypt (*Egypte*): (3) 172, 331, 372
Elijah (*Helias*), the prophet: (1) 502
Elisha (*Eliseu*), the prophet: (1) 505
Eloy, name of God: (6a) 21
Enemy, i.e. devil (*Adversier, Adverser*): (1) 1105; (3) 506
Envy (*envie*), a deadly sin: (1) 737
Eregius, a compiler of *Suidas*: (2) 610: 11
Eugenius, a compiler of *Suidas*: (2) 610: 10
Eusebius (*Eusebius Panfile*), bishop of Caesarea: (2) 612: 32–33
Eve (*Eve, Evain*), the first woman: (1) 59, 1211

Father (*Pere, Pater*), i.e. God the Father: (1) Prol., 1352, 1433, 1482, 1486, *etc.*; (4) 41, 214; (6a) 3, 4, 12, 14, 25 *etc.*; (6b) 31, 68; (6e) 3
Father (*Pere*), i.e. Jesus: (1) Prol., 514, 1363, 1379, 1446, 1449, *etc.*
Frondise, governor of Sotinen (city to which the Holy Family fled): (3) 343, 361, 381

Galilee, region of Palestine: (1) 1246; (2) 612: 1; (4) 50, 110
Generosity (*largesce*), one of the seven virtues: (1) 742
Gluttony (*glotunie*), a deadly sin: (1) 738
God (*Deu, Deus, Dé*): (1) 10, 21, 25, 41, 44, *etc.*; (2) 612: 30, 42; (3) 41, 53, 76, 82, 131, *etc.*; (4) 37, 40, 52, 68, 76, 95, *etc.*; (5) 19, 38, 50, 57, *etc.*; (6a) 1, 3, 4, 5, 11, *etc.*; (6b) 4, 8, 20, 68, 141, 160 *etc.*; (6c) 1, 5; (6f) 254: 6, 258: 17, 260: 8

God the Father (*Deu le Pere, Perre*): (1) 7, 461, 879; (6a) 38; (6e) 1; (6f) 258: 31; *see also* Father
God the Son (*Deus le Fiz, Fiz,*), i.e. second person of the Trinity, God the Son: (1) 7, 462, 1352, 1433, 1486; (4) 41, 214; *see also* Son of God
Golgotha, place of the Crucifixion: (4) 48, Greeks (*Gregeis*): (4) 10
Habakkuk (*Abacuc*), the prophet: (1) 502
Hail Mary (*Ave Marie, Ave*), a prayer: (6a) 38; (6d) 15; (6e) 3
Hebron: (1) 75
Hendenus, a compiler of *Suidas*: (2) 610: 10
Henry (*Henrie, Henri*), King Henry III: (5) 49, 296, 346
Heradius, a compiler of *Suidas*: (2) 610: 10
Herod (*Herode, Herodes*), ruler of Galilee: (3) 65, 97, 113, 144, 152 *etc.*; (6f) 258: 1
Holy Communion (*seinte Communion*), Eucharist of the Mass: (6e) 1
Holy Spirit (*Deus li Seinz Espiriz, Seint Espirit, Seintime Espirit, Seint Esspirit*): (1) 8, 463, 1352, 1434, 1486; (2) 612: 3; (3) 1604; (4) 30, 41, 214; (6a) 18, 38; (6e) 1
Holy Trinity (*Seinte Trinité*): (1) 77; (2) 610: 1; (6a) 37
Hugh (*Huchon, Huet*), St. Hugh of Lincoln: (5) 4, 201, 237, 278
Humility (*humilité*), one of the seven virtues: (1) 736

Isaiah (*Ysaïe, Ysaÿe*), the prophet: (1) Prol., 54, 504, 508, 549, 1337, 1356; (2) 612: 38; (3) 191

Jacob, a relative of Jesus: (3) 1767
Jeremiah (*Jeremie*), the prophet: (1) 503
Jericho (*Jerico, Jericho*): (3) 1049, 1101, 1158
Jerusalem: (2) 611: 20, 36, 612: 32; (3) 1786; (4) 54, 62, 76, 94, 101 *etc.*
Jesus (*Jesu, Jesum, Jesus, Jhesu, Jhesus, Jhesum*): (1) 841, 899, 975, 1005, *etc.*; (2) 611: 27, 35, 39, 42; 612: 4, *etc.*; (3) 162, 221, 236, 237, 277, *etc.*;

Index

(4) 1, 84, 91, 102, 110, 162, *etc.*; (5) 75, 83, 106; (6a) 1, 2, 6, 13, 14 *etc.*; (6b) 14, 273; (6d) 8, 12, 15; (6e) 1

Jesus Christ (*Jhesu Crist, Jesu Crist*): (1) Prol., 849, 1242, 1307, 1375 *etc.*; (2) 611: 2, 4, 5, 9, 17, *etc.*; (3) 7, 20, 33, 313, 349, *etc.*; (4) 16, 42, 59, 151, *etc.*; (5) 36; 65, 131, 347; (6a) 7, 8, 9, 10, 11, *etc.*; (6b) 2, 123, 164, 192, *etc.* (6c) 1, 3, 4, 5; (6d) 1; (6e) 1, 3; (6f) 254, 1; 256: 8, 19, 25; 258: 5, 24, *etc. See also* Counselor, God the Son, Lord, Marvellous, Mighty One, Prince of Peace, Son of God

John, apostle and evangelist: (6a) 25, 26, 28; (6f) 260: 3

John (*Johan*), poet-artist: (3) 2011

Jonah (*Jonas, Jonam*), the prophet: (1) 501; (4) 207

Jopin (*Jopin*), sold Hugh to his killer, confessed the crime: (5) 73, 80, 308, 344, 351, *etc.*

Joseph, husband of Mary: (2) 611: 35; (3) 166, 178, 204, 205 *etc.*; (6a)18

Joseph, a rich man raised from the dead: (3) 1661, 1665, 1685, 1714

Joseph, a relative of Jesus who was bitten by a snake: (3) 1721, 1725, 1731, 1736, 1747, 1752, *etc.*

Joseph, a relative of Jesus: (3) 1768

Joseph of Arimathea (*Arimatie, Arymathie*): (4) 103, 105, 109, 161; (6f) 260: 29

Josephus, Flavius Josephus (*Josephus, Joseph*): (2) 612: 32, 35

Joy (*leesce*), one of the seven virtues: (1) 745

Judas Iscariot (*Judas Scariot, Judas*): (6f) 254: 2; 256: 9, 19

Jude (*Judee*), a relative of Jesus: (3) 1768

Judea (*Judee*), region of Palestine: (4) 5, 8, 10, 15, 46, 51, *etc.*

Julius, a compiler of *Suidas*: (2) 610: 11

Justinian, the emperor: (2) 610: 12

Justice (*Justice, Dreit*), a daughter of God: (1) Prol., 233, 311, 321, 329, 333, 338, *etc.*

Justice, a cardinal virtue: (1) 706

Lady (*Dame*), i.e. Mary: (1) 794, 795; (3) 445; (6a) 25, 26, 27, 32, 33, 34, 35

Lazarus (*Lazere, Lazarum*), man raised by Jesus from the dead: (1) 1265, 1270; (4) 18, 168

Lechery (*lecherie*), a deadly sin: (1) 739

Levi, one of the masters who instructs Jesus: (3) 621, 629, 637, 860, 864, 869, 882

Levi, the Patriarch: (2) 611: 31

Libourne (*Lure*), city near Bordeaux: (4) 7, 45

Lincoln (*Nichole, Nichol*): (5) 2, 5, 38, 42, 46, *etc.*

Longinus (*Longis, Longieus*), soldier who lanced Jesus on the Cross: (1) 1416; (6f) 260: 25

Lord, i.e. God or Jesus Christ (*Sire, Seignur, Domine*): (1) 490, 491, 860, 1020, 1563; (2) 611: 9, 612: 38; (4) 33, 36, 203, 205, 223; (6a) 3, 7, 8, 9, 10, 12, 13, *etc.*; (6d) 1, 3; (6e) 1, 2, 3; (6f) 256: 8, 19, 24, 25, *etc.*; *see also* Our Lord, Lord God

Lord God (*Dampnedeu, Damnedeu*): (1) 656, 997, 1553, 1724, 1753; (4) 215; (6a) 5, 18, 21, 28, 37; (6c) 4

Lucifer, the fallen angel: (1) 985

Luke, evangelist: (2) 612: 37; 613: 1

Marvelous (*Merveillus*), i.e. Jesus Christ: (1) Prol., 513, 520

Mary (*Marie*), the Virgin, the mother of Jesus: (1) Prol., 666, 672, 1174, 1195, 1665, 1719; (2) 610: 5; 611: 35; 612: 6, 7, 9, 13; (3) 36, 165, 177, 181, *etc.*; (6a) 18, 25, 29, 30, 32, *etc.*; (6b) 167; *see also* Lady, Mother of God, Queen, Virgin

Mary (*Marie*), mother of Joseph: (3) 1769–72

Mary Cleophas (*Marie Cleophé*): (3) 1769–70

Mary Magdalen (*la Magdalene*): (6c) 5

Mass (*Messe*), liturgy: (6e) 1

Mercy (*Misericorde*): (1) Prol., 230, 249, 284, 291, 297, *etc.*

Mighty One (*Fort*), i.e. Jesus Christ: (1) Prol., 514

Mohammed (*Mahoun*), the prophet: (3) 109

Moses (*Moysen, Moyses*), the Patriarch: (1) 195, 501

Mother of God (*Mere, Mere Deu*), i.e. Mary: (1) 1174, 1195, 1664; (6f) 258: 21, 260: 3, 33

Mother of Mercy (*Mere de misericorde*): (6a) 32, 35

Nathan, son of Nahum, messenger from Pilate to Tiberias: (4) 5, 9, 14, 26, 39

Nazareth (*Nazarez, Nazareth*), home of Jesus: (3) 974, 1813

Nicodemus (*Nichodemus, Nichodeme, Nicodeme*): (4) 103, 104, 162; (6f) 260: 29

Noah (*Noé*): (1) 363

Our Father (*Pater noster, Pater*), the Lord's Prayer: (6a) 22, 38; (6d) 15; (6e) 1, 3

Our Lady (*Nostre Dame*): (6a)28, 29; (6c) 2, 3

Our (My) Lord (*Nostre Seigneur, Nostre Sire, Nostre Synur, Mun Seigneur*): (1) 860, 1563; (2) 612: 20, 612: 39; (4) 86, 121, 137, 140, 179, 181, *etc.*; (6f) 254: 4; 256: 6

Pallion, a compiler of *Suidas*: (2) 610: 11.

Panfilius, a compiler of *Suidas*: (2) 610: 11

Patience (*patience*), one of the seven virtues: (1) 743

Paul (*Pol*), author of New Testament Epistles: (6a) 21

Peace (*Pès*), a daughter of God: (1) Prol., 234, 322, 353, 355, 370, *etc.*

Peitevin (*Peitevin, Partenin*), Jew of Lincoln who kidnapped Hugh: (5) 7, 312

Pharaoh (*Pharaon*), drowned in the Red Sea: (3) 369

Philip (*Phelipe argenter, Phelipes*), 6th-century Christian silversmith: (2) 610: 14; 611: 1, 613: 1

Pilate (*Pilate, Pilat, Pylat*): (4) 10, 57, 61, 87, 118, *etc.*; (6f) 256: 26, 29; 258: 1, 4, 9, 12, *etc.*

Pity (*Pité*): (1) 340, 370, 1175

Pride (*Orgoil*), a deadly sin: (1) 733

Prince of Peace (*Prince de Pès*), i.e. Jesus: (1) Prol., 516, 1496, 1610, 1647, 1763

Prudence, cardinal virtue: (1) 706

Queen (*Reïne*), i.e. Mary: (1) 789, 795, 1173, 1716

Robert Grosseteste, (*Robertum Grossetests*), Bishop of Lincoln: (1) Prol.

Rome (*Rume*): (4)1, 6, 10, 89, 149

Sadness (*tristesce*), a deadly sin: (1) 742

Samuel, the prophet: (1) 504

Satan (*Sathanas, Sathan*), the devil: (1) 1019; (3) 414; (6b) 215

Savior (*Sauveur, Salvator*): (1) 1112; (4) 113; (6a) 17; (6b) 4; (6e) 1, 3

Simeon (*Siméon*), the priest at the Presentation in the Temple: (1) 1178; (3) 47; (4) 114

Simeon (*Siméoun*), a relative of Jesus: (3) 1767

Sinai (*Synaïs*), mountain in Palestine: (1) 194

Solomon (*Slomo*), a Jewish child: (3) 1031, 1042

Solomon, as author of the *Song of Songs*: (6a) 18

Son (*Fiz*), i.e. Jesus: (1) Prol., 832; (6a) 4, 27, 37

Son of God (*Filz Deu, filius dei*), Son of God: (1) 1016, 1352, 1431; (2) 612: 2, 10, 13, 16, 19, *etc.*; (4) 97, 106, 115–16 119, 133; (6a) 2, 3, 5, 6, 11, 15, 16; (6f) 256: 33, 260: 22

Sotinen, city in Egypt to which the Holy Family fled: (3) 336

Star of the Sea (*Estele de mer*), i.e Mary: (6a) 29

Strength (*Force*), cardinal virtue: (1) 705

Suidas (*Suda*): (2) 613: 4

Sylvester (*Silvestre*), a disciple of Jesus: (4) 211, 213

Temperance, cardinal virtue: (1) 705
Theodosius (*Theodosii, Theodosius, Theodose*), a 6th-century Jewish leader: (2) 610: 9–10, 12; 611: 1; 613: 1
Thomas, the apostle: (1) 1412, 1418
Tiber (*Teivre*), river in Rome: (4) 149
Tiberias (*Tyberius, Tyberii, Tiberio, Tyberium*), emperor of Rome: (4) 1, 2, 3, 6, 14, 32, *etc.*
Tiberias (*Tyberiade, Tyberiaden*), city in Galilee: (2) 612: 19, 21
Titus (*Tytus, Tyti, Tyto, Tyte,*), king of Aquitaine: (4) 2, 7, 12, 25, 32, 59, 64, 75, *etc.*
Truth (*Verité*), a daughter of God: (1) Prol., 232, 283, 288, 294, 298, 321, *etc.*
Tullius the sophist, a compiler of *Suidas*: (2) 610: 11

Velosian (*Velosianum, Velosianus, Velosiane*), the emperor's messenger: (4) 90, 92, 97, 99, 118, *etc.*

Veronica (*Veronices*): (4) 86, 116, 121, 125, 135, *etc.*
Vespasian (*Vespasianum, Vaspasiani, Vaspasiano, Vaspasiane*), brother of the emperor: (4) 43, 59, 64, 75, 79, *etc.*
Vienne (*Vigenne*), city south of Lyons in France where Pilate was imprisoned: (4) 227
Virgin (*Pucele, Virgine*), i.e. Mary: (1) 666, 681, 724, 751, 789, *etc.*; (6a) 4, 15, 38; (6c) 4

Wicked One (*Malfé, Maufé*), i.e. devil: (1) 1297, 1331; (3) 341, 352

Zachary (*Zakarie*), one of Jesus's teachers: (3) 526, 565, 601
Zapathon, a compiler of *Suidas*: (2) 610: 11
Zeb, a boy pushed down a flight of steps: (3) 1027, 1029
Zonomanus, a compiler of *Suidas*: (2) 610: 11